AJAX and Flash Development with OpenLaszlo

A Tutorial

Chris Coremans

AJAX and Flash Development with OpenLaszlo : A Tutorial
©2006 by Brainy Software
First Edition: October 2006

International Standard Book Number: 0-9752128-6-9

Book and Cover Designer: Mona Setiadi

Technical Reviewer: Paul Deck
Indexer: Chris Mayle

Warning and Disclaimer

Table of Contents

Introduction

Welcome to *AJAX and Flash Development with OpenLaszlo: A Tutorial.* This book teaches you OpenLaszlo, an exciting technology for writing AJAX and Flash applications. AJAX, for Asynchronous JavaScript and XML, is slated to be the technology for developing the next generation of Web applications. Flash, as you likely have known, is a popular technology for writing highly interactive Web applications that normally involve movies, animation, or games. More appealingly, unlike Macromedia Flash that costs a few hundred dollars, OpenLaszlo is free and open-sourced, licensed under the Common Public License (CPL) version 1.0 (http://www.opensource.org/licenses/cpl.php). Authored by IBM, CPL provides flexibility for commercial reuse of source code. No wonder companies like Yahoo, Earthlink, and many others rely on OpenLaszlo as their development platform.

OpenLaszlo comes with an Application Programming Interface (API) that includes built-in classes and a rich set of user interface components. These classes and components allow you to draw shapes, create animation, lay out components, bind data, communicate with the server, make movies and games, and do practically anything a mature programming language would allow you to do. With the OpenLaszlo suite at your disposal, you have everything a rich client programmer has ever needed. In addition, an Integrated Development Environment (IDE) for rapid OpenLaszlo development is available through the OpenLaszlo Eclipse plug-in.

The rest of this introduction discusses AJAX, Flash, and OpenLaszlo. It also prepares you with prerequisite software installation and provides an overview of each chapter in this book.

AJAX

AJAX is a new name coined by Jesse James Garrett of Adaptive Path for two old technologies: JavaScript and XML. Basically, AJAX applications asynchronously connect to the server to collect more data that can be displayed in the current Web page. As a result, new information can be shown without page refresh. Google was the first to popularize this strategy with their Gmail and Google Maps applications. However, Google was not the first to make full use of the engine that makes asynchronous connections possible: the XMLHttpRequest object. Microsoft added it to Internet Explorer 5 and seasoned developers discovered ways to reap its benefits. Soon afterwards Mozilla browsers also had their own version of this object. Prior to XMLHttpRequest, people used DHTML and HTML frames and iframes to update pages without refresh.

Despite advance in client-side technologies, writing JavaScript code, hence AJAX applications, is still intimidating. Even though IDEs are available for writing JavaScript scripts, programmers still have to overcome the biggest challenge in writing client-side applications: browser compatibility. It is a fact of life that every browser implements JavaScript slightly differently from each other. Even the same browser does not interpret JavaScript in the same way in different operating systems. As a result, you have to test your script in various operating systems using various browsers and write multiple versions of code that work in all browsers.

This is where OpenLaszlo comes to rescue. With OpenLaszlo, you only need to write and test once and let it worry about browser compatibility. Needless to say, using OpenLaszlo as your AJAX platform saves an awful lot of time. Support for AJAX started since OpenLaszlo 4.0 (code-named Legals). Prior to this release, OpenLaszlo could only generate Flash. Now you can choose between AJAX and Flash.

Flash

Flash is a technology to jazz up static Web sites. Its history started when talented software developer Jonathan Gay launched FutureSplash Animator in May 1996. As the name implies, this product was focused on animation. At that time, the only way to play back animation in a Web browser was through animated GIF files and Java applets. Gay's product was initially based on a Java applet and it was, as Gay later admitted, awfully slow. Yet, it was interesting because it provided easy animation without programming.

Gay's luck came in August 1996 when he closed a deal with Microsoft, who was smitten by FutureSplash Animator's capability to create, as Gay puts it, "the most TV-like experience on the Internet." Gay was amazed that Microsoft launched MSN that was dependent on a new animation technology from a six-person company!

Another success story followed when Gay signed up Disney Online, who would be using FutureSplash Animator to develop the Disney Daily Blast, a site for small children. In November 1996 Macromedia bought this product and in December 1996 FutureSplash Animator became Macromedia Flash 1.0. Soon Macromedia turned it into one of the most successful software products in history. Macromedia Flash became synonymous with Internet animation. Adobe must still be banging its head against the wall for turning down Gay who offered to sell FutureSpalsh Animator prior to his rendezvous with Microsoft.

Note

More details on the Flash history can be found here:
http://www.macromedia.com/macromedia/events/john_gay/

When first launched, Flash was used solely for producing animation that could play in Web browsers. Its competitor for creating animation without programming was animated GIF files, but Flash movies loaded faster and could be programmed to provide interactivity. Flash took off in no time and has since grown into a full-blown general-purpose programming platform that can be used to take user input, connect to the database, create games and e-learning sites, and many others. Internally, Flash uses vector graphics so image quality is not affected when they are resized.

Today, Flash players (currently at version 8) are available in most browsers, including in Internet Explorer, Netscape Navigator, and Mozilla Firefox. In total, more than 95% browsers in use today can play Flash without manually reinstalling the player. The list of browsers that include the Flash player can be found here:

http://www.macromedia.com/cfusion/knowledgebase/index.cfm?id=
tn_14159

Mozilla FireFox 1.5, the latest version of this open source browser, blocks Flash by default, however. The reason: many people are annoyed with too much animation. However, support for Flash in this browser is still available because a user can simply click on blocked animation if he/she wants to let it run.

> **Note**
>
> If your browser does not support Flash, you can download a Flash player from http://www.macromedia.com/downloads/

Flash is deployed as a ShockWave Format (swf) file and this format specification can be obtained from Macromedia by agreeing to their specification license, which allows software developers to use the ShockWave Format to create applications that generate Flash files. The licensing agreement does not grant you the right to make a Flash player, however. You can view the license here:

```
http://www.macromedia.com/licensing/developer/fileformat/license/
```

OpenLaszlo is possible thanks to this licensing agreement. It is now challenging Macromedia by providing free software for writing Flash.

OpenLaszlo

OpenLaszlo was invented by Laszlo Systems, a company based in San Mateo, California. The main difference between OpenLaszlo and Macromedia Flash is that OpenLaszlo is modeled as an application development suite, rather than a tool for producing movies.

OpenLaszlo comes with a language called LZX, which is based on the familiar XML and JavaScript. As a result, many beginners to OpenLaszlo already feel at home even before they start. An object-oriented programming language, LZX is case-sensitive and event-driven. JavaScript is primarily used for writing event handlers.

An LZX application generates a Flash file or dynamic HTML (DHTML). Choose the latter if you want to deploy your program as an AJAX application. You can write animation, play MP3 files, create e-commerce applications, develop Web Services clients, and so on with it. You can view demos by visiting www.openlaszlo.com In addition, LaszloMail (www.laszlomail.com) is a sleek Web mail application written entirely in LZX.

OpenLaszlo provides a compiler that can convert lzx source files to Flash or DHTML. This compiler was written in Java but understanding Java is not necessary to write LZX applications. All you need to do is install Java and the OpenLaszlo suite. In addition, for smooth compilation, OpenLaszlo uses Apache Tomcat, an open source servlet/JSP container. You can find more information on Tomcat on its Web site:

```
http://tomcat.apache.org/
```

Java Installation

As mentioned previously, the OpenLaszlo compiler is based on Java. Therefore, before you can start compiling LZX programs, you need to download and install the Java Development Kit (JDK) as well as configure some system environment variables.

Downloading and Installing the JDK

The JDKs for Windows, Linux, and UNIX can be downloaded from this URL:

```
http://java.sun.com/j2se/1.5.0/download.jsp
```

Note
The link above will download Java version 5. If you like, you can also use Java 6, which is also already available.

Once you click the link, you'll be redirected to a page that lets you select an installation for your platform: Windows, Linux, or Unix. The 64 bit versions for certain platforms are available. Also, note that the same link also provides the Java Runtime Environment (JRE). However, you need the JDK, and the JDK includes the JRE.

Note
For Macintosh, download the JDK from this URL:
http://developer.apple.com/java/download/

After obtaining the JDK, you need to install it. Installation varies from one operating system to another. These subsections detail the installation process.

Installation on Windows

Installation on Windows is easy. Simply double-click the icon of the executable file you downloaded and follow the instructions.

Installation on UNIX and Linux

On these platforms, the JDK is available in two installation formats.

- Self-extracting binary file. This format can be used to install the JDK in a location you choose and you do not need to be a root user.
- Packages. A compressed file containing packages to be installed.

If you are using the self-extracting binary installation, follow these steps.

1. Use **chmod** to give the file the execute permissions:

   ```
   chmod +x shFile
   ```

   Here, *shFile* is the downloaded sh file for your platform.
2. Change directory to the location where you would like the files to be installed.
3. Run the self-extracting binary. Execute the downloaded file with the path prepended to it. For example, if the file is in the current directory, prepend it with "./" (necessary if "." is not in the PATH environment variable):

   ```
   ./shFile
   ```

If you downloaded the JDK in the package format, see the following URLs:

```
http://java.sun.com/j2se/1.5.0/install-linux.html
http://java.sun.com/j2se/1.5.0/install-solaris.html
```

Configuring System Environment Variables

After you install the JDK, you can start compiling and running Java programs. However, you can only invoke the compiler and the JRE from the location of the **javac** and **java** programs or by including the installation path in your command. To make compiling and running programs easier, it is important that you set the **PATH** environment variable on your computer so that you can invoke **javac** and **java** from any directory.

Setting the Path Environment Variable on Windows

To set the **PATH** environment variable on Windows NT, Windows 2000, and Windows XP, do these steps:

1. Click **Start, Settings, Control Panel**.
2. Double-click **System**.
3. on Windows NT, select the **Environment** tab. On Windows 2000 and Windows XP select the **Advanced** tab and then click on **Environment Variables**.
4. Locate the **Path** environment variable in the **User Variables** or **System Variables** panes. The value of **Path** is a series of directories separated by semicolons. Now, add the full path to the **bin** directory of your Java installation directory to the end of the existing value of **Path**. The directory looks something like:

   ```
   C:\Program Files\Java\jdk1.5.0_<version>\bin
   ```

5. Click **Set**, **OK**, or **Apply**.

Setting the Path Environment Variable on UNIX and Linux

Set the path environment variable on these operating systems depends on the shell you use.

For the C shell, add the following to the end of your **~/.cshrc** file:

```
set path=(path/to/jdk/bin $path)
```

where *path/to/jdk/bin* is the bin directory under your JDK installation directory.

For the Bourne Again shell, add this line to the end of your **~/.bashrc** or **~/.bash_profile** file:

```
export PATH=/path/to/jdk/bin:$PATH
```

Here, *path/to/jdk/bin* is the **bin** directory under your JDK installation directory.

Testing the Installation

To confirm that you have installed the JDK correctly, type **javac** on the command line from any directory on your machine. If you see instructions on how to correctly run **javac**, then you have successfully installed it. On the other hand, if you can only run **javac** from the **bin** directory of the JDK installation directory, your **PATH** environment variable was not configured properly.

Downloading and Installing OpenLaszlo

You can download OpenLaszlo from this site:

```
http://www.openlaszlo.org/download/
```

Both binary and source are available here. For testing and running the examples in this book, you need the binary. The binary comes with installers for different operating systems: Windows, Macintosh, and Linux/Unix.

Note

The OpenLaszlo Development Kit includes Tomcat, an open source servlet/JSP container, that by default runs on port 8080. Make sure that nothing is running on this port prior to installation.

Installation on Windows

OpenLaszlo Windows distribution includes an installer that makes installation nice and easy. The distribution file has the name of openlaszlo-x.y.z-windows.exe, where x.y.z is the version number. For example, the distribution file of OpenLaszlo 4.0 is **openlaszlo-4.0.x-windows.exe**.

To install OpenLaszlo, run the installer and follow the instructions. The installer also creates shortcuts to start and stop the OpenLaszlo servers.

Installation on Linux/Unix

Before you proceed with installation, make sure your browser has Flash. Here is where to download and install it:

```
http://www.macromedia.com/shockwave/download/download.cgi
```

The distribution of OpenLaszlo for Unix/Linux is a gz-compressed tar file. Its name is something like openlaszlo-x.y.z-unix.tar.gz. For example, for version 4.0.0, the name would be openlaszlo-4.0.0-unix.tar.gz. To install, follow these steps.

- Extract the distribution file to a working directory
- Run **the startup.sh** file in the **Server/tomcat-*a.b.c*/bin** directory. Here *a.b.c* is the version of Tomcat included with OpenLaszlo.

Installation on Mac OS X

OpenLaszlo for Macintosh is distributed as a dmg file. Its name is something like openlaszlo-x.y.z-osx-dev-install.dmg, where x.y.z is the version number. For instance, the distribution for version 4.0.0 is the openlaszlo-4.0.0-osx-dev-install.dmg.

The Directory Structure

As shown in Figure I.1, there are three directories created following successful installation.

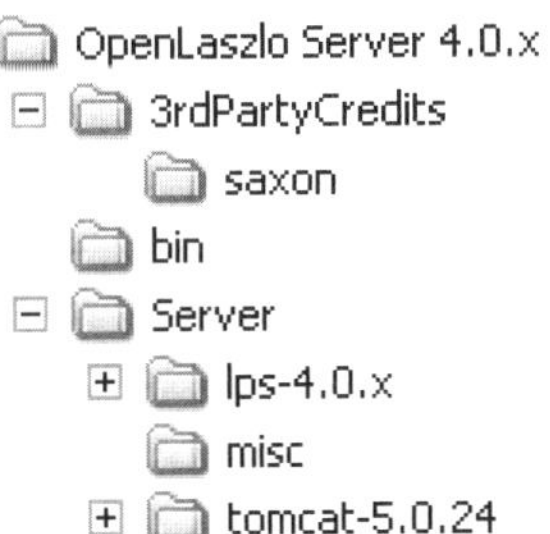

Figure I.1: The directory structure of OpenLaszlo installation

These directories are:

- **3rdPartyCredits**. Contains licenses of open source projects used by the OpenLaszlo server.
- **bin**. Contains scripts for setting environment variables. OpenLaszlo uses these scripts internally and you don't have to deal directly with them.
- **Server**. Contains the OpenLaszlo development kit.

The Server directory has two subdirectories:

- **lps-*x.y.z***, where *x.y.z* is the OpenLaszlo version.
- **misc**. This directory stores various icon files for OpenLaszloe.
- **tomcat-*a.b.c***. Here, *a.b.c* is Tomcat version used to run the OpenLaszlo servlet/JSP application to compile your scripts.

Testing the Installation

To test your installation, start the OpenLaszlo server and direct your browser to this URL:

```
http://localhost:8080/lps-x.y.z/laszlo-explorer/index.jsp
```

Note that you need to replace the *lps-x.y.z* part with the version of OpenLaszlo you downloaded. For example, if you downloaded version 4.0.x, the URL would be

```
http://localhost:8080/lps-4.0.x/laszlo-explorer/index.jsp
```

You will see the OpenLaszlo welcome page as shown in Figure I.2.

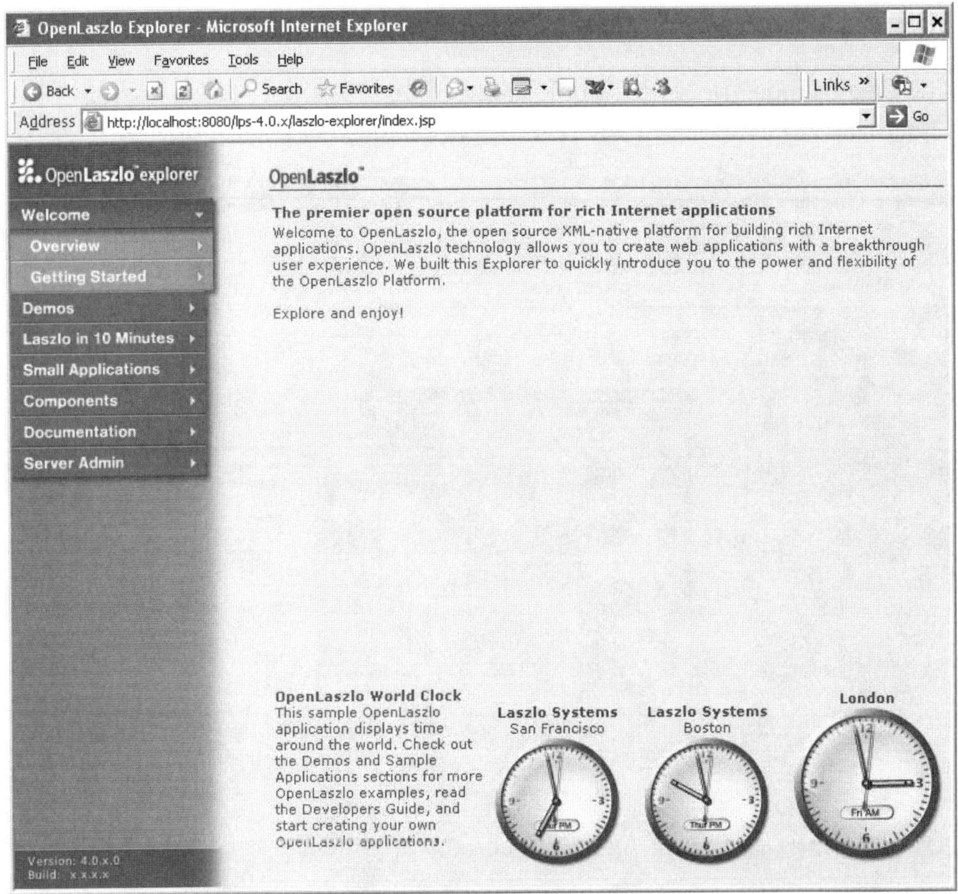

Figure I.2: The OpenLaszlo welcome page

Exploring OpenLaszlo

The OpenLaszlo server comes with sample applications and documentation. It is a good idea to take a tour on what OpenLaszlo can do. Start now by clicking the menu on the left. Each menu is given below.

Demos

The Demos menu presents sample applications that shows off the features in OpenLaszlo. The Demos page is shown in Figure I.3.

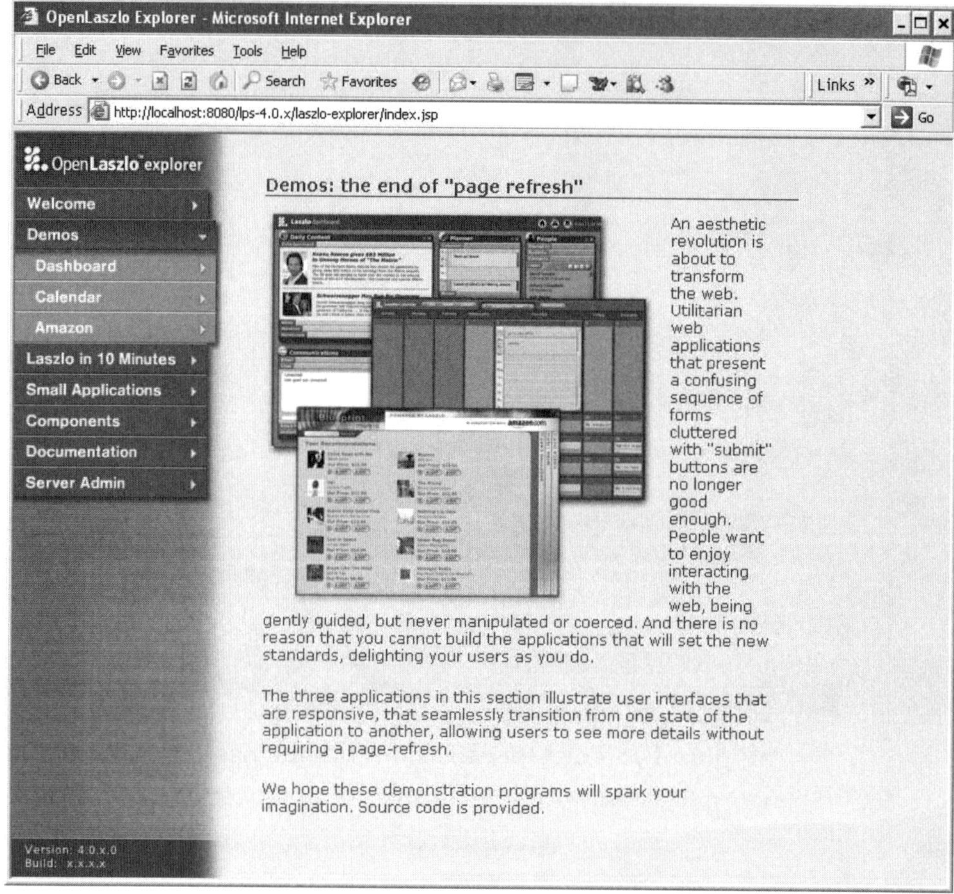

Figure I.3: The Demos page

Currently, Demos presents these full-featured applications.

- Dashboard
- Calendar
- Amazon

Try them to see for yourself the power of OpenLaszlo and be ready to be amazed.

Laszlo in 10 Minutes

Laszlo in 10 Minutes, shown in Figure I.4, allows you to develop applications on the fly. This is explained in Chapter 1, "Starting OpenLaszlo."

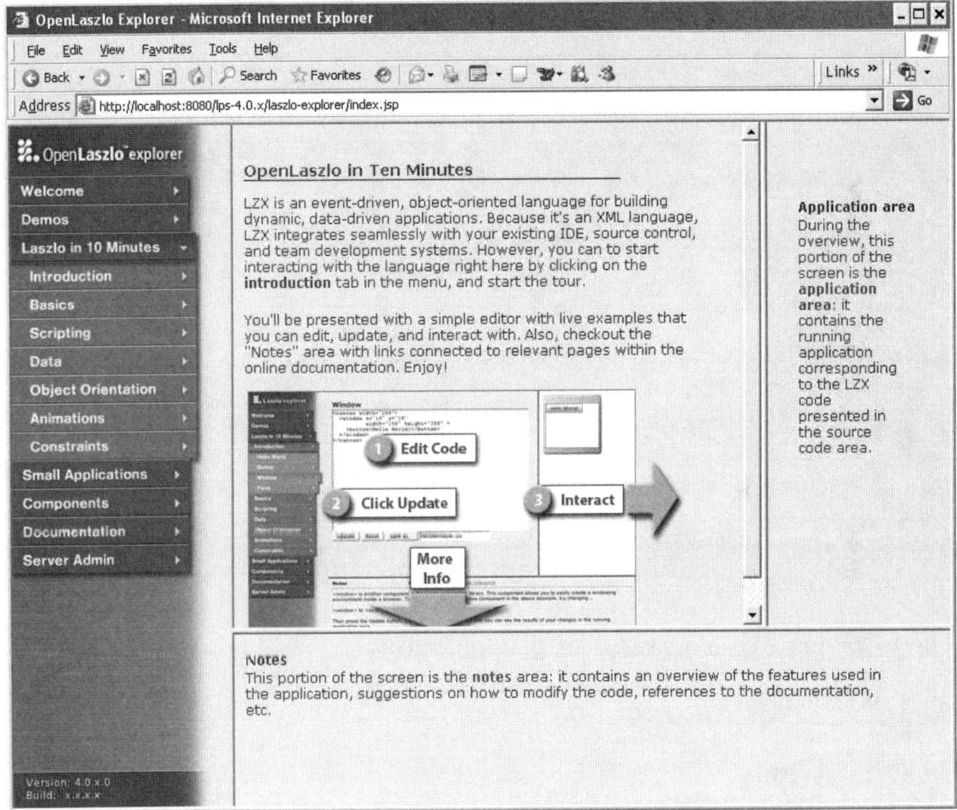

Figure I.4: Laszlo in 10 Minutes

Small Applications

This section features small OpenLaszlo applications. The page is shown in Figure I.5.

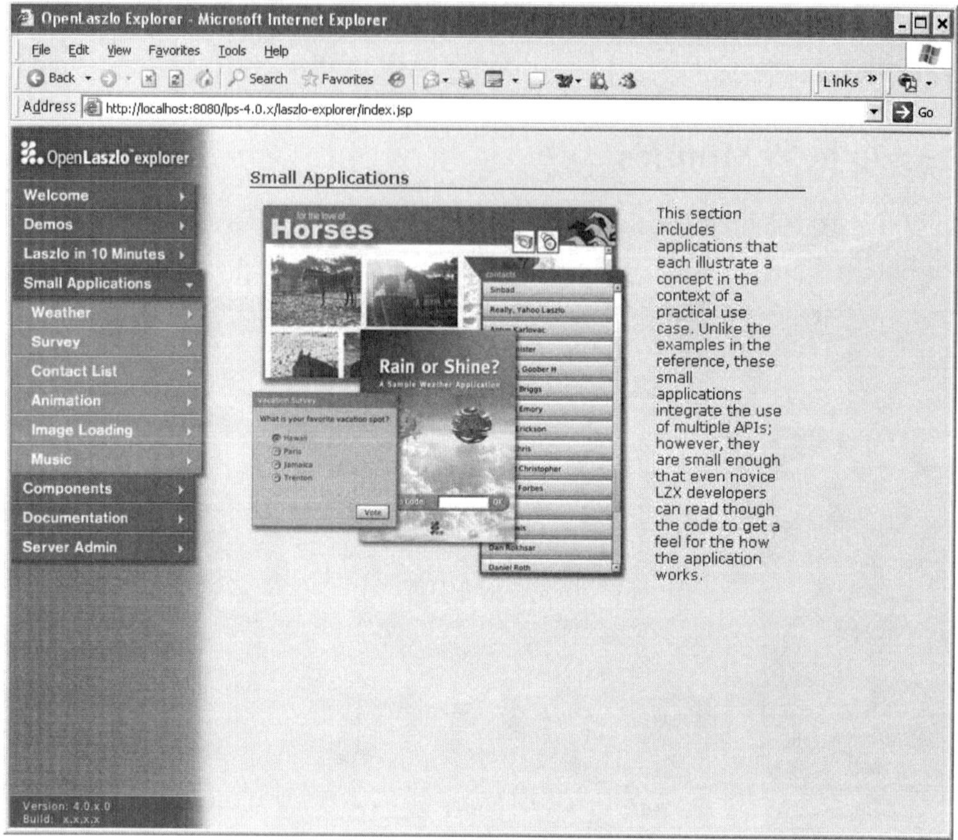

Figure I.5: Small Applications

The following are the featured small applications:

- Weather
- Survey
- Contact List
- Animation
- Image Loading
- Music

Again, you should try these to familiarize yourself with what OpenLaszlo can do.

Components

OpenLaszlo provides built-in components that make programming more rapid. The Components menu, displayed in Figure I.6, shows some of these components.

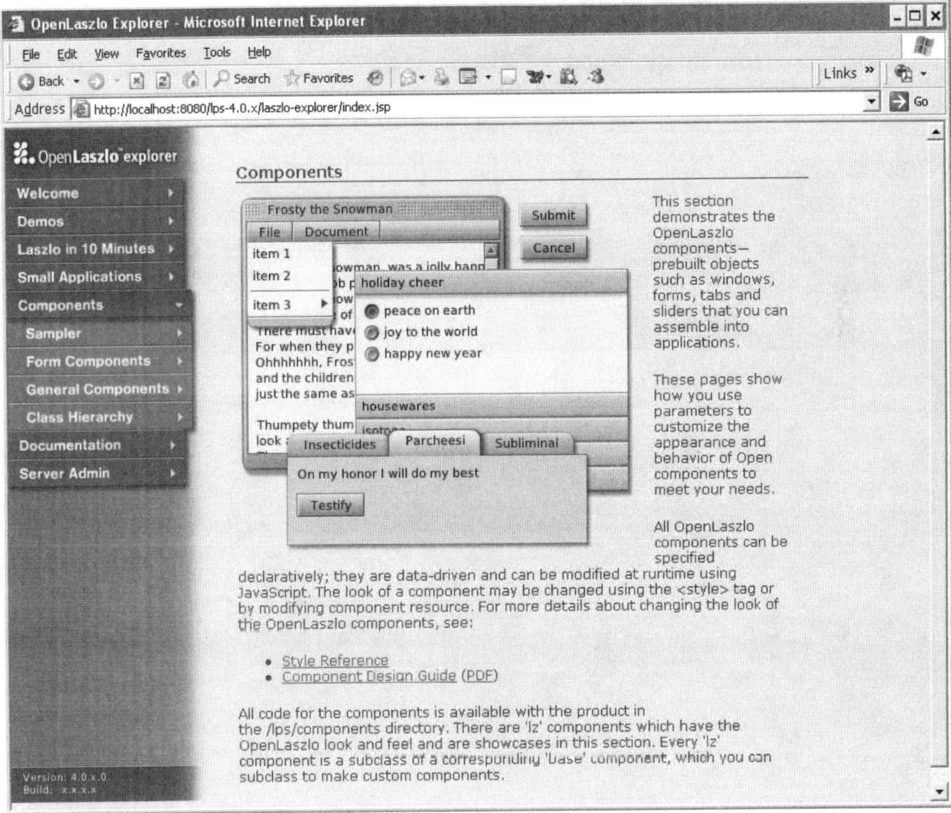

Figure I.6: Components

Various components are available, from the simple Button to the more complex DatePicker. All these components and how to use them will be explained in the chapters to follow.

Documentation

OpenLaszlo is a mature project with plenty of documentation. Documentation is available for software developer and system administrator. In addition, there are also the LZX reference manual and components guide. Figure I.7 shows various types of documentation available in OpenLaszlo.

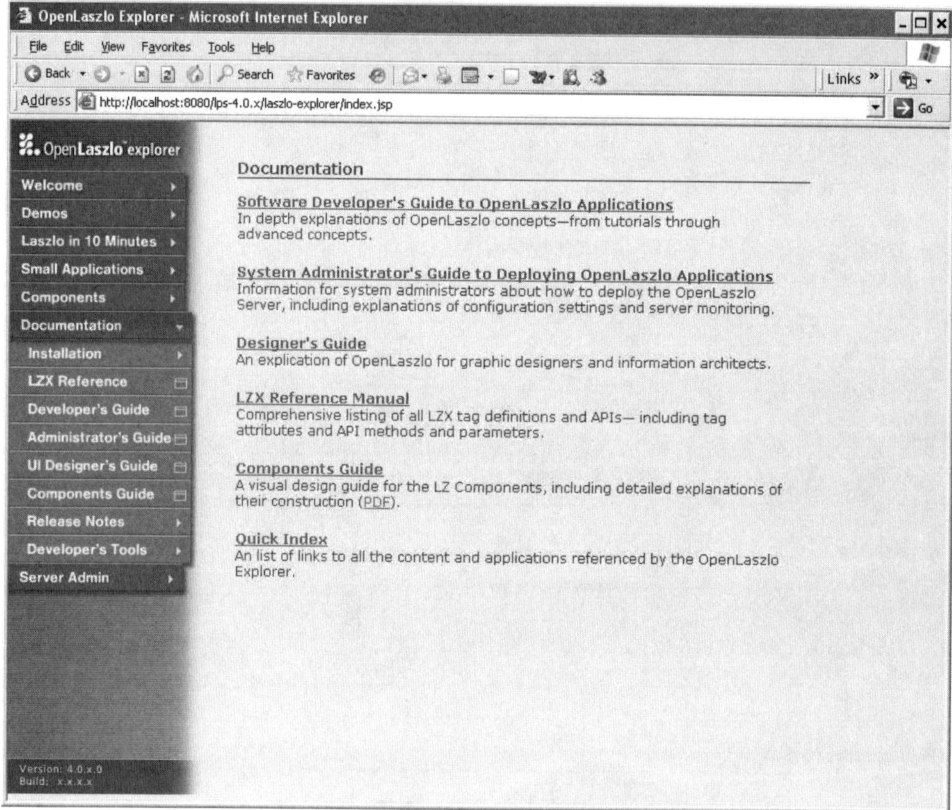

Figure I.7: Documentation

Server Admin

The last menu item within OpenLaszlo Explorer provides tools for administering the OpenLaszlo server. Figure I.8 shows these tools.

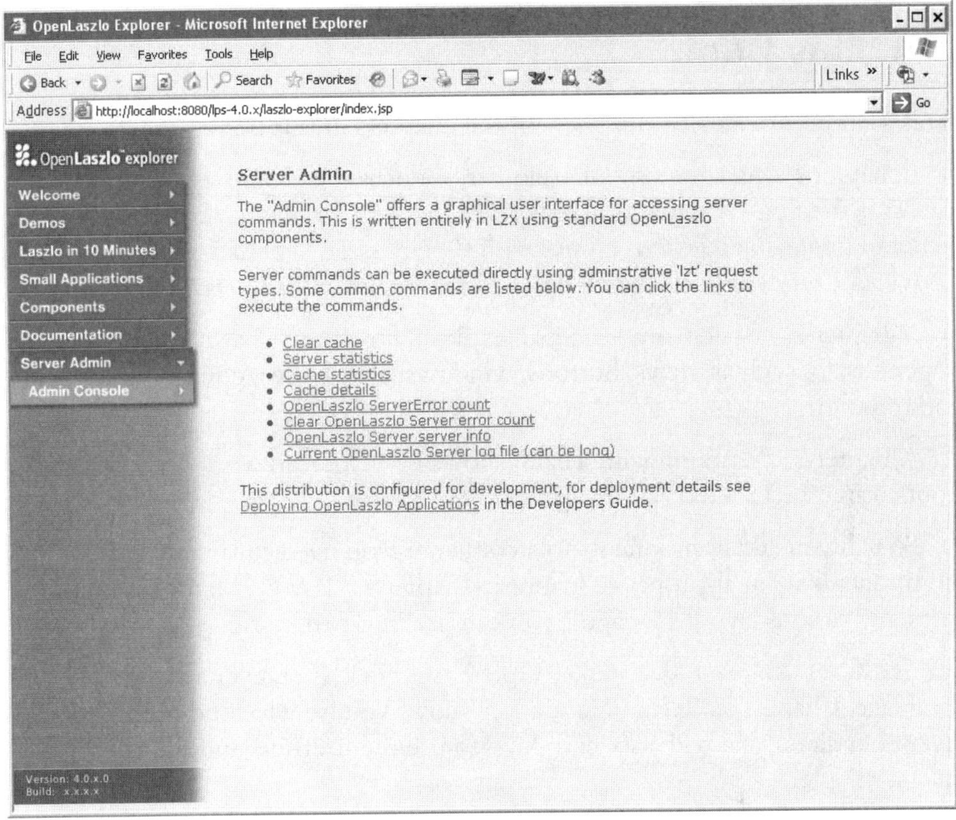

Figure I.8: Server Admin

OpenLaszlo Forum

OpenLaszlo is a popular project that has attracted Flash and AJAX developers from all over the world. A communication forum for these developers has also been created by Laszlo Systems. You can access the forum here:

```
http://www.laszlosystems.com/developers/community/forums/
```

In this forum you can get programming help, find professional OpenLaszlo developers to help with your projects, post applications, or look for an OpenLaszlo job.

About This Book

This section provides an overview of the chapters in this book.

Chapter 1, "Starting OpenLaszlo," introduces the OpenLaszlo server, presents the first OpenLaszlo application that you write and run, and the LZX programming language that comes with OpenLaszlo. OpenLaszlo also provides a set of classes that all descend from the **LzNode** class.

Chapter 2, "Basic Components," explains how to use basic components in OpenLaszlo, such as views, buttons, windows, alert boxes, combo boxes, and radio buttons.

Chapter 3, "Working with Text," shows how you can work with text and fonts using the **LzText**, **LzInputText**, and **LzFont** classes.

When you add components to a container, you need to lay out those components in an appropriate manner. Chapter 4, "Layout Management," presents various layout managers you can use in OpenLaszlo.

LZX, the language that makes OpenLaszlo tick, is an event-based language. Chapter 5, "Event Handling," shows you how to bind objects with event handlers. You will also learn how to use the **method** and **handler** tags in this chapter.

In OpenLaszlo a constraint is the evaluation value of an expression and a state is a conditional constraint. Both provide an easy way to monitor a dynamic value and assign the value to an attribute. Chapter 6, "Constraints and States," explains constraints and states.

Chapter 7, "Animation," discusses how you can make animation in OpenLaszlo using the **animator** and **animatorGroup** tags. In this chapter you will also learn how to use the **LzTimer** class to create a timer.

Chapter 8, "Working with Data," explains how you can access and manipulate data using XPath and the following OpenLaszlo classes: **LzDataset**, **Grid**, and **LzDataPointer**.

Chapter 9, "Working with Menus," teaches you to create and use menu bars, menus, and menu items in OpenLaszlo applications. Menus are handy because they take only little space out of the user screen real estate.

Chapter 10, "Custom Drawing," teaches how you can draw custom shapes using the **LzDrawView** class. Custom drawing is useful in the cases where using standard components is not sufficient.

Chapter 11, "Rich Components," features richer components than those covered in Chapter 2. They include the following classes: **Slider**, **DatePicker**, **ScrollBar**, **Tabs**, **Tabpane**, and **Tree**.

OpenLaszlo comes with hundreds of classes that make up the framework. However, there are circumstances where you need to add more functions to an existing class or change the behavior of a class through inheritance. Chapter 12, "Extending Classes," shows how you can achieve this.

Chapter 13, "Communicating with the Browser," is for those who would like to deploy their OpenLaszlo applications as Flash. This chapter discusses the wrapper HTML page that embeds the Flash file and explains how to call the browser from LZX programs.

Chapter 14, "Debugging and Deployment," explains two topics in OpenLaszlo development process. First, it teaches you how to activate the Debugger window and evaluate variable values and expressions. Second, it explains how you can easily deploy OpenLaszlo applications.

Chapter 15, "Google Maps Application," presents a sample application that uses the Google Maps API to show various location maps.

Appendix A, "Introduction to XML," provides a brief introduction to XML and XML document validation with DTDs and schemas.

Appendix B, "Introduction to JavaScript" provides an introduction to JavaScript.

Downloading Program Examples

The program examples accompanying this book can be downloaded from this location:

```
http://www.brainysoftware.com/download/openLaszloSamples.zip
```

Extract the zip file to the **Server/lps-*x.y.z*** directory under the OpenLaszlo installation directory. Figure I.9 shows where you should extract the sample applications to.

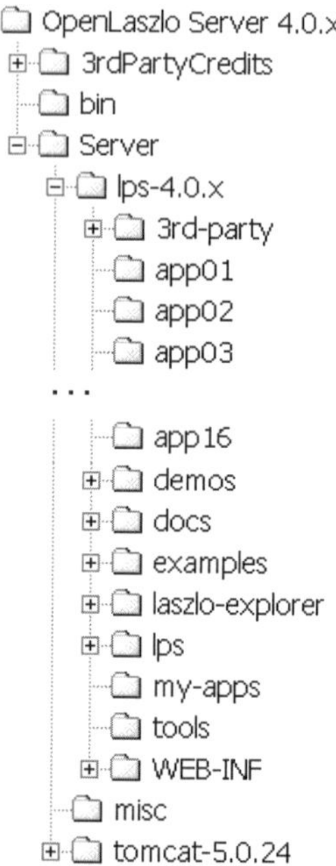

Figure I.9: The OpenLaszlo installation directory after the sample applications are extracted

Chapter 1
Starting OpenLaszlo

OpenLaszlo programs are XML documents, so you can use any text editor to write one. Then, you can use the LZX compiler to convert it to an SWF file or DHTML. A convenient way to pass an OpenLaszlo program to the compiler is by sending a message to the OpenLaszlo Server via a Web browser. Compiling an OpenLaszlo program this way saves time because the OpenLaszlo Server will send the result directly to the browser that will then execute the generated Flash/DHTML.

Because of the importance of the OpenLaszlo Server, we will take time to examine it, learn how to install it, and understand its architecture. The OpenLaszlo Server is the first topic of discussion in this chapter. Afterwards, I will introduce you to LZX, the language used to write OpenLaszlo programs. LZX is an object-oriented programming (OOP) language and OpenLaszlo comes with hundreds of built-in LZX classes that help you write applications more rapidly. All these classes are directly or indirectly derived from the **LzNode** class. As such, the language lesson in this chapter starts by presenting an OOP tutorial followed by a thorough look at the **LzNode** class.

The OpenLaszlo Server

The OpenLaszlo Server is a Java servlet/JSP application. This server makes LZX application development process a breeze. You compile your code by directing your Web browser to the OpenLaszlo server. The server examines the URL and compiles the appropriate source code (LZX file). It then sends the generated output to the browser so that you can view your application. If compilation fails, the server sends a compile error, telling you which line or lines of code caused the error. If there is an error but compilation can continue, the server generates output and sends warning messages.

Because the OpenLaszlo Server is a servlet/JSP application, you need a servlet/JSP engine, which is more often referred to as the servlet/JSP container. You do not need to know about servlet programming to develop LZX applications, but you need to know how to install and run a servlet/JSP container.

There are several free servlet/JSP containers available in the market. Jetty and Tomcat are two of them. The developers of OpenLaszlo have chosen Tomcat as their servlet/JSP container, even though other products can also be used. Alternatively, you can use a J2EE application server to run the OpenLaszlo Server. A J2EE application server always includes a servlet/JSP container but is much more powerful than a servlet/JSP container. The following are examples of J2EE application servers.

- BEA's WebLogic
- IBM's WebSphere
- Sun Microsystems' Sun Java Application Server
- Oracle's 10g Application Server
- GlassFish
- JBoss
- Jonas
- Apache Geronimo

JBoss, Jonas, and Geronimo are open source application servers. They have different licenses, though, so make sure you read them before using the products.

The OpenLaszlo Server can be used in two different environments:

1. As a development platform for easy and fast compilation of OpenLaszlo applications.
2. As a deployment platform to rapidly dispatch and run OpenLaszlo applications.

Note that, albeit more difficult, you can also compile your OpenLaszlo scripts without the OpenLaszlo Server.

The architecture of the OpenLaszlo development platform is given in Figure 1.1. The diagram shows a client that requests output to be sent as a Flash file. For DHTML no Flash player needs to be present in the browser.

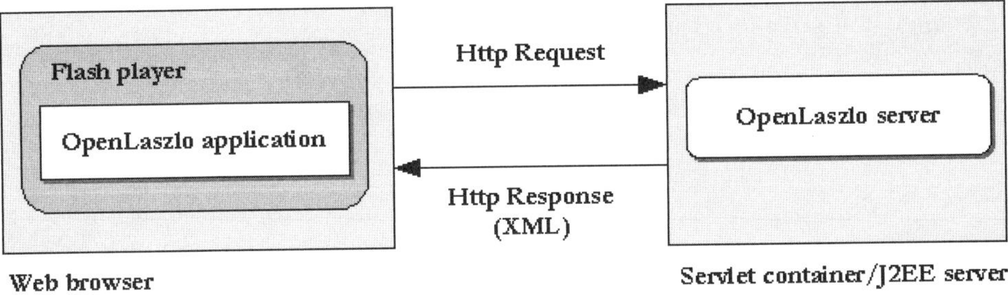

Figure 1.1: The OpenLaszlo development platform architecture

The development process can be summarized as follows. You write your code and save it as an lzx file in the specified directory. You then use a Web browser to send an HTTP request to the OpenLaszlo Server, which in turn compiles your code and generates a Flash file. The OpenLaszlo Server sends the Flash file to the browser and the browser automatically plays it.

Let's now create an OpenLaszlo application to get the feel of the development process.

Your First OpenLaszlo Application

The steps for developing an OpenLaszlo application are as follows.

1. Write your OpenLaszlo program (in XML and JavaScript) using a text editor.
2. Save the file as an lzx file.
3. Compile the lzx file to an swf file or DHTML, either manually or by using the OpenLaszlo server.

You can then run the output in a Web browser.

The steps are described in the following subsections.

Writing an OpenLaszlo Application

As mentioned before, an OpenLaszlo application is an XML document. Therefore, you can use any text editor to write your code. The code in Listing 1.1 is a simple LZX application.

Listing 1.1: A simple example

```
<canvas height="150" width="200" bgcolor="yellow" >
    <view width="150" height="100" bgcolor="white">
        <button text="OpenLaszlo"
                onclick="setAttribute('text', 'rocks')"/>
    </view>
</canvas>
```

Saving the Source File

Now, save the script as the **firstLaszlo.lzx** file. The file must be saved in the **Server/lps-4.0.x** directory under the OpenLaszlo Server installation directory or a directory under it. If you have downloaded the zip file that contains sample applications for this book and extracted them as explained in Introduction, you already have subdirectories under the **Server/lps-4.0.x** directory. You can find the **firstLaszlo.lzx** file under the **app01** subdirectory.

Compiling and Running the Script

The easiest way to compile an lzx file is by using the OpenLaszlo Server. Make sure that Tomcat is running on your computer, and then direct your browser to the following URL:

```
http://localhost:8080/lps-4.0.x/path
```

Here, *path* is the path to the lzx file relative to the **Server/lps-4.0.x** directory under the OpenLaszlo Server installation directory. For example, if your script is saved as the **firstLaszlo.lzx** file under the **app01** directory under **Server/lps-4.0.x** directory, you use this URL to compile your OpenLaszlo application.

```
http://localhost:8080/lps-4.0.x/app01/firstLaszlo.lzx
```

The servlet container will pass your HTTP request to the OpenLaszlo Server. The latter opens and compiles the correct lzx file, generates the output, and saves it in a temporary directory. The OpenLaszlo Server then sends the generated output to the browser.

If the application is compiled as Flash, the generated swf file and related files are cached, so subsequent requests for the same unmodified lzx file will be much faster because no recompilation needs to be performed. If the compilation failed, an error message will be displayed on the browser.

For this OpenLaszlo application, you will see a Flash application displayed in your browser, as shown in Figure 1.2.

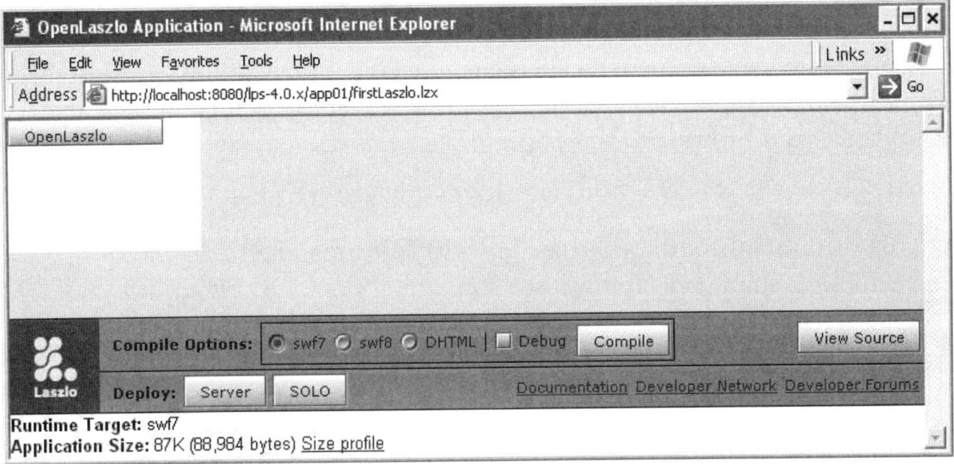

Figure 1.2: Your first OpenLaszlo program

There are two parts in the browser window. The top part is the output of your application. There is a button that says "OpenLaszlo" on top of a white rectangle, placed inside a bigger yellow rectangle. If you click the button, the text on it will change to "rocks."

The bottom part is a development tool containing buttons that allow you to view your OpenLaszlo source code, deploy your application, recompile the source code, and perform other functions. There is also some information at the bottom of Figure 1.2 that says that the runtime target is Flash 7 and the size of the Flash file is 88,984 bytes.

To save space, the bottom part will not be shown for other applications in this book.

On-the-Fly Development

Laszlo Systems, the company that invented OpenLaszlo, provides the on-the-fly development mode. In this mode you do not even need to write your code in an lzx file or install Tomcat. You just need to open a Web page and type your code there.

To test the on-the-fly development mode, direct your Web browser to this URL.

```
http://www.laszlosystems.com/lps/laszlo-in-ten-minutes/
```

The on-the-fly development mode is also available locally if you have installed Tomcat and the OpenLaszlo Server. Make sure that Tomcat is running and then direct your browser to this page:

```
http://localhost:8080/lps-4.0.x/laszlo-explorer/index.jsp
```

On the menu on the left, click **Laszlo in 10 Minutes**, then click its **Introduction** submenu. You will see something similar to Figure 1.3.

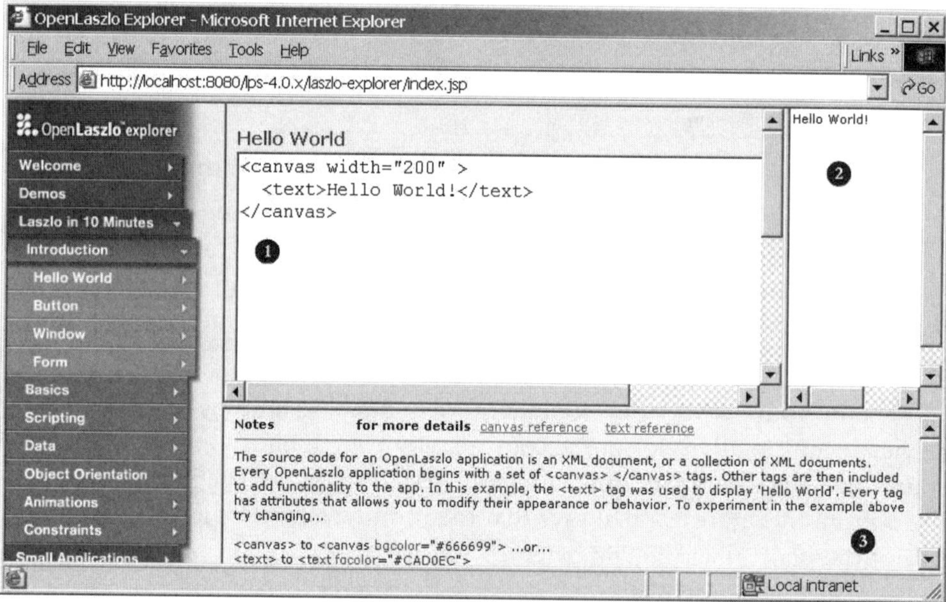

Figure 1.3: On-the-fly development

You will see three panes, numbered 1, 2, and 3. In the first pane, you write your script. Once you are finished, click the Update button at the bottom of the first pane. This will send an HTTP request to the server that will then compile your code. The result will be displayed on the second pane. Make sure you save your script every now and then by clicking the Save as button.

The third pane provides a quick reference on OpenLaszlo language syntax.

An Overview of Object-Oriented Programming

Now that you've seen how easy it is to write an OpenLaszlo application, let's take a look at OOP. Because LZX is an OOP language, OOP skills are crucial to creating effective OpenLaszlo applications.

Object-oriented programming (OOP) works by modeling applications on real-world objects. Three principles of OOP are encapsulation, inheritance, and polymorphism. LZX supports all the three.

The benefits of OOP are real. These are the reason why most modern programming languages, including LZX, are object-oriented (OO). I can even cite two well-known examples of language transformation to support OOP: The C language evolved into C++ and Visual Basic was upgraded to Visual Basic.NET.

This section explains the benefits of OOP and provides an assessment of how easy or hard it is to learn OOP.

The Benefits of OOP

The benefits of OOP include easy code maintenance, code reuse, and extendibility. These benefits are detailed below.

1. **Ease of maintenance.** Modern software applications tend to be very large. Once upon a time, a "large" system comprised a few thousand lines of code. Now, even those consisting of one million lines are not considered that large. When a system gets larger, it starts giving its developers problems. Bjarne Stroustrup, the father of C++, once said something like this. A small program can be written in anything, anyhow. If you don't quit easily, you'll make it work, at the end. But a large program is a different story. If you don't use techniques of "good programming," new errors will emerge as fast as you fix the old ones. The reason for this is there is interdependency among different parts of a large program. When you change something in some part of the program, you may not realize how the change might affect other parts. OOP makes it easy to make applications modular, and modularity makes

maintenance less of a headache. Modularity is inherent in OOP because a class, which is a template for objects, is a module by itself. A good design should allow a class to contain similar functionality and related data. An important and related term that is used often in OOP is coupling, which indicates the degree of interaction between two modules. Loosely coupling among parts make code reuse—another benefit of OOP—easier to achieve.

2. **Reusability**. Reusability means that code that has previously been written can be reused by the code writer and others who need the same functionality provided by the original code. It is not surprising, then, that an OOP language often comes with a set of ready-to-use libraries. In the case of LZX, the language is accompanied by hundreds of built-in classes that have been carefully designed and tested. It is also easy to write and distribute your own library. Support for reusability in a programming platform is very attractive, because it shortens the time taken to develop an application.

   One of the main challenges to class reusability is creating good documentation for the class library. How fast can a programmer find a class that provides the functionality he/she is looking for? Is it faster to find such a class or write a new one from scratch? Fortunately, LZX core classes come with decent documentation and examples.

   Reusability does not only apply to the coding phase through the reuse of classes and other types; when designing an application in an OO system, solutions to OO design problems can also be reused. These solutions are called design patterns. To make it easier to refer to each solution, each pattern is given a name. The early catalog of reusable design pattern can be found in the classic book *Design Patterns: Elements of Reusable Object-Oriented Software*, by Erich Gamma, Richard Helm, Ralph Johnson, and John Vlissides.

3. **Extendibility**. Every application is unique. It has its own requirements and specifications. In terms of reusability, sometimes you cannot find an existing class that provides the exact functionality that your application requires. However, you will probably find one or two that provide part of the functionality. Extendibility means that you can still use those classes by extending them so that they suit your need. You still save time, because you don't have to write code from scratch.

   In OOP, extendibility is achieved through inheritance. You can extend an existing class, add some methods or data to it, or change the behavior of the methods you don't like. If you know the basic functionality that will be used in many cases, but you don't want your class to provide very specific functions, you can provide a generic class that can be extended later to provide functionality specific to an application.

What Is an LZX Object?

When developing an application in an OOP language, you create a model that resembles a real-life situation to solve your problem. Take for example a company payroll application, which can calculate the take home pay of an employee and the amount of income tax to be paid. An application like this would have a **Company** object to represent the company using the application, **Employee** objects that represent the employees in the company, **Tax** objects to represent the tax details of each employee, and so on. Before you can start programming such applications, however, you need to understand what objects are and how to create them.

Let's begin with a look at objects in life. Objects are everywhere, living (persons, pets, etc) and otherwise (cars, houses, streets, etc); concrete (books, televisions, etc) and abstract (love, knowledge, tax rate, regulations, and so forth). Every object has two features: attributes and actions the object is able to perform. For example, the following are some attributes of a car:

- color
- number of tires
- plate number
- number of valves

Additionally, a car can perform these actions:

- run
- brake

As another example, a dog has the following attributes: color, age, type, weight, etc. And it also can bark, run, urinate, sniff, etc.

An LZX object also has attributes(s) and can perform actions. In LZX methods are called functions. In other languages, attributes are often called fields.

Both attributes and methods are optional, meaning that some LZX objects may not have attributes but have methods and some others may have attributes but not methods. Some, of course, have both attributes and methods and some have neither.

How do you create LZX objects? This is the same as asking, "How do you make cars?" Cars are expensive objects that need careful design that takes into account many things, such as safety and cost-effectiveness. You need a good blueprint to make good cars. To create LZX objects, you need similar blueprints: classes.

LZX Classes

A class is a blueprint or a template to create objects of identical type. If you have an **Employee** class, you can create any number of **Employee** objects. To create **Street** objects, you need a **Street** class. A class determines what kind of objects you get. For example, if you create an **Employee** class that has **age** and **position** attributes, all **Employee** objects created out of this **Employee** class will have **age** and **position** attributes as well. No more no less. The class determines the object.

In summary, classes are an OOP tool that enables programmers to create the abstraction of a problem. In OOP, abstraction is the act of using programming objects to represent real-world objects. As such, programming objects do not need to have the details of real-world objects. For instance, if an **Employee** object in a payroll application needs only be able to work and receive a salary, then the **Employee** class needs only two methods, **work** and **receiveSalary**. OOP abstraction ignores the fact that a real-world employee can do many other things including eat, run, kiss, and kick.

Classes are the fundamental building blocks of an OpenLaszlo program. All program elements in LZX must reside in a class and every class must be saved as an lzx file. You need to consider three things when writing a class:

- the class name
- the attributes
- the methods

In the first few chapters of this book, you will learn how to use standard classes that come with the LZX compiler. Chapter 12, "Extending Classes" discusses how to write your own classes.

Note

In UML class diagrams, a class is represented by a rectangle that consists of three parts: the topmost part is the class name, the middle part is the list of attributes, and the bottom part is the list of methods. (See Figure 1.4) The attributes and methods can be hidden if showing them is not important.

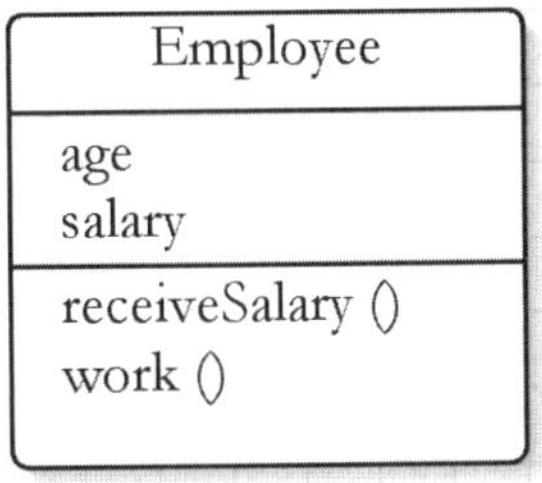

Employee

age
salary

receiveSalary ()
work ()

Figure 1.4: The Employee class in the UML class diagram

Attributes

Attributes are variables. For example, the **Employee** class in Figure 1.4 has two attributes, **age** and **salary**. An attribute can reference a simple data type such as an integer or a complex type such as an object.

Methods

Methods define actions that the objects (or instances) of a class can do. A method has a declaration part and a body. The declaration part consists of a return value, the method name, and a list of arguments. The body contains code that perform the action.

To declare a method, use the **method** tag.

```
<method name="methodName" [args="listOfArguments"]>
```

The **args** attribute is optional.

For example, here is a method named **addNumbers** that accepts two arguments.

```
<method name="add" args="a,b">
    return (a + b);
</method>
```

Note

Actually, there are two other class members in LZX, events and handlers, which will be explained in Chapter 5, "Event Handling."

Class Members in UML Class Diagrams

Figure 1.4 depicts a class in a UML class diagram. The diagram provides a quick summary of all attributes and methods. You could do more in UML. UML allows you to include attribute types and method signatures. For example, Figure 1.5 presents the **Book** class with five attributes and one method.

```
                        Book
________________________________________________
height  : Integer
isbn  : String
numberOfPages  : Integer
title  : String
width  : Integer
________________________________________________
getChapter (Integer chapterNumber) : Chapter
```

Figure 1.5: Including class member information in a class diagram

Note that in a UML class diagram a colon separates an attribute and its type. A method's argument list is presented in parentheses and its return type is written after a colon.

Case Sensitivity

OpenLaszlo 4 applications can be compiled into swf7, swf8, or DHTML. If the version is not specified, swf7 will be used. Identifiers in LZX programs are case-sensitive. For example, having two global variables called **myData** and **MyData** will generate a compile error.

LZX Programs

An LZX program is also a valid XML document. If you are not familiar with XML, please take time to read and understand Appendix A, "Introduction to XML."

Inside an LZX program, you use programming syntax similar to JavaScript. Appendix B provides a brief tutorial on JavaScript.

Creating an Object

There are two ways to create an object in LZX, by using the tag associated with a class and by using the **new** keyword in a JavaScript script. For example, every application must have exactly one canvas, to which all other components are added. To create a canvas, you use the **canvas** tag like this.

```
<canvas>

</canvas>
```

You can nest tags to create an object within an object. For example, the following code creates a canvas and then a view component inside the canvas.

```
<canvas>
    <view bgcolor="0x00ffdd">
    </view>
</canvas>
```

In this case, the view will be a child of the canvas.

Note
The root of an LZX application must be **canvas**.

You can use the **script** tag to write JavaScript code. Note that the **script** tag can only be nested within the **canvas** tag. It is a compile error to write it as a child tag of other tags. For example, Listing 1.2 shows an LZX application that uses a script to change the background color of a view from lime to red.

Listing 1.2: Using scripts

```
<canvas width="400">
    <view name="v1" width="150" height="100" bgcolor="lime"/>
```

```
    <script.>
        canvas.v1.setAttribute("bgcolor", 0xFF0000);
    </script>
</canvas>
```

You can compile and run this program by using this URL:

```
http://localhost:8080/lps-4.0.x/app01/scriptTest.lzx
```

To create an object programmatically, you can use the **new** keyword with a class's constructor:

```
var obj = new LzView();
```

For example, the code in Listing 1.3 shows how to create a view using the **new** keyword.

Listing 1.3: Using the new keyword to create an object

```
<canvas width="400">
    <script>
        var v1 = new LzView(canvas, {width: 200, height: 50,
                bgcolor: green, name: "myView"});
        myView.setX(100);
    </script>
</canvas>
```

To test this program, use this URL:

```
http://localhost:8080/lps-4.0.x/app01/newKeywordTest.lzx
```

Because an LZX source must be a valid XML document, you must encode XML special characters, such as < and >, that occur in your scripts. An easier way is to enclose scripts with **<![CDATA[** and **]]>**. For example, Listing 1.4 is a rewrite of the code in Listing 1.3.

Listing 1.4: Securing scripts with a special block

```
<canvas width="400">
    <script>
    <![CDATA[
        var v1 = new LzView(canvas, {width: 200, height: 50,
                bgcolor: green, name: "myView"});
        myView.setX(100);
    ]]>
    </script>
</canvas>
```

As you read through this chapter and the next, you will find more about programming with LZX.

Using the attribute Tag

You can set an object's attribute by specifying the attribute name and value in the object's tag. For example, the following **view** tag specifies the **width** attribute.:

```
<view width="50"></view>
```

You can also use the **attribute** tag to set an attribute. The **view** tag above can be rewritten as:

```
<view>
    <attribute name="width" value="50"/>
</view>
```

Note that you use the **name** and **value** attributes inside the **attribute** tag to specify the name and value of the attribute, respectively. To access and set an attribute from a method, you use the **getAttribute** and **setAttribute** methods of the **LzNode** (See the next section, "The LzNode Class").

Using the Debug Tool

OpenLaszlo provides a helpful debugging tool. You can display the value of a variable and display any runtime error messages. To use the debug tool, use the debug attribute of the **canvas** tag:

```
<canvas debug="true">
```

Using the **debug** attribute will display the Debugger window as shown in Figure 1.6.

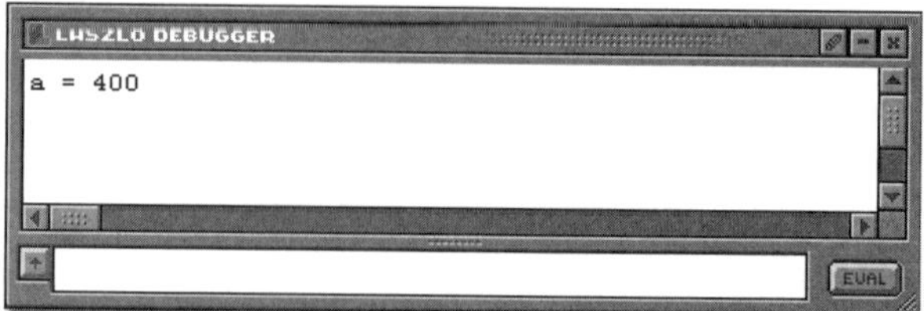

Figure 1.6: The Debugger window

You can configure the Debugger window by using the **debug** tag. For example, this **debug** tag sets the width and the height of the Debugger window that will be displayed.

```
<debug width="400" height="130"/>
```

Bear in mind that the **debug** tag can only be written as a direct child tag of the **canvas** tag.

From inside an LZX application, you can write to the Debugger window by using its **write** method:

```
Debug.write("a = " + a);
```

The Debugger window will be discussed further in Chapter 14, "Debugging and Deployment."

The LzNode Class

The **LzNode** class is the ultimate parent of all LZX classes. It defines attributes, methods, and events that are inherited by all LZX objects. Here is the **LzNode** class's constructor:

```
LzNode(parent, args)
```

Here, *parent* is the parent of the new **LzNode** object and *args* is a collection of attribute name/value pairs that are to be applied to the new object.

The more important child classes of **LzNode** are shown in Figure 1.7.

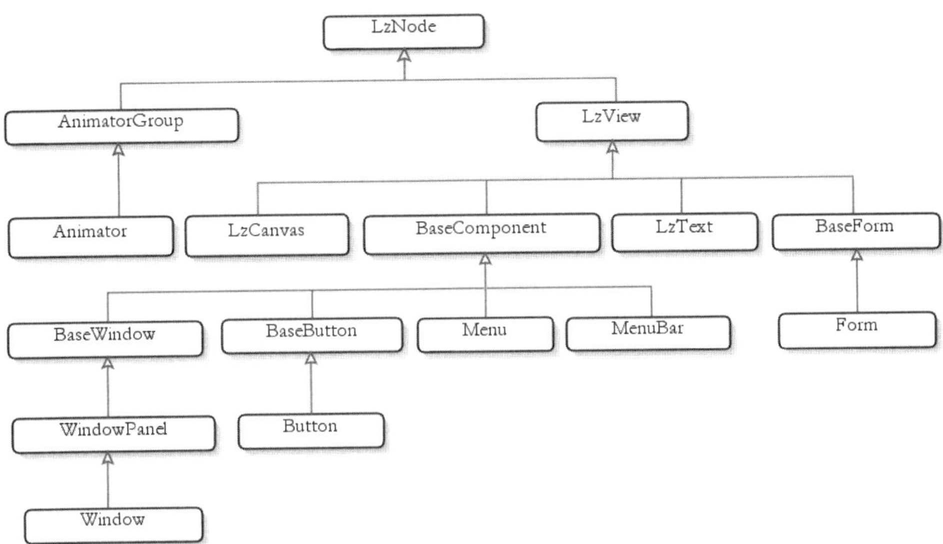

Figure 1.7: The more important subclasses of LzNode

These classes will be discussed in Chapter 2 and subsequent chapters.

We will now examine the attributes and methods of the **LzNode** class. Table 1.1 lists the attributes of the **LzNode** class. You will use this as a reference, so don't worry if you do not understand them the first time you read this. For now, bear in mind there are two important attributes that identify an **LzNode** object: **id** and **name**. The **id** attribute must be unique throughout the application and provides a convenient way of referencing an object. The **name** attribute must be unique within a context and you must qualify its parents to reference it.

Note

JS in the Usage column in Table 1.1 indicates Javascript.

Name	Usage	Type	Default	Accessibility
classroot	JS only	LzNode		read-only
	Description. A reference to the instance of the **class** tag in which this node is defined. This is a convenient shortcut to access a node from another node nested deep in the node hierarchy. For example, instead of writing **parent.parent.parent.aMethod**, you can use **classroot.aMethod**.			
cloneManager	JS only	LzNode		read-only

	Description. The **LzReplicationManager** that controls this node upon replication.			
datapath	Tag and JS	LzDataPath		read-only
	Description. A pointer to the **LzDataPath** object attached to this node, if one exists.			
defaultplacement	Tag and JS	string		read-only
	Description. A non-null value forces this node to run its **determinePlacement** method for any subnodes of this node. If a subnode has a different **placement** attribute, **determinePlacement** will be invoked with that value.			
id	Tag and JS	string		read-only
	Description. A global identifier for this node that must be unique throughout the whole application. Compare it with the **name** attribute that must be unique only in a context.			
ignoreAttribute	JS only	boolean		read-only
	Description. Setting an argument attribute to this value in the construct routine of a subclass of **LzNode** will prevent further processing of the attribute.			
immediateparent	JS only	LzNode		read-only
	Description. The immediate parent of this node. **immediateparent** is different from the **parent** attribute in that when a class uses **placement** or **defaultplacement** to assign a subnode a specific place. For instance, you always use immediateparent to obtain the mouse position of a view.			
initstage	Tag only		normal	Final
	Description. Determines the execution of the **init** method. The valid values are as follows: **immediate.** The init method is called immediately as the last phase of instantiation. **early.** The init method is called immediately after the view and its children have been instantiated. **normal.** The init method is called when this node's parent is initialized. **late.** The init method is called during idle time. After the init method is called, the **isinited** property is set to **true**. **defer.** The **init** method will not be called unless specifically invoked by the **completeInstantiation** method.			
name	Tag and JS	string		read-only
	Description. An identifier for this node that must be unique within a context. Compare with the **id** attribute that must be unique throughout the application.			

nodeLevel	JS only	number		read-only
	Description. The depth of this node in the node hierarchy.			
onconstruct	JS only	script		event handler
	Description. The event handler for the **construct** event, which is triggered at the end of the instantiation process but before any subnode is created or any reference resolved.			
oninit	Tag only	script		event handler
	Description. This event handler is called after the element's sub-elements have been initialized. This handler is only called once.			
parent	JS only	LzNode		read-only
	Description. The parent of this node. If this node is created by using the tag, the parent is the tag enclosing the tag.			
placement	Tag only	String		final
	Description. Defines the placement of this node within its container's internal hierarchy.			
subnodes	JS only	array		read-only
	Description. An array of all subnodes.			

Table 1.1: The attributes of the LzNode class

Here are the methods of the **LzNode** class

```
animate(property, to, duration, isRelative, args)
```
Animates a property. The parameters are as follows.
- *property*. Specifies the property to animate.
- *to*. The end value of the animation.
- *duration*. The duration of the animation in milliseconds.
- *isRelative*. Specifies if the value of the to argument is applied relative to the current value.
- *args*. A dictionary of attributes to pass to the **LzAnimator** constructor.

See Chapter 7, "Animation" for a complete discussion of animation.

```
applyConstraint(property, cFunction, dep)
```
Applies a constraint to the specified attribute. The arguments are as follows.
- *property*. The attribute to which this constraint is to be applied.
- *cFunction*. The function that specifies the constraint.
- *dep*. An array of attribute pairs on which the constraint depends.

```
applyData(data)
```

Invoked on this **LzNode** if its datapath matches a terminal selector, such as **text()** or **@***attribute* when the matching data changes.

`childOf(`*`node`*`)`

Tests if the specified node is a parent (either direct or indirect) of this node. Returns either **true** or **false**.

`completeInstantiation()`

Ensures this node's children have been created and this node initialized.

`construct(`*`parent, args`*`)`

This method is the first method to be called when this **LzNode** is constructed. If you override this method, you must call **super.construct(*parent, args*)**.
The arguments are as follows.

- *parent*. The parent of this node, i.e. the node to which to attach this node.
- *args*. A dictionary of attribute name/value pairs used to initialize this node.

`createChildren(`*`children`*`)`

Instantiates the subnodes. The argument *children* is an array of children.

`dataBindAttribute(`*`attribute, path`*`)`

Binds the named attribute to the specified path, relative to this node's datapath. This method is called when the $path{} constraint is present. The arguments are as follows.

- *attr*. The name of the attribute to bind to the specified path.
- *path*. The xpath to which to bind the attribute.

`destroy(`*`recursive`*`)`

Deletes the node and all the subnodes. The *recursive* argument is either **true** or **false** and is for internal use only.

`determinePlacement(`*`subnode, placement, args`*`)`

Returns the immediate parent of the specified subnode, which must be a direct or an indirect child of this node. The arguments are

- *subnode*. The subnode whose immediate parent is to be determined.
- *placement*. The placement attribute for the returned subnode.
- *args*. A dictionary of attribute name/value pairs for the returned subnode.

`getAttribute(`*`attribute`*`)`

Returns the value of the specified attribute.

```
getOption(key)
```
Returns the value of the specified key.

```
getUID()
```
Returns this node's unique identifier.

```
init()
```
This method is invoked when the **oninit** event is raised.

```
lookupSourceLocator(sourceLocator)
```
Returns the **LzNode** that matches the *sourceLocator* argument. If no match was found, returns **undefined**.

```
searchSubnodes(attribute, value)
```
Returns the subnode that matches the specified attribute and value.

```
setAttribute(attribute, value)
```
Assigned the specified value to the specified attribute.

```
setDatapath(xpath)
```
Sets the datacontext for the node to the specified xpath.

```
setID(id)
```
Assigns the specified identifier to this node.

```
setName(name)
```
Sets the name of this node.

```
setOption(key, value)
```
Sets the specified key with the specified value.

Including Libraries

OpenLaszlo allows a program to be divided into smaller files for the sake of modularity. It achieves this by introducing the **include** tag. The resource that is to be included in another file must have the **library** tag as its topmost tag. For example, the code in Listing 1.5 includes the code in Listing 1.6.

Listing 1.5: Using the include tag

```
<canvas height="100">
    <include href="include.lzx"/>
</canvas>
```

Listing 1.6: The included resource

```
<library>
    <radiogroup>
        <radiobutton text="New York"/>
        <radiobutton text="Chicago"/>
        <radiobutton text="Seattle"/>
    </radiogroup>
</library>
```

It is effectively the same as the following code:

```
<canvas height="100">
    <radiogroup>
        <radiobutton text="New York"/>
        <radiobutton text="Chicago"/>
        <radiobutton text="Seattle"/>
    </radiogroup>
</canvas>
```

Note that changes to an include file will be reflected the next time the LZX
application is invoked.

Comments

Proper commenting helps code readability. There are three types of comments
you can use in your LZX applications.

1. XML comments: <!--   -->
2. OpenLaszlo comments <?ignore ... ?>
3. Script comments (used in scripts), which are the same as JavaScript
   comments:

```
// or /* */
```

For example, the code in Listing 1.7 uses two of the three comment types:

Listing 1.7: Using comments

```
<!-- the main file -->
<canvas height="100">
    <?ignore you can select one of three cities ?>
    <radiogroup>
        <radiobutton text="New York"/>
```

```
        <radiobutton text="Chicago"/>
        <radiobutton text="Seattle"/>
    </radiogroup>
</canvas>
```

Summary

This chapter provides an introduction to LZX programming. It also showed how to write an LZX application and presented a tutorial on OOP. Towards the end, it discussed the **LzNode** class, the **include** tag, and three comment types.

Chapter 2
Basic Components

OpenLaszlo comes with a set of classes that represent simple and rich components that make LZX programming easier and more rapid. Because of the sheer number of these components, discussion has to be divided into several chapters. This chapter explains basic components that you use most often. Chapter 3, "Working with Text" focuses on working with text and fonts and Chapter 11, "Rich Components" discusses more complex components that are more powerful but not used that often.

The discussion in this chapter starts with the **LzView** class, a class that represents a visible rectangular area that can contain other components. Afterwards, the **LzCanvas** class is discussed. Then, the **Basecomponent** class is explained. The latter is the parent class of all OpenLaszlo components. Basic components covered in this chapter include **Window**, **Button**, **RadioButton**, **ComboBox**, and **List**.

View

A view represents a rectangular area that can display text and other elements. You can create a view using the **view** tag or by instantiating the **LzView** class. Because **LzView** is the superclass of every LZX component class, it is important to learn all its methods and attributes. Table 2.1 lists the attributes of the **LzView** that you can use within the **view** tag.

Name	Usage	Type	Default	Accessibility
align	Tag only	string	left	final
	Description. The alignment for subviews. The valid values are **left**, **center**, and **right**.			
bgcolor	Tag and JS	color value	0x000000	read-write
	Description. The background color of this view. See the sidebar "Color Values."			
clickable	Tag and JS	boolean	false	read-write
	Description. Determines whether this view is clickable. A clickable view can raise the **onclick** event and respond to a mouse click.			
clip	Tag only	boolean	false	final
	Description. If this attribute is set to **true**, the resource and children of this view will only be displayed to this view's width and height.			
cursor	Tag and JS	string		read-write
	Description. References a resource, such as an icon, that will be displayed as the cursor when the mouse pointer is over this view.			
fgcolor	Tag and JS	color value		read-write
	Description. The foreground color.			
focusable	Tag and JS	boolean	false	read-only
	Description. If this attribute is set to **true**, this view can receive focus and therefore can raise focus-related events.			
focustrap	Tag and JS	boolean		read-write
	Description. If this attribute is set to **true**, this view can trap the focus.			
font	Tag and JS	string		read-write
	Description. The font to draw text element in this view.			
fontsize	Tag and JS	number	8	read-write
	Description. The pixel size to use to render text in this view.			
fontstyle	JS only	string	plain	read-write
	Description. The style for the font used to draw text elements in this view. The valid values are **plain**, **bold**, **italic**, and **bolditalic**.			
frame	Tag and JS	number	0	read-write
	Description. Specifies the frame being displayed by the resource referenced by this view.			
framesloadratio	JS only	number		read-only
	Description. The ratio of the loaded frames and the number of frames. The value must be between 0 and 1 (inclusive).			
hassetwidth	JS only	boolean		read-only

	Description. A value of **true** indicates that the **setHeight** method has been called on this view and the view will not be resized to fit its contents.			
hassetwidth	JS only	Boolean		read-only
	Description. A value of **true** indicates that the **setWidth** method has been called on this view and the view will not be resized to fit its contents.			
height	Tag and JS	number		read-write
	Description. The height of this view.			
layout	Tag and JS	string		read-write
	Description. The layout manager used to lay out subviews. See the discussion of the layout manager in Chapter 4.			
loadratio	JS only	number		read-only
	Description. The ratio of the loaded bytes to the number of bytes of the resource associated with this view. The value is between 0 and 1 (inclusive).			
mask	JS only	LzView		read-only
	Description. Reference to the closest masked view in the hierarchy above this view.			
onblur	Tag only	script		event handler
	Description. The script assigned to this attribute is invoked when the **onblur** event fires.			
onclick	Tag only	script		event handler
	Description. The script assigned to this attribute is invoked when the **onclick** event is raised.			
ondata	Tag and JS	script		event handler
	Description. The script assigned to this attribute is invoked when the **ondata** event fires.			
ondblclik	Tag only	script		event handler
	Description. The script assigned to this attribute is invoked when the **ondblclick** event fires.			
onfocus	Tag only	script		event handler
	Description. The script assigned to this attribute is invoked when the **onfocus** event fires.			
onkeydown	Tag and JS	script		event handler
	Description. The script assigned to this attribute is invoked when the **onkeydown** event fires.			
onkeyup	Tag and JS	script		event handler
	Description. The script assigned to this attribute is invoked when the **onkeyup** event fires.			

onmousedown	Tag only	script		event handler
	Description. The script assigned to this attribute is invoked when the **onmousedown** event is raised.			
onmouseout	Tag only	script		event handler
	Description. The script assigned to this attribute is invoked when the **onmouseout** event fires.			
onmouseover	Tag only	script		event handler
	Description. The script assigned to this attribute is invoked when the **onmouseover** event fires.			
onmouseup	Tag only	script		event handler
	Description. The script assigned to this attribute is invoked when the **onmouseup** event fires.			
onselect	Tag and JS	script		event handler
	Description. The script assigned to this attribute is invoked when the **onselect** event fires.			
opacity	Tag and JS	number	1.0	read-write
	Description. The opacity of this view. A value of 0.0 makes this view completely transparent.			
options	Tag only	css		final
	Description. A list of CSS property names and values that configure the behavior of corresponding objects, such as data binding and view layout, that operate on this view.			
pixellock	Tag only	boolean	false	final
	Description. A value of **true** turns on the snap-to-grid feature.			
play	Tag and JS	boolean	true	read-write
	Description. A value of **true** causes this view to play the attached resource.			
resource	Tag and JS	string		read-write
	Description. The name of the resource associated with this view.			
resourceheight	JS only	number		read-only
	Description. The height of the resource associated with this view.			
resourcewidth	JS only	number		read-only
	Description. The width of the resource associated with this view.			
rotation	Tag and JS	number	0	read-write
	Description. The rotation value in degrees. The value must be between 0 and 360 (inclusive).			
selected	JS only			read-only
	Description. Setting this attribute calls the **setSelected** method.			

selectiontype	Tag and JS	string	any	read-write
	Description. The selection type for this view. The value can be one of the following: **none, single, toggle, multi, range**.			
showhandcursor	Tag and JS	boolean		read-write
	Description. Shows or hides the handcursor for this view, if this view is clicable.			
source	JS only	string		read-write
	Description. The URL from which to load the resource for this view.			
stretches	Tag and JS	string	any	read-write
	Description. Determines how the view should stretch to fit the resource and subviews. Valid values are **width**, **height**, **both**, and **any**. A value of **any** causes stretching to be disabled.			
subviews	JS only			read-only
	Description. Returns an array of subviews.			
totalframes	JS only	number		read-only
	Description. The number of frames for this view's resource.			
unstretchedheight	JS only	number		read-only
	Description. The height, in pixels, of the view if stretching were turned off.			
unstretchedwidth	JS only	number		read-only
	Description. The width, in pixels, of the view if stretching were turned off.			
valign	Tag and JS	string	top	read-write
	Description. The vertical alignment. The valid values are top, middle, and bottom.			
visible	Tag and JS	boolean	true	read-write
	Description. Indicates if this view is visible.			
width	Tag and JS	number		read-write
	Description. The width of this view.			
x	Tag and JS	number		read-write
	Description. The x position of this view.			
xoffset	Tag and JS	number	0	read-write
	Description. The left margin of this view from the container.			
xscale	Tag and JS	number	1.0	read-write
	Description. The horizontal scaling applied to the view's resource.			
y	Tag and JS	number	0	read-write
	Description. The y position of this view.			
yoffset	Tag and JS	number	0	read-write

	Description. The top margin of this view from the container.			
yscale	Tag and JS	number	1.0	read-write
	Description. The vertical scaling applied to the view's resource.			

Table 2.1: The LzView class's attributes

Color Codes

You will be working with colors all the time when programming OpenLaszlo. You will set a component's background and foreground colors, the color of the text component, of a border, and so on. It is therefore crucial to understand how OpenLaszlo translates a value into color representation. If you have worked with HTML, this is nothing new to you.

A color is composed of three components: red, green, and blue (RGB). Each component may have one of 256 intensity levels, represented by the hexadecimal numbers 00 to FF. A color is the combination of these three components. For instance, black is a color whereby its components all have an intensity level of 0, i.e. 0x000000. White is where all have the maximum intensity level or 0xFFFFFF. There are therefore 256 x 256 x 256 or 1.67 million colors possible in OpenLaszlo.

Because it is easier to work with color names than with numbers, OpenLaszlo defines the following constants that you can use:

- black 000000
- green 008000
- silver C0C0C0
- lime 00FF00
- gray 808080
- olive 808000
- white FFFFFF
- yellow FFFF00
- maroon 800000
- navy 000080
- red FF0000
- blue 0000FF
- purple 800080
- teal 008080
- fuchsia FF00FF

> - aqua 00FFFF
>
> Therefore, instead of writing 0xFF0000, you can simply say "red."

The following are methods defined in the **LzView** class.

addProxyPolicy(*function*)
Adds a function that decides how the media referenced by a given URL will be loaded. The function argument specifies the function that takes a URL and returns one of the following: "server", "none" or null. "server" indicates that the request should be proxied by the LPS server; "none" indicates that it should be made directly to the server. Null indicates that the request should be passed to the next policy function in the list.

addSubview(*subview*)
Adds the specified subview to this view.

bringToFront()
Causes this view to be the frontmost subview of its parent.

containsPt(*x, y*)
Returns **true** if the coordinate (x, y) is within this view.

getAttributeRelative(*attribute, referenceView*)
Sets the **width/height/x/y** attribute to match the corresponding attribute of *referenceView*.

getBounds()
Returns an object with the following **x, y, width, height, xoffset**, and **yoffset** properties that reflect this view's bounds.

getColor()
Returns a number that describes the RGB components of the view's color. For example, 0x00ff00 is green.

getColorTransform()
Returns an object that represents the color transformation applied to this view. This object has the following keys:

- **o.ra**. The percentage alpha for the red component (-100 to 100)
- **o.rb**. The offset for the red component (-255 to 255)
- **o.ga**. The percentage alpha for the green component (-100 to 100)
- **o.gb**. The offset for the green component (-255 to 255)

- **o.ba**. The percentage alpha for the blue component (-100 to 100)
- **o.bb**. The offset for the blue component (-255 to 255)
- **o.aa**. The overall percentage alpha (-100 to 100)
- **o.ab**. The overall offset (-255 to 255)

`getCurrentTime()`

> Returns the time that has elapsed since the view's resource started to play.

`getDepthList()`

> Returns an array of subviews in depth order.

`getHeight()`

> Returns the height of the view.

`getID3()`

> If this view's resource is associated with an MP3 file loaded with the proxy turned off, this method returns an object containing the media's id3 tag.

`getMouse(axis)`

> If axis is x, returns the horizontal position of the mouse relative to this view. If axis is y, returns the vertical position of the mouse relative to this view.

`getPan()`

> Returns a number between −100 and 100 that represents the pan level of the associated resource.

`getTotalTime()`

> Returns the amount of time to play the resource.

`getVolume()`

> Returns a number between 0 to 100 that represents the volume level of the associated resource.

`getWidth()`

> Returns this view's width.

`init()`

> This method is called at initialization, right before the view is displayed.

`measureHeight()`

> Returns the height of the contents of the view.

`measureWidth()`

> Returns the width of the contents of the view.

`play(`*`frame, relative`*`)`

Start playing the associated resource. The optional frame argument indicates the starting frame. If it is not specified, the resource will play at the current frame. If the *relative* argument is **true**, *frame* is relative to the current frame. Otherwise, it is relative to the first frame.

`removeProxyPolicy(`*`function`*`)`

Removes the specified proxy policy function.

`searchParents(`*`property`*`)`

Search parent views having the named property and returns the first one found as an **LzView** object.

`searchSubviews(`*`property, value`*`)`

Search all subviews having the specified property name and value and returns the first one.

`seek(`*`seconds`*`)`

Skips the associated resource forward or backward in seconds. A negative value of seconds indicates a skip backward.

`sendBehind(`*`anotherView`*`)`

Sends this view behind the specified view. The specified view must be a sibling of this view.

`sendInFrontOf(`*`anotherView`*`)`

Sends this view in front of the specified view, which must be a sibling of this view.

`sendToBack()`

Sends this view behind all its siblings.

`setAlign(`*`align`*`)`

Sets this view's alignment. The value can be one of "left", "center", and "right".

`setAttributeRelative(`*`property, refView`*`)`

Assigns the value of the specified property of *refView* to the same property of this view.

`setBGColor(`*`color`*`)`

Sets the background color of this view.

`setClickable(`*`clickable`*`)`

The *clickable* argument is a boolean. A value of **true** makes this value clickable, a value of **false** makes it not clickable.

`setColor(color)`

Sets the color of this view and its subviews.

`setColorTransform(dictionary)`

Transforms this view colors, except its background color, using the specified dictionary. The dictionary must have the following keys:

- **o.ra**. The percentage alpha for the red component (-100 to 100)
- **o.rb**. The offset for the red component (-255 to 255)
- **o.ga**. The percentage alpha for the green component (-100 to 100)
- **o.gb**. The offset for the green component (-255 to 255)
- **o.ba**. The percentage alpha for the blue component (-100 to 100)
- **o.bb**. The offset for the blue component (-255 to 255)
- **o.aa**. The overall percentage alpha (-100 to 100)
- **o.ab**. The overall offset (-255 to 255)

`setContextMenu(contextMenu)`

Adds menu items that will be displayed upon the user clicking the right-mouse button.

`setCursor(cursor)`

Sets the cursor to the given resource when the mouse is over this view. The cursor argument specifies the name of the resource that will be used.

`setHeight(height)`

Sets this view's height.

`setLayout(layout)`

Sets the layout manager of this view. The *layout* argument specifies a dictionary of attributes that describe the layout. See Chapter 4 on layout management for more information about the layout manager.

`setOpacity(opacity)`

Sets this view's opacity. The opacity argument must be a number between 0.0 and 1.0.

`setPan(pan)`

Sets the pan of the associated resource.

`setPlay(start)`

If start is **true**, starts playing the associated resource. If *start* is **false**, stops playing the associated resource.

`setResource(resourceName)`

Sets the resource of this view.

`setResourceNumber(number)`

This method takes effect if called on a view whose associated resource has multiple frames. The number argument specifies the index of the frame to be displayed.

`setRotation(angle)`

Sets the rotation of the view.

`setShowHandCursor(show)`

If *show* is **true**, shows the hand cursor. If *show* is **false**, hides the hand cursor.

`setSource(url, cache, headers)`

Causes this view to load its media from the specified URL at runtime. The *cache* argument controls the caching behavior. Its value is one of "none", "clientonly", "serveronly" and "both" (the default). The *headers* argument is a string to send with the request.

`setValign(vAlign)`

Sets the vertical alignment of this view. The *vAlign* argument can be one of these: "top", "middle", and "bottom".

`setVisible(visible)`

If the *visible* argument is **true**, causes this view to be visible. If the *visible* argument is **false**, causes this view to be invisible.

`setVolume(volume)`

Sets the volume level of the associated resource. The *volume* argument must be a number between 0 and 100 (inclusive).

`setWidth(width)`

Sets the width of this view.

`setX(x)`

Sets the x position of this view.

`setY(y)`

Sets the y position of this view.

`stop(frameIndex, relative)`

Stops playing the associated resource. If the *frameIndex* argument is present, stops playing at the specified frame. If the *relative* argument is **true**, the *frameIndex* argument is relative to the current frame. If it is **false**, the *frameIndex* argument is relative to the first frame.

```
stretchResource(axis)
```
Stretches the view to the height and/or the width of the associated resource. The axis argument is either "x" or "y". If the axis argument is not presents, stretches the view in both direction.

```
unload()
```
Unloads the associated resource.

```
updateResourceSize()
```
Forces the view to update its size.

In addition to attributes and methods, the **LzView** class also defines several events. These events will be discussed in Chapter 5, "Event Handling."

As an example, Listing 2.1 displays an LZX application that uses the **view** tag.

Listing 2.1: The viewTest1.lzx file

```
<canvas width="300" bgcolor="#ddddee">
    <view align="center" bgcolor="white" width="200"
          height="150"/>
</canvas>
```

You can call this application by using this URL:

```
http://localhost:8080/lps-4.0.x/app02/viewTest1.lzx
```

Figure 2.1 shows the output generated from the **viewTest1.lzx** file.

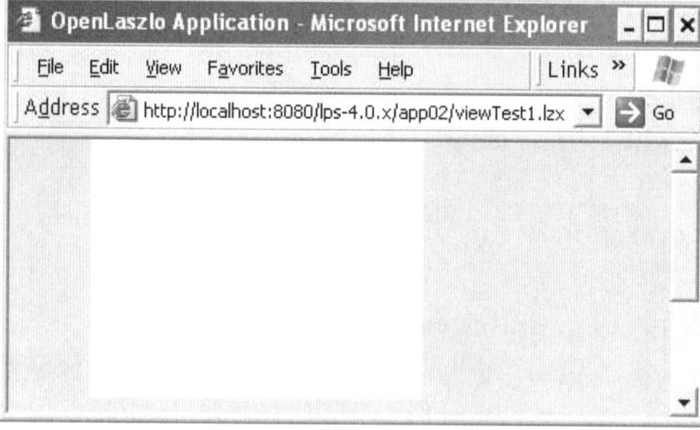

Figure 2.1: Using View

As you can see in Figure 2.1, the view appears as a white rectangle.

Nested Views

In a typical LZX application, you often use multiple views, nested within each other. Listing 2.2 shows an LZX application with nested views.

Listing 2.2: Nested views

```
<canvas height="370">
    <view width="150" height="150" bgcolor="black">
        <view width="100" height="100" bgcolor="white">
            <view width="50" height="50" bgcolor="gray"/>
        </view>
    </view>
</canvas>
```

Invoke the LZX application by directing your browser to this URL:

```
http://localhost:8080/lps-4.0.x/app02/viewTest2.lzx
```

Figure 2.2 shows the nested views.

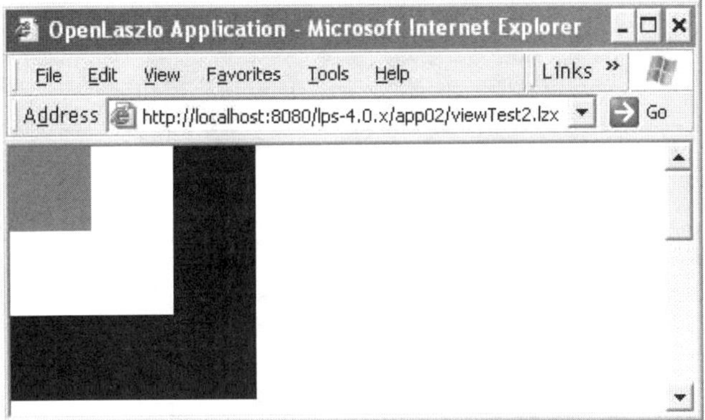

Figure 2.2: Nested views

The first view has a width and a height of 150 pixels. It is black in color. The second view is drawn on top of the first view, white and 100 x 100 pixels in size. The third view, the gray one, is on top of the second view.

Displaying External Resources

You can use the **view** tag to display or play external resources, such as images, MP3 files, and other Flash files. The media types supported are JPG (JPEG),

GIF, PNG, MP3, and SWF. Note that support for MP3 is limited to audio files sampled at 44.1 khz, 22 Khz, 11 Khz, 8khz, and 5.5Khz.

For example, Listing 2.3 shows an LZX application that uses **view** to display an image.

Listing 2.3: Displaying an image

```
<canvas height="360" bgcolor="white">
    <view align="center" resource="panda.jpg"/>
</canvas>
```

Invoke the LZX application using this resource locator:

```
http://localhost:8080/lps-4.0.x/app02/viewTest3.lzx
```

Figure 2.3 shows the generated Flash file.

Figure 2.3: Displaying an image

The **resource** attribute in Listing 2.3 is assigned a relative URL. In this case, the file **panda.jpg** must be in the same directory as the lzx file. You can, however, assign an absolute URL to a resource on the Internet.

As another example, the code in Listing 2.4 is an LZX application that uses **view** to play a Flash file.

Listing 2.4: Playing Flash

```
<canvas height="360" bgcolor="white">
    <view align="center"
          resource="logo.swf"/>
</canvas>
```

Use this URL to compile and run the code in Listing 2.4:

```
http://localhost:8080/lps-4.0.x/app02/viewTest4.lzx
```

The result is shown in Figure 2.4.

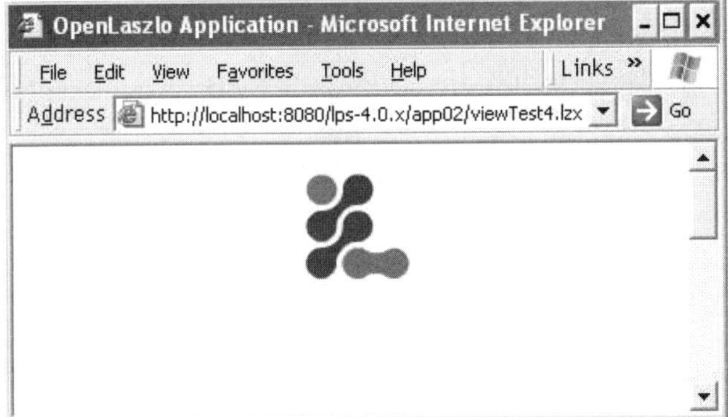

Figure 2.4: Playing an external Flash

Canvas

The **canvas** tag represents the topmost container for all views and elements in an LZX application and there is exactly one canvas for each LZX application. The **LzCanvas** class is the class that will be instantiated when the LZX compiler encounters the **canvas** tag. This class is a subclass of **LzView**.

Table 2.2 lists the attributes defined in the **LzCanvas** class.

Name	Usage	Type	Default	Accessibility
build	JS only	string		read-only
	Description. The build number of the LPS that generated this Flash. For .lzo files, this attribute specifies the server that generated the optimized file, not the one that served it.			
dataloadtimeout	Tag and JS	number		read-only
	Description. The number of milliseconds the application will wait for data loading before it times out.			
datasets	JS only			read-only
	Description. The dictionary of all named datasets in this application.			
debug	Tag and JS	boolean	false	read-write
	Description. Indicates if debugging is enabled. The Debug window will be displayed if debugging is enabled.			
embedfonts	Tag and JS	boolean	true	read-write
	Description. Indicates if the fonts used in this application should be embedded.			
expires	JS only	string		read-only
	Description. The expiration date of this application.			
libraries	Tag and JS	string		read-write
	Description. A list of names of libraries included in this application.			
lpsrelease	JS only	string		read-only
	Description. The release number of the LPS that generated this application. For .lzo files, this is the release number of the server that generated the optimized the file, not the one serving it.			
lpsversion	JS only	string		read-only
	Description. The version number of the LPS that generated this application. For lzo files, it is the version number of the server that generated the optimized file, not the one serving it.			
maxtextheight	Tag and JS	number		read-write
	Description. The maximum height of any output text field in pixels.			
maxtextwidth	Tag and JS	number		read-write
	Description. The maximum width of any output text field in pixels.			
medialoadtimeout	Tag and JS	number		read-only
	Description. The number of milliseconds the application will wait the media loading operation before it times out.			
onpercentcreated	JS only			read-only

	Description. Invoked when the number of created nodes changes.			
percentcreated	JS only			read-only
	Description. A number between 0 and 1 (inclusive) that represents the percentage of the application that has been instantiated.			
proxied	Tag and JS	boolean		read-only
	Description. Indicates whether or not runtime requests should be proxied.			
title	Tag and JS	string	Laszlo Application	read-write
	Description. The title of the browser that plays the generated Flash.			
validate	Tag and JS	boolean	true	read-write
	Description. Indicates if the application source will be validated against the schema during compilation.			
version	Tag and JS	string		read-only
	Description. The version for this LZX application.			

Table 2.2: The attributes defined in the LzCanvas class

The following are methods defined in the **LzCanvas** class:

```
compareVersion(version, anotherVersion)
```
Compares two version strings. It returns -1 if the *version* argument is less than *anotherVersion*, 0 if *version* is equal to *anotherVersion*, and 1 if *version* is larger than *anotherVersion*.

```
setContextMenu(cMenu)
```
Sets *cMenu* as the right click menu for the canvas.

```
setDefaultContextMenu(cMenu)
```
Sets *cMenu* as the right click menu on the canvas and the default menu for all views.

For example, the code in Listing 2.5 shows how to use the canvas tag and some of its attributes.

Listing 2.5: Using the canvas tag

```
<canvas title="Testing Canvas" width="300" height="200"
        bgcolor="#ddddee">
    <text>OpenLaszlo is cool.</text>
</canvas>
```

You can use a double quote or a single quote to enclose an attribute value. However, for consistency, the double quote will be used throughout this book.

You can compile and run the code in Listing 2.5 by using this URL:

```
http://localhost:8080/lps-4.0.x/app02/canvasTest1.lzx
```

The result is shown in Figure 2.5.

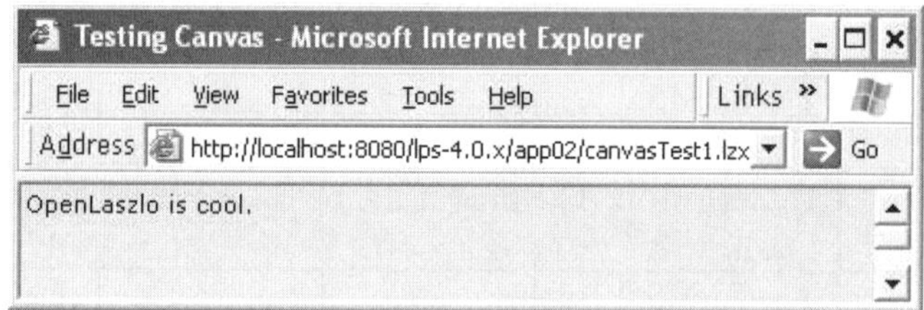

Figure 2.5: Using canvas

Note that the **canvas** tag in Listing 2.5 specifies the string "Testing Canvas" as the value of its title attribute. This value is displayed as the browser title.

The background of the HTML page follows the canvas background color. As such, the right border is not visible here. However, if you reduce the width to 100, you will see the text truncated.

If the width is not specified, the generated output will occupy the whole width of the browser. If the height attribute is not present, the generated output will fill the whole height of the browser.

The BaseComponent Class

The **BaseComponent** class is a subclass of **LzView** and the superclass of all LZX components. It is therefore worthwhile to spend some time examining its attributes and methods.

The attributes defined in the **BaseComponent** class are given in Table 2.3.

Name	Usage	Type	Default	Accessibility
doesenter	Tag and JS	boolean	false	read-write
	Description. If set to **true**, the component manager will call the **doEnterDown** and **doEnterUp** methods on this component.			
enabled	Tag and JS	boolean	true	read-write
	Description. Indicates if the component is enabled. An enabled component is also clickable and a disabled component is not clickable.			
hasdefault	Tag and JS	boolean	false	read-write
	Description. Indicates if this component can receive enter key events.			
isdefault	Tag and JS	boolean	false	read-write
	Description. Indicates if this component will be the default and therefore will receive the enter key.			
style	Tag and JS	boolean		read-write
	Description. If the value of this attribute is null, the style is set to the inherited style from the parent component.			
styleable	Tag and JS	boolean	true	read-write
	Description. Indicates if style should be applied to this component.			
text	Tag and JS	html		read-write
	Description. The label or title of this component.			

Table 2.3: The attributes of the BaseComponent class

The following are methods added to the **BaseComponent** class.

```
doEnterDown()
```
Called when the enter key goes down and the component has the focus and its **doesenter** attribute is set to **true**.

```
doEnterUp()
```
Called when the enter key goes up and the component has the focus and its **doesenter** attribute is set to **true**.

```
doSpaceDown()
```
Called when the space bar goes down and the component has the focus.

```
doSpaceDown()
```
Called when the space bar goes up and the component has the focus.

```
setStyle(style)
```
Sets this component's style.

```
setTint(subview, color, brightness)
```
> Tints a view so that 50% gray appears as the given color with shades of the color darker or lighter. The brightness argument must be a number between −255 and 255 (inclusive).

```
updateDefault()
```
> Forces the default button to update.

Window

A **Window** object represents a resizable window. The **Window** class is a subclass of **WindowPanel**, which itself is a subclass of **BaseWindow**. **BaseWindow** is a direct child of **BaseComponent**. The class hierarchy is shown in Figure 2.6.

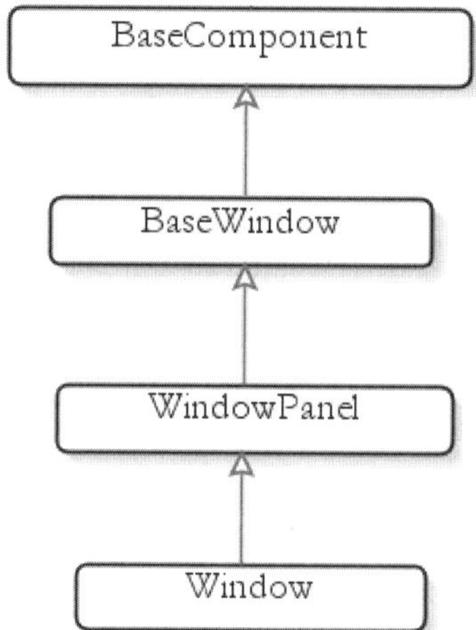

Figure 2.6: The hierarchy of the Window class

Tables 2.4, 2.5, and 2.6 present the attributes of the **BaseWindow** class, **WindowPanel** class, and **Window** class, respectively.

Name	Usage	Type	Default	Accessibility
datacontrolsvisibility	Tag only	boolean	false	final
	Description. Indicates if the datapath associated with this window will cause the window to be invisible if it matches no data or visible if it matches data.			

haswindowfocus	Tag and JS	boolean	false	read-write
	Description. Indicates if this window has the focus.			
minheight	Tag only	number	50	final
	Description. The minimum height of this window in pixels.			
minwidth	Tag only	number	60	final
	Description. The minimum width of this window in pixels.			
state	Tag and JS	number	1	read-only
	Description. The stat of this window. The value is one of these: 1 (selected), 2 (not selected), 3 (dragging), 4 (disabled), and 5 (resizing).			

Table 2.4: The attributes of the BaseWindow class

Name	Usage	Type	Default	Accessibility
closeable	Tag and JS	boolean	false	read-write
	Description. Indicates if this window panel can be closed.			
inset_bottom	Tag and JS	number	20	read-write
	Description. The bottom inset for the content area in pixel.			
inset_left	Tag and JS	number	6	read-write
	Description. The left inset for the content area in pixel.			
inset_right	Tag and JS	number	11	read-write
	Description. The right inset for the content area in pixel.			
inset_top	Tag and JS	number	22	read-write
	Description. The top inset for the content area in pixel.			
title	Tag and JS	string		read-write
	Description. The title of this window panel.			
titlearea_inset_top	Tag and JS	number	6	read-write
	Description. The top inset for the window title area in pixel.			

Table 2.5: The attributes of the WindowPanel class

Name	Usage	Type	Default	Accessibility
resizable	Tag and JS	boolean	false	read-write
	Description. Indicates if this window can be resized. A resizable window has a handle it its lower-right corner that the user can drag to resize the window.			

Table 2.6: The attributes of the Window class

The **BaseWindow** class adds three methods:

```
close()
```
  Hides the window, the same as setting the **visible** attribute to **false**.

`open()`

Shows the window, the same as setting the **visible** attribute to **true**.

`setVisible(visible)`

Sets the **visible** attribute.

The **WindowPanel** and **Window** classes do not add new methods.

The **windowTest1.lzx** file in Listing 2.6 features an LZX application that displays a resizable window.

Listing 2.6: A resizable window

```
<canvas height="200" width="400">
    <window resizable="true" width="200" height="200">
        <text>OpenLaszlo is cool!</text>
    </window>
</canvas>
```

You can invoke the LZX application using this URL:

```
http://localhost:8080/lps-4.0.x/app02/windowTest1.lzx
```

The generated output is shown in Figure 2.7.

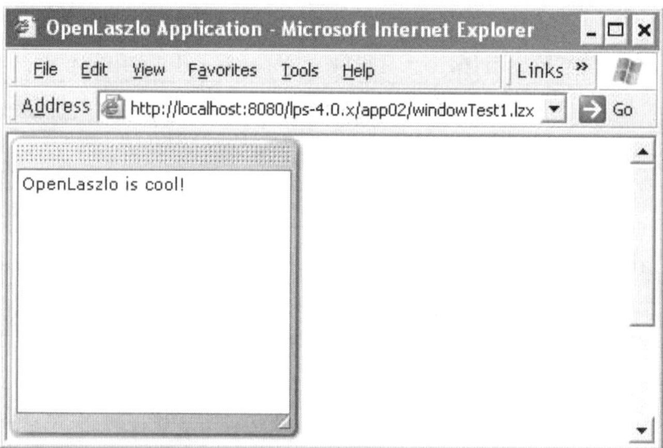

Figure 2.7: A Window object

You can resize the window by dragging the arrow at the right bottom corner. You can also draw the window around the canvas. If the window is nested inside a container, such as a view, the window can move beyond the container.

Alert

An **Alert** object represents a modal dialog box to display a message. An **Alert** box comes equipped with an **OK** button and by default is not displayed. You must call its **open** method to make it visible.

The **Alert** class is a subclass of the **ModalDialog** class, which is derived from **WindowPanel**. A **ModalDialog** object represents a moveable floating view. When a modal dialog is open, no other part of the application is accessible, until the user closes the dialog.

Figure 2.8 shows the **Alert** class hierarchy.

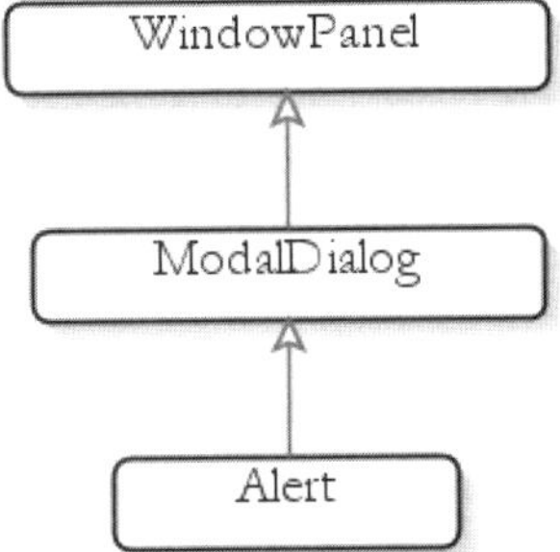

Figure 2.8: The Alert class hierarchy

Table 2.7 shows the attributes of the **ModalDialog** class and Table 2.8 presents those of the **Alert** class.

Name	Usage	Type	Default	Accessibility
content_inset_bottom	Tag and JS	number	10	read-write
	Description. The bottom inset for the content in pixels.			
content_inset_left	Tag and JS	number	14	read-write
	Description. The left inset for the content in pixels.			
content_inset_right	Tag and JS	number	14	read-write
	Description. The right inset for the content in pixels.			
content_inset_top	Tag and JS	number	10	read-write
	Description. The top inset for the content in pixels.			

Table 2.7: The attributes defined in the ModalDialog class

Name	Usage	Type	Default	Accessibility
button1	Tag and JS	string	OK	read-write
	Description. The text to be displayed on the first button on the Alert box.			
button2	Tag and JS	string		read-write
	Description. The text for the second button on the Alert box.			
maxtextwidth	Tag and JS	number		read-write
	Description. The maximum length of a line of text before it wraps. The default is one third of the parent's width – the width of the window dressing and margin.			
onresult	Tag and JS	expression	null	read-write
	Description. Invoked when a button is pressed.			
result	Tag and JS	boolean		read-write
	Description. The value of this attribute is set after the user closes this **Alert** box. The value is **true** is the user pressed the first button, and **false** if the user pressed the second button.			
text_x	Tag and JS	number	0	read-write
	Description. The x position of the button text.			
text_y	Tag and JS	number	0	read-write
	Description. The y position of the button text.			

Table 2.8: The attributes defined in the Alert class

There are two methods defined in the **ModalDialog** class:

```
close()
```
Closes this dialog.

```
open()
```
Opens the dialog and makes it visible.

For example, the code in Listing 2.7 shows how to use the **Alert** box.

Listing 2.7: Using the Alert box

```
<canvas>
    <alert name="warning">Press OK to continue.</alert>
    <script>
        canvas.warning.open();
    </script>
</canvas>
```

To test this application, invoke the following URL:

```
http://localhost:8080/lps-4.0.x/app02/alertTest1.lzx
```

The generated output is shown in Figure 2.9.

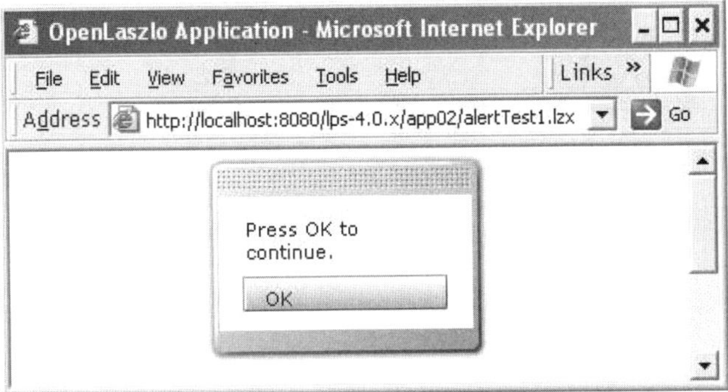

Figure 2.9: The Alert box

As another example, the code in Listing 2.8 shows an Alert box with two buttons, the Yes button and the No button. If the OK button is pressed, "You said 'Yes'" is displayed. Otherwise, "You said 'No'" is shown. Note that the code in Listing 2.3 uses an event handler, which we will discuss in Chapter 5, "Event Handling"

Listing 2.8: An Alert box with two buttons

```
<canvas>
    <alert name="warning" button1="Yes" button2="No">
        Do you want to continue?
        <handler name="onresult">
            if (this.result) {
                parent.message.setText("You said 'Yes'");
            } else {
                parent.message.setText("You said 'No'");
            }
        </handler>
    </alert>
    <script>
        canvas.warning.open();
    </script>
    <text name="message">What do you think?</text>
</canvas>
```

You can run the application by directing your browser to this URL:

```
http://localhost:8080/lps-4.0.x/app02/alertTest2.lzx
```

The result is shown in Figure 2.10:

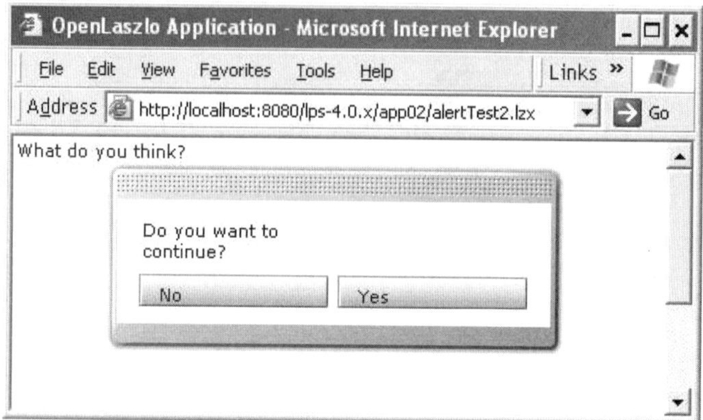

Figure 2.10: An Alert box with two buttons

Button

A **Button** object represents a clickable button. A button is also used to raise an event, so that you can perform an action upon a click on the button. We will discuss event handling in Chapter 5, "Event Handling."

The **Button** class is the template for creating **Button** objects. This class is a subclass of **BaseButton**, which in turn is a subclass of **BaseComponent**. The class hierarchy is shown in Figure 2.11.

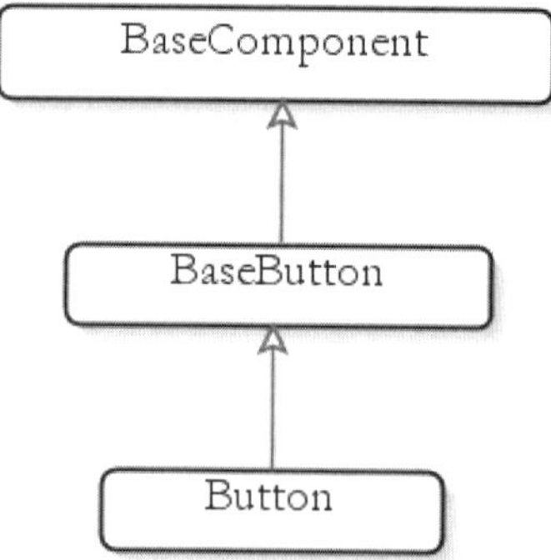

Figure 2.11: The hierarchy of the Button class

The attributes of **BaseButton** and those of **Button** are listed in Tables 2.7 and 2.8, respectively.

Name	Usage	Type	Default	Accessibility
disabledResourceNumber	Tag only	number	4	final
	Description. The resource for the disabled state. Use 0 if the resource has at least four frames and there is no disabled state.			
downResourceNumber	Tag only	number	3	final
	Description. The resource for the mouse down state. Use 0 if the resource has at least three frames and there is no down state.			
maxframes	Tag only	number		final
	Description. The maximum number of frames to use.			
normalResourceNumber	Tag only	number	1	final
	Description. The resource for the mouse up state, and the initial state of the button.			
onresourceviewcount	Tag and JS	boolean		read-write
	Description. This event is raised when the value of **resourceviewcount** changes.			
overResourceNumber	Tag and JS	boolean		final
	Description. This event is raised when the resourceviewcount changes.			
reference	Tag only	string		final
	Description. The target of mouse events.			
resourceviewcount	Tag and JS	number	0	read-write
	Description. The number of the first subviews that will respond to mouse events by changing the resource's frame number.			
respondtomouseout	Tag and JS	boolean	true	read-write
	Description. Indicates if this button responds to onmouseout or onmousedragout events.			

Table 2.7: The attributes of the BaseButton class

Name	Usage	Type	Default	Accessibility
text_padding_x	Tag and JS	number	11	read-write
	Description. The amount of space to add horizontally when resizing button to its text.			
text_padding_y	Tag and JS	number	4	read-write

	Description. The amount of space to add vertically when resizing button to its text.			
text_x	Tag and JS	number		read-write
	Description. The x position of the button text. The default is centered.			
text_y	Tag and JS	number		read-write
	Description. The y position of the button text. The default is centered.			

Table 2.8: The attributes of the Button class

The **BaseButton** class defines the following methods:

doSpaceDown()

Shows the down state. This method only takes effect if the space bar is down.

doSpaceUp()

Shows the up state. This method will only take effect if the space bar is up.

setResourceViewCount(*resourceViewCount*)

Sets the **resourceviewcount** attribute.

showDown(*sd*)

Called when the button's visible state should appear to be down. The argument *sd* is not used.

showOver(*sd*)

Called when the button's visible state should appear to be raised, to indicate it can be clicked.

showUp(*sd*)

Called when the button's visible state should appear to be up.

The following are methods defined in the **Button** class.

doEnterDown()

Called by the button manager when this button is the default.

doEnterUp()

Called by the button manager when this button is the default.

The **buttonTest1.lzx** file in Listing 2.9 presents an LZX application that uses a button. The button's text says, "Click Here."

Listing 2.9: Using a button

```
<canvas width="150">
    <button>Click Here</button>
</canvas>
```

To compile the LZX application, direct your browser here to this URL:

```
http://localhost:8080/lps-4.0.x/app02/buttonTest1.lzx
```

Figure 2.12 shows the generated output.

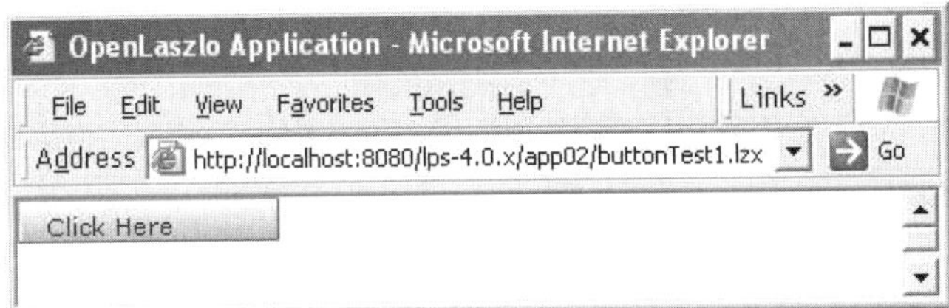

Figure 2.12: Using button

ComboBox

The **ComboBox** class represents a combo box. This class is a direct subclass of **BascComboBox**, which extends **BaseFormItem**. **BaseFormItem** is derived from the **BaseValueComponent** class, which itself is a direct subclass of **BaseComponent**. The class hierarchy is shown in Figure 2.13.

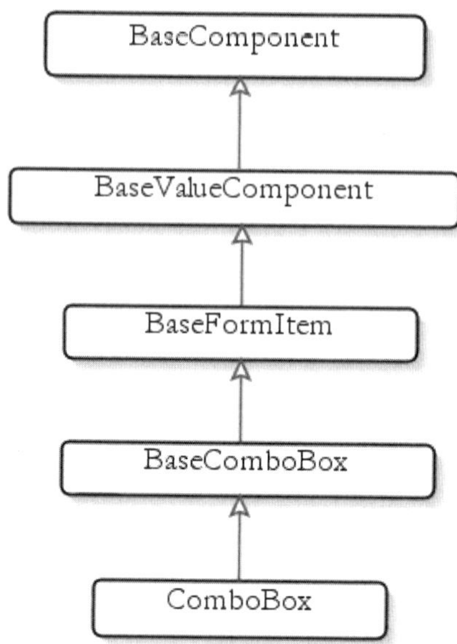

Figure 2.13: The hierarchy of the ComboBox class

Tables 2.9, 2.10, and 2.11 list the attributes defined in the
BaseValueComponent class, the **BaseFormItem** class, and the
BaseComboBox class, respectively. The **ComboBox** class does not add new
attributes..

Name	Usage		Type	Default	Accessibility
value	Tag and JS	any		null	read-write
	Description. The value represented by this item.				

Table 2.9: The attribute defined in the BaseValueComponent class

Name	Usage		Type	Default	Accessibility
submit	Tag and JS	boolean		true	read-write
	Description. Indicates whether or not the value of this element will be submitted with the containing form.				
submitname	Tag and JS	string			read-write
	Description. The parameter name used for this value when the containing form is submitted.				

Table 2.10: The attributes defined in the BaseFormItem class

Name	Usage	Type	Default	Accessibility
attachoffset	Tag and JS	number	-1	read-write
	Description. The vertical offset, in pixels, of the floating list attached to this combo box.			
autoscrollbar	Tag and JS	boolean	true	read-write
	Description. Indicates whether or not a scroll bar should be displayed when there are more items than the value of the shownitems attribute.			
bordersize	Tag and JS	number	1	read-write
	Description. The border size of the popup list in pixels.			
dataoption	Tag and JS	string	none	read-write
	Description. One of "lazy", "resize", "pooling", and "none".			
defaultselection	Tag and JS	number		read-write
	Description. The number of the item initially selected.			
editable	Tag and JS	boolean	true	read-write
	Description. Indicates whether or not the items in this combo box are editable.			
isopen	Tag and JS	boolean	false	read-write
	Description. Indicates whether or not the popup list is showing.			
itemclassname	Tag and JS	string		read-write
	Description. The name of the class to instantiate when itemdatapath is assigned.			
ondefaultselection	Tag and JS	expression		read-write
	Description. Invoked when the default selection is set.			
shownitems	Tag and JS	number	-1	read-write
	Description. The number of items shown at a time.			
spacing	Tag and JS	number	0	read-write
	Description. The spacing between items in the popup list in pixels.			
text_width	Tag and JS	number		read-write
	Description. The text width. By default it is the width of this combo box − 19.			
text_x	Tag and JS	number	2	read-write
	Description. The x position of the text.			
text_y	Tag and JS	number	2	read-write
	Description. The y position of the text.			

Table 2.11: The attributes defined in the BaseComboBox class

The **BaseValueComponent** class adds one method, **getValue**. Its signature is as follows:

`getValue()`
> Returns the value contained by the **BaseValueComponent** object.

The **BaseFormItem** class does not add new methods.

The **BaseComboBox** class adds the following methods:

`addItem(`*text,* *value*`)`
> Adds the specified text/value pair. The *text* argument is of type string and the *value* argument is of type **Object**.

`clearSelection()`
> Clear the selection list.

`getItem(`*value*`)`
> Return the specified value as Object; returns null if the combo box does not contain the specified value.

`getItemAt(`*index*`)`
> Returns the item at the specified index.

`getSelection()`
> Returns the current selection.

`getText()`
> Returns the displayed text.

`getValue()`
> Returns the value for the combo box.

`removeItem(`*value*`)`
> Removes the specified item.

`removeItemAt(`*index*`)`
> Removes the item at the specified index.

`select(`*item*`)`
> Selects the specified item.

`selectItem(`*value*`)`
> Selects an item by value.

`selectItemAt(`*index*`)`
> Selects the item at the specified index.

`setDefaultSelection(`*position*`)`
> Sets the item in the specified position.

`setItemclassname(`*name*`)`

Specifies the name of the class to instantiate in the floating list when necessary.

```
setOpen(open, withKey)
```
Sets the open/cloase state of the popup list. Both the open and withKey arguments are boolean.

```
setText(text)
```
Sets the displayed text.

```
toggle(withKey)
```
Toggles the open/close state of the popup list.

The **ComboBox** class does not add new methods.

As an example, the code in Listing 2.10 shows an LZX application that uses the **combobox** tag to create a **ComboBox** object.

Listing 2.10: Using a combo box (comboboxTest1.lzx)

```
<canvas width="150" height="150">
    <combobox id="genre" x="5" y="3" width="100" editable="false">
        <textlistitem text="Jazz"/>
        <textlistitem text="Pop"/>
        <textlistitem text="Blues"/>
    </combobox>
</canvas>
```

To invoke the LZX application, use this URL:

```
http://localhost:8080/lps-4.0.x/app02/comboboxTest1.lzx
```

The generated output is shown in Figure 2.14.

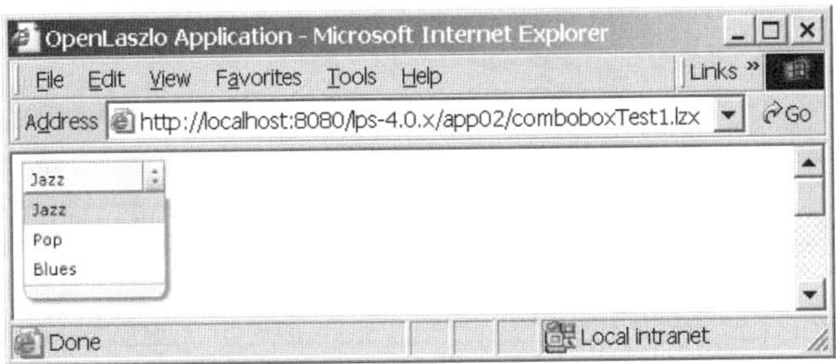

Figure 2.14: Combo box

You can also use the **value** attribute in a **textlistitem** element if the value of an item is different than the display text, as demonstrated in Listing 2.11.

Listing 2.11: Using the value attribute of textlistitem

```
<canvas width="150" height="150">
    <combobox id="genre" x="5" y="3" width="100" editable="false">
        <textlistitem text="Jazz" value="1"/>
        <textlistitem text="Pop" value="2"/>
        <textlistitem text="Blues" value="3"/>
    </combobox>
</canvas>
```

List

A **List** object represents a list of items that the user can select. The **List** class is derived from **BaseList**, which is a subclass of **BaseFormItem**. The class hierarchy for **List** is shown in Figure 2.15

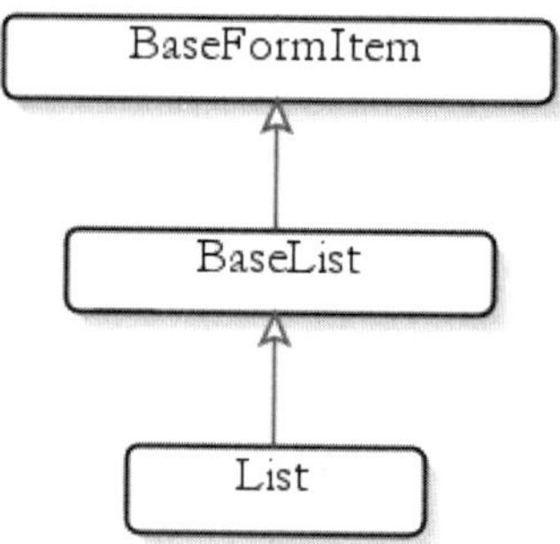

Figure 2.15: The class hierarchy for List

Tables 2.12 and 2.13 present the attributes of the **BaseList** and **List** classes, respectively.

Name	Usage	Type	Default	Accessibility
dataoption	Tag and JS	string	none	read-write
	Description. One of "lazy", "resize", "pooling", and "none".			
defaultselection	Tag and JS	Object	null	read-write
	Description. The index of the default selected item.			
itemclassname	Tag and JS	string		read-write

	Description. The name of the class to instantiate when the addItem method is invoked.			
multiselect	Tag and JS	boolean	false	read-write
	Description. Indicates if multiple selection is allowed.			
toggleselected	Tag and JS	boolean	false	read-write
	Description. Indicates whether or not a click toggles a selection.			

Table 2.12: The attributes defined in the BaseList class

Name	Usage	Type	Default	Accessibility
autoscrollbar	Tag and JS	boolean	true	read-write
	Description. Indicates whether or not a scroll bar should be displayed when there are more items than the value of the shownitems attribute.			
border_bottom	Tag and JS	number		read-write
	Description. The size of the bottom border in pixels.			
border_left	Tag and JS	number	none	read-write
	Description. The size of the left border in pixels.			
border_right	Tag and JS	number		read-write
	Description. The size of the right border in pixels.			
border_top	Tag and JS	number		read-write
	Description. The size of the top border in pixels.			
bordersize	Tag and JS	number	1	read-write
	Description. The border size for this list in pixels.			
minheight	Tag and JS	number	24	read-write
	Description. The minimum height of the list in pixels.			
scrollable	Tag and JS	boolean	false	read-write
	Description. Indicates if this List is scrollable.			
shownitems	Tag and JS	number	-1	read-write
	Description. The number of items shown at a time.			
spacing	Tag and JS	number	0	read-write
	Description. The spacing between items in the popup list in pixels.			
tracking	Tag and JS	boolean	false	read-write
	Description. Indicates if mousedown tracking is enabled.			

Table 2.13: The attributes defined in the List class

Both **BaseList** and **List** define new methods. Here are methods defined by **BaseList**.

```
addItem(text, value)
```

Adds the specified text/value pair. The *text* argument is of type string and the *value* argument is of type **Object**.

`clearSelection()`
Clear the selection list.

`getItem(value)`
Return the specified value as Object; returns null if the combo box does not contain the specified value.

`getItemAt(index)`
Returns the item at the specified index.

`getNumItems()`
Returns the number of items in the list.

`getSelection()`
Returns the current selection.

`getText()`
Returns the displayed text.

`getValue()`
Returns the value for the list.

`moveSelection(direction)`
Moves the selection to the next view if *direction* is -1, or to the previous view if *direction* is 1.

`removeItem(value)`
Removes the specified item.

`removeItemAt(index)`
Removes the item at the specified index.

`select(item)`
Selects the specified item.

`selectItem(value)`
Selects an item by value.

`selectItemAt(index)`
Selects the item at the specified index.

`selectNext()`
Select the next item.

`selectPrev()`
Select the previous item.

```
setHilite(view)
```
>   Highlights the specified view.

The following are methods added in the List class:

```
ensureItemInView(item)
```
>   Scrolls the list so that the specified item will appear at the top of the list.

```
select(view)
```
>   Selects the specified view.

Listing 2.12 shows an LZX application that uses a **List** object.

Listing 2.12: Using list (listTest1.lzx)

```
<canvas height="150">
    <list shownitems="3">
        <textlistitem>Jazz</textlistitem>
        <textlistitem>Pop</textlistitem>
        <textlistitem>Heavy Metal</textlistitem>
        <textlistitem>Fusion</textlistitem>
        <textlistitem>Rock</textlistitem>
    </list>
</canvas>
```

Use this URL to compile and run the LZX application in Listing 2.12..

```
http://localhost:8080/lps-4.0.x/app02/listTest1.lzx
```

Figure 2.16 shows the generated application.

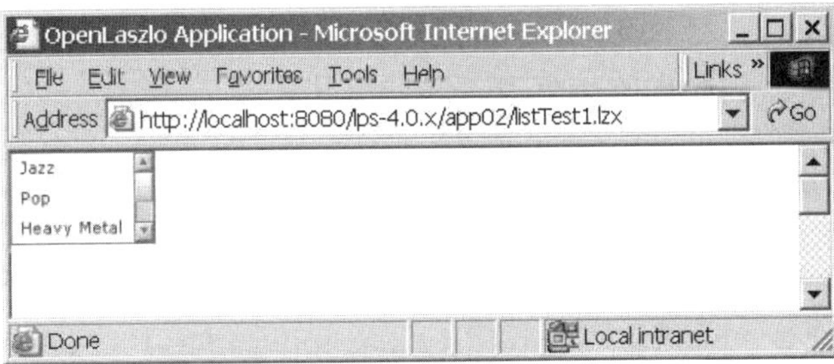

Figure 2.16: A list

Note that the list in Figure 2.16 has five items but is only showing three items because the **showitems** attribute of the list was given the value of 3.

RadioButton

A **RadioButton** object represents a radio button. The **RadioButton** class is a subclass of **BaseListItem**, which is derived from **BaseValueComponent**. The class hierarchy for **RadioButton** is shown in Figure 2.17.

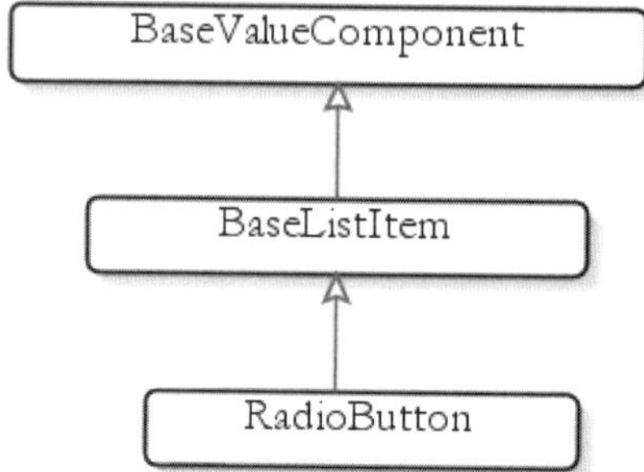

Figure 2.17: The class hierarchy for RadioButton

Table 2.14 shows the attribute defined in the **BaseListItem** class and Table 2.15 shows the attribute defined in **RadioButton**.

Name	Usage	Type	Default	Accessibility
onselected	Tag and JS	expression	null	read-write
	Description. Invoked when this item is selected.			

Table 2.14: The attribute in the RadioButton class

Name	Usage	Type	Default	Accessibility
text_y	Tag and JS	number	centered	read-write
	Description. The y position of the text label.			

Table 2.15: The attribute in the RadioButton class

No new methods are defined in **BaseListItem** and **RadioButton**.

The code in Listing 2.13 shows an LZX application that uses **RadioButton**. Note that you can create a **RadioButton** by using the **radiobutton** tag. The **radiogroup** tag is used to group radio buttons in the same selection.

Listing 2.13: Using RadioButton

```
<canvas height="150">
    <radiogroup>
```

```
        <radiobutton text="Red"/>
        <radiobutton text="Green"/>
        <radiobutton text="Blue"/>
    </radiogroup>
</canvas>
```

You can invoke the code in Listing 2.13 using this URL:

```
http://localhost:8080/lps-4.0.x/app02/radioTest1.lzx
```

The generated output is shown in Figure 2.18.

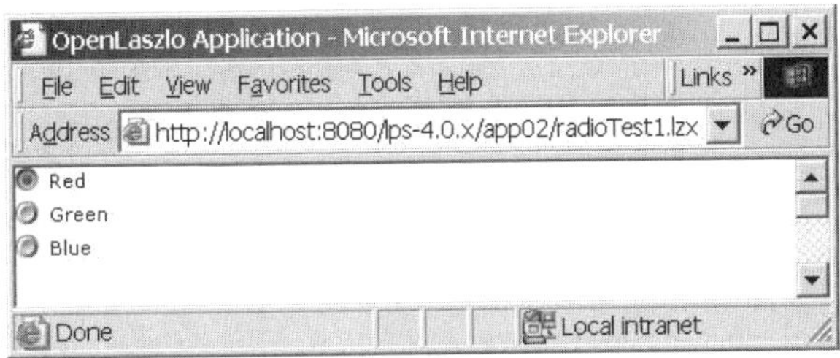

Figure 2.18: Using radios

The resource Tag

You have seen that the **LzView** class has the **resource** attribute that can be assigned the URL to an external attribute. Using this attribute, you can assign an image or a Flash. However, its use is quite limited. The **resource** attribute, for example, cannot play MP3 song.

The **resource** tag is similar in functionality to the **LzView** class's **resource** attribute. However, it gives you more flexibility and power. For one, when used with frames, you can associate a resource with multiple images, each image linked to a frame. Secondly, the **resource** tag can be used to play MP3 songs, something the **LzView** class cannot do.

The **resource** tag has two attributes, listed in Table 2.16.

Name	Usage	Type	Default	Accessibility
name	Tag only	string		final
	Description. An identifier for this resource.			
src	Tag only	string		final

	Description. The URL to an external file to be associated with this resource.

Table 2.16: The resource tag's attributes

Listing 2.14 shows an LZX application that uses the **resource** tag to link an MP3 file.

Listing 2.14: Playing MP3 song

```
<canvas height="150">
    <simplelayout axis="x"/>
    <resource src="mySong.mp3" name="mp3"/>
    <button text="Play"
            onclick="LzAudio.playSound('mp3');"/>
    <button text="Stop"
            onclick="LzAudio.stopSound('mp3');"/>
</canvas>
```

Note that the **resource** tag in Listing 2.14 is linked to the **mySong.mp3** file. This file in not deployed with the zip file that contains the sample applications for this book. To test the application, find an MP3 file and reassign the src attribute.

To run the application in Listing 2.14, use this URL:

```
http://localhost:8080/lps-4.0.x/app02/resourceTest1.lzx
```

Figure 2.19 shows the result for successful compilation. Click the Play button to play the MP3 song, and the Stop button to stop the song.

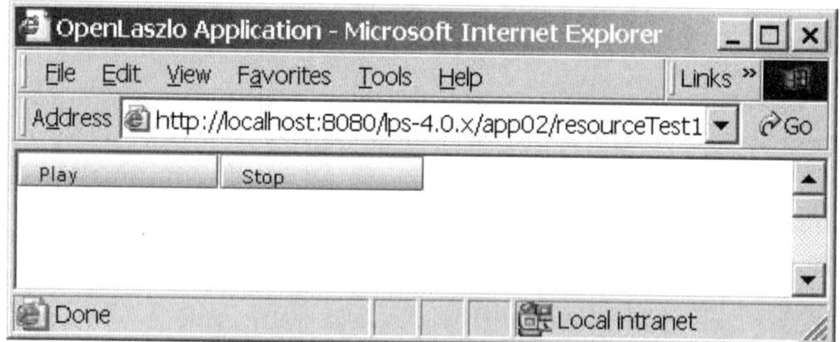

Figure 2.19: Playing MP3 Files

Note

See also the section "The frame Tag" for more use of the **resource** tag.

The frame Tag

The **frame** tag is used within the **resource** tag to define a single frame of a multiframe resource. The attributes of the **frame** tag are presented in Table 2.17.

Name	Usage	Type	Default	Accessibility
name	Tag only	string		final
	Description. An identifier for this frame.			
src	Tag only	string		final
	Description. The URL to an external file to be associated with this frame.			

Table 2.17: The frame tag's attributes

The LZX application in Listing 2.15 shows how to use the **resource** tag with two frames.

Listing 2.15: Using frames

```
<canvas>
    <resource name="arrow">
        <frame src="arrow1.gif"/>
        <frame src="arrow2.gif"/>
    </resource>

    <view resource="arrow"
        onmousedown="setResourceNumber(2)"
        onmouseup="setResourceNumber(1)"
    />
</canvas>
```

The **view** tag in Listing 2.15 is linked to the resource tag named **arrow**. The **setResourceNumber** method accepts an index number and assigns the frame at the specified index to the view. As a result, when you click the view, the second frame will be used. When you release the mouse, the first frame is used.

To test the application, direct your browser to this URL:

```
http://localhost:8080/lps-4.0.x/app02/frameTest1.lzx
```

The result is shown in Figure 2.20.

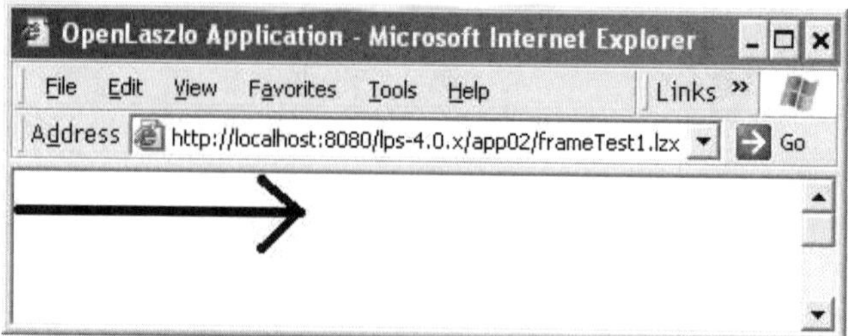

Figure 2.20: Using frames

Summary

OpenLaszlo comes with standard classes for rapid AJAX and Flash development. This chapter showed some of the classes that represent basic component you will often use. Chapter 11, "Rich Components" discusses more components.

Chapter 3
Working with Text

Just like other GUI-based platforms, OpenLaszlo provides a way to display text. A piece of text is represented by an **LzText** object. Not only that, you can use any font available to render your text. The default font is Tahoe and the default size is 10px.

This chapter discusses several text-related classes: **LzText**, **LzInputText**, and **LzFont**.

The LzText Class

An **LzText** object represents a non-editable text component. The **LzText** class is a direct subclass of **LzView**. You can use the **text** tag to create an instance of **LzText**. Table 3.1 shows the attributes of the **LzText** class.

Name	Usage	Type	Default	Accessibility
embedfonts	Tag and JS	boolean		read-write
	Description. Indicates whether fonts are embedded.			
label	Tag and JS	string		read-write
	Description. The label of this **LzText** object.			
maxlength	Tag and JS	number		read-only
	Description. The maximum number of characters allowed in this field.			
multiline	Tag only	boolean	false	final
	Description. Indicates if this text supports multiline.			
pattern	Tag and JS	string		read-only
	Description. The regular expression that describes a set of characters allowed in this field.			
resize	Tag and JS	boolean	false	read-only
	Description. Indicates whether to resize this field width to adjust to the text.			

selectablc	Tag and JS	boolean	false	read-write
Description. Indicates if the text can be selected.				
text	Tag and JS	string		read-write
Description. The text of this field.				

Table 3.1: The attributes of the LzText class

Here are the methods defined in the **LzText** class:

`addText(text)`
> Appends the specified string to the current text.

`clearText()`
> Clears this text field.

`escapeText(string)`
> Escapes the specified string.

`getSelectionPosition()`
> Returns the position of the cursor within the text. It returns -1 if the text cursor is currently not in this field.

`getSelectionSize()`
> Returns the number of characters selected in this object. It returns -1 if the text cursor is currently not inside this object.

`getText()`
> Returns the text in this object.

`getTextHeight()`
> Returns the text height.

`getTextWidth()`
> Returns the text width.

`setColor(color)`
> Sets the text color.

`setMultiline(multiline)`
> Sets the multiline attribute.

`setResize(resize)`
> Sets the resize attribute.

`setSelectable(selectable)`
> Sets the selectable attribute.

`setSelection(start, end)`
> Selects part of or the whole text starting from *start* to *end*.

```
setText(text)
```
Sets the text.

```
setXScroll(x)
```
Sets the x scroll position of the text field.

```
setYScroll(y)
```
Sets the y scroll position of the text field.

The **LzText** class adds one event: **ontext**. This event is raised when the text changes.

For example, the code in Listing 3.1 is an LZX application that uses the **text** tag.

Listing 3.1: Using text

```
<canvas>
    <simplelayout axis="y"/>
    <view height="200" width="100">
        <text>This is an LzText object</text>
    </view>
</canvas>
```

To test this application, direct your browser to this URL:

```
http://localhost:8080/lps-4.0.x/app03/textTest1.lzx
```

Figure 3.1 shows the generated output.

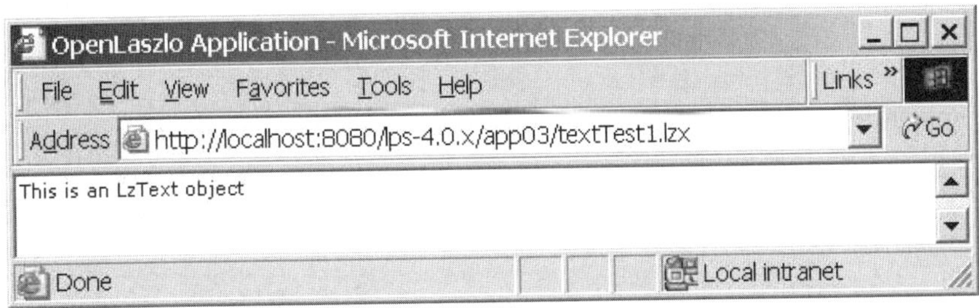

Figure 3.1: Displaying text with the text tag

Note that the content of the text component appears as the text of the **text** tag. You can, however, use the **text** attribute instead:

```
<text text="This is an LzText object"/>
```

The **text** tag understands HTML and will correctly interpret HTML tags. For example, the following **text** tag will display its text in italic.

```
<text><i>Italicized text</i></text>
```

By default the **text** tag can only display a single line of text. To display multiple line text, set the **text** tag's **multiline** attribute to **true**. The code in Listing 3.2 shows a multiline text component.

Listing 3.2: Multiline text

```
<canvas>
    <simplelayout axis="y"/>
    <view height="200" width="50">
        <text width="50" multiline="true">This is a very very long
      piece of text</text>
    </view>
</canvas>
```

Note that when using the **multiline** attribute, you must also specify the **width** attribute. Otherwise, no wrapping will occur.

To test the multiline text example, direct your browser to this URL:

```
http://localhost:8080/lps-4.0.x/app03/textTest2.lzx
```

The result is given in Figure 3.2.

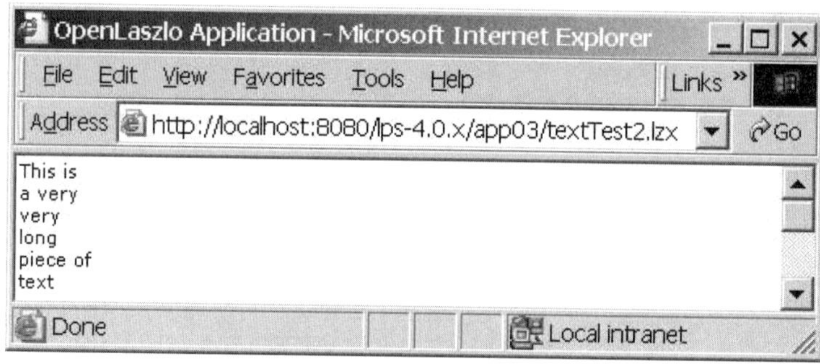

Figure 3.2: Multiline text

LzInputText

The **LzInputText** class is a direct descendant of **LzText**. An **LzInputText** object represents an editable text component. You can create an **LzInputText** object using the **inputtext** tag and you can set its **password** attribute to **true** to construct a password box.

Table 3.2 shows the attributes defined in the **LzInputText** class.

Name	Usage	Type	Default	Accessibility
password	Tag and JS	Boolean	false	read-write
	Description. Indicates whether or not this input text masks each of its character as an asterisk.			
resizable	Tag and JS	Boolean	false	read-write
	Description. Indicates if this input text is resizable.			

Table 3.2: The attributes defined in the LzInputText class

The **LzInputText** class defines four methods:

```
setEnabled(enabled)
```
Specifies whether or not this input text is enabled. The user can edit the text of an enabled text input.

```
setHTML(html)
```
Sets the HTML flag on this text view.

```
setText(text)
```
Sets the text to display.

```
updateData()
```
Retrieves the contents of the text field for use by a datapath.

For example, Listing 3.3 shows an input text named **inputField** with a script that highlights the text in it.

Listing 3.3: Highlighting text

```
<canvas>
    <simplelayout axis="y"/>
    <view height="20" width="140" bgcolor="yellow" clip="true">
        <inputtext id="nameField">[Enter your name]</inputtext>
    </view>
    <script>
        var length = nameField.getText().length;
```

```
        nameField.setSelection(0, length);
    </script>
</canvas>
```

To run the program, use this URL:

```
http://localhost:8080/lps-4.0.x/app03/textTest3.lzx
```

The generated output is shown in Figure 3.3.

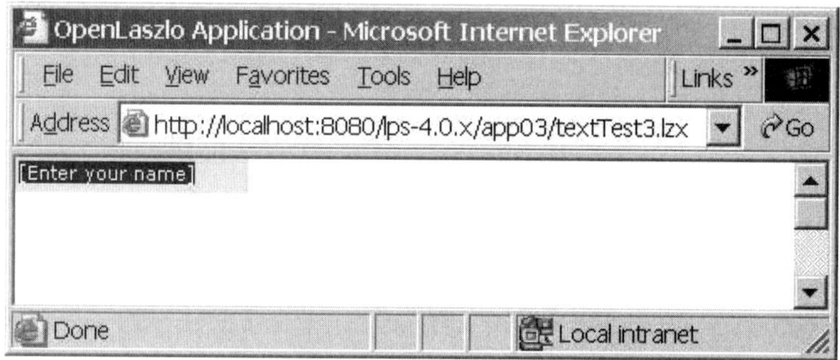

Figure 3.3: Using inputtext

As another example, the code in Listing 3.4 shows an input text component used as a password box.

Listing 3.4: Using password

```
<canvas>
    <view height="20" width="140" bgcolor="silver">
        <inputtext password="true">secret</inputtext>
    </view>
</canvas>
```

Try this example by directing your browser here:

```
http://localhost:8080/lps-4.0.x/app03/textTest4.lzx
```

The output is shown in Figure 3.4

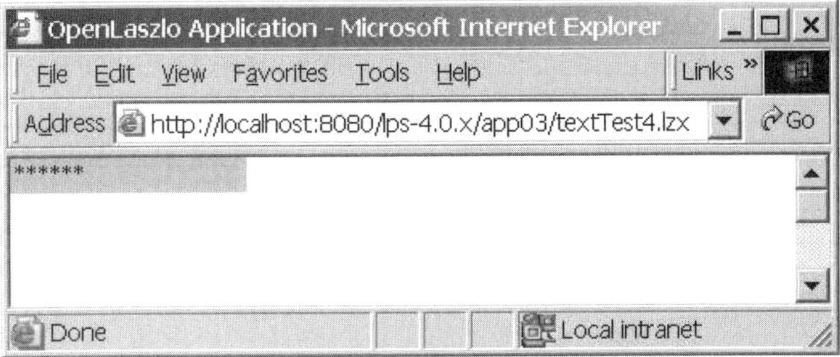

Figure 3.4: The password box

LzFont

An **LzFont** object represents a font. You can create an instance of the **LzFont** class using the **font** tag. The **font** tag must be a direct child of the **canvas** tag or the **library** tag.

Table 3.3 presents the attributes of the **LzFont** class.

Name	Usage	Type	Default	Accessibility
advancetable	JS only	array of numbers		read-only
	Description. An array of character widths indexed by character codes (normally ASCII).			
ascent	JS only	number		read-only
	Description. The ascent of this font above the baseline in pixels.			
descent	JS only	number		read-only
	Description. The descent of this font below the baseline in pixels.			
height	JS only	number		read-only
	Description. The height of this font in pixels.			
lsbtable	JS only	array of numbers		read-only
	Description. An array of character left-side bearings indexed by character codes (normally ASCII).			
name	Tag and JS	string		read-only
	Description. The identifier for this font.			
rsbtable	JS only	array of numbers		read-only
	Description. Array of character right-side-bearings indexed by character codes (normally ASCII).			

src	Tag only	string		read-write
	Description. The path to font file relative to the lps/fonts directory under the installation directory.			
style	Tag and JS	string	plain	read-only
	Description. The style for this font. The value is one of "bold", "italic", "bold italic", "italic bold", and "plain".			

Table 3.3: The attributes defined in the LzFond class

For example, the code in Listing 3.5 shows how to use the **font** tag:

Listing 3.5: Using a font

```
<canvas height="50" fontsize="18">
    <font src="lztahoe8.ttf" name="tahoe"/>
    <text font="tahoe">
        You can use any TTF font
        as long as you have the source
    </text>
</canvas>
```

To test and run this program, direct your browser to this URL:

```
http://localhost:8080/lps-4.0.x/app03/fontTest1.lzx
```

You will see in your browser something similar to Figure 3.5.

Figure 3.5: Using a font

OpenLaszlo will search the **lps/fonts** directory for font files. Therefore, you can specify the following in your code:

```
<font src="congab.ttf" name="Conga"/>
```

Note that you do not need to specify the path to the **congab.ttf** file because this file resides in the **lps/fonts** directory. However, if a font file lives in a directory under fonts, you need to include the folder too.

For instance:

```
<font src="verity/verity9.ttf" name="Verity"/>
```

This indicates to the OpenLaszlo Server that the **verity9.ttf** file can be found under the **lps/fonts/verity** folder.

If a component specifies an unidentified font name in its **font** attribute, OpenLaszlo will send a runtime error message. However, compilation will continue and the default font will be used.

As another example, the button in the code in Listing 3.6 uses the verity font.

Listing 3.6: Using a different font in a button

```
<canvas height="50" fontsize="12">
    <font src="verity/verity9.ttf" name="verity"/>
    <button font="verity" text="Register"/>
</canvas>
```

You can invoke the application by using this URL:

```
http://localhost:8080/lps-4.0.x/app03/fontTest2.lzx
```

Figure 3.6 shows the result.

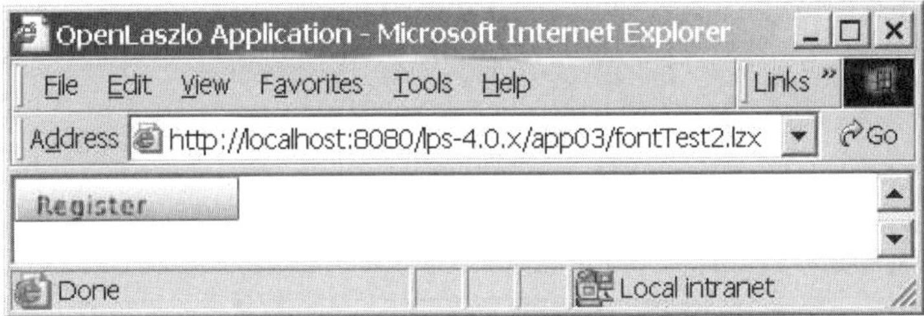

Figure 3.6: A button that uses a non-default font

Summary

Text is an important component of any GUI application. **OpenLaszlo** allows you to display text by providing the **LzText** class and its subclasses. **LzText** is a template for non-editable text components. For editable text, you use

LzInputText. In addition, you can render your text in any font you wish, by using the **LzFont** class.

Chapter 4
Layout Management

If you are familiar with Java Swing, you probably have worked with layout managers to lay out components in a container. OpenLaszlo supports a similar notion through the **LzLayout** class. In this chapter we examine this class and its various subclasses and see how different layout managers manage components differently.

Absolute Positioning

All views and components have the **x** and **y** attributes that specify their position in the container's coordinate space. Changing the value of **x** and **y** changes a view's or a component's position. However, while this positioning strategy is flexible, it is not always the best or easiest approach. For one, you have to calculate the width and height of each component so that they don't overlap. In addition, the views maintain their absolute positions when the container is resized. For example, consider the LZX application in Listing 4.1.

Listing 4.1: Absolute positioning

```
<canvas height="60">
    <view x="0" y="0" bgcolor="silver" width="20" height="20"/>
    <view x="40" y="0" bgcolor="gray" width="20" height="20"/>
    <view x="80" y="0" bgcolor="black" width="20" height="20"/>
</canvas>
```

To test this application, direct your browser to this URL:

```
http://localhost:8080/lps-4.0.x/app04/absolutePositionTest1.lzx
```

The generated application is shown in Figure 4.1.

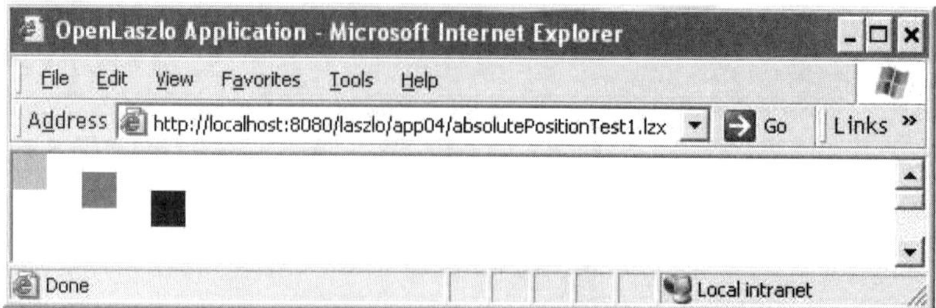

Figure 4.1: Absolute positioning

When the Web browser is resized, however, some of the components may not be visible anymore. Clearly, we need a different approach.

The LzLayout Class

The **LzLayout** class is a subclass of **LzNode** that is responsible for laying out views. The **LzLayout** class is a base class that provides this functionality. You never instantiate this class directly, but always create an instance of its subclass. Subclasses of **LzLayout** are shown in Figure 4.2.

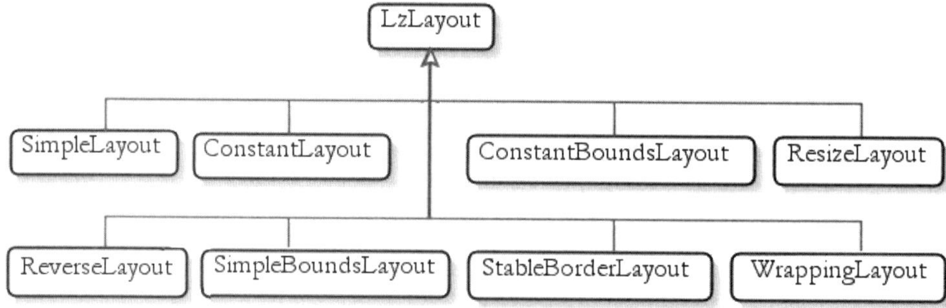

Figure 4.2: The subclasses of LzLayout

The attributes defined in the **LzLayout** class are given in Table 4.1.

Name	Usage	Type	Default	Accessibility
delegates	JS only	array of **LzDelegate** objects		read-only
	Description. All the delegates used by the layout.			
locked	Tag and JS	boolean		read-write
	Description. Indicates whether or not the layout is locked from updates.			
subviews	JS only	array of views		read-only
	Description. All the views managed by this layout.			
updateDele gate	JS only	**LzDelegate**		read-only
	Description. A delegate responsible for updating the layout.			

Table 4.1: The attributes defined in the LzLayout class

The following are methods defined in the **LzLayout** class.

`addSubview(`*`subview`*`)`
> Adds the specified subview.

`ignore(`*`subview`*`)`
> Ignores the specified subview.

`lock()`
> Locks the layout so no updates are allowed.

`releaseLayout()`
> Removes the layout from the view and deregisters the delegates that the layout uses.

`removeSubview(`*`subview`*`)`
> Removes the specified subview.

`setLayoutOrder(`*`subView1, subView2`*`)`
> Reorders so that *subView2* immediately follows *subView1*.

`swapSubviewOrder(`*`subView1, subView2`*`)`
> Swaps the positions of *subView1* and *subView2*.

`unlock()`
> Unlocks the layout so that updates are allowed.

You can specify a layout by using the **layout** attribute of the **LzView** class or, as demonstrated in the later sections, by instantiating a subclass of **LzLayout**.

SimpleLayout

You use **SimpleLayout** to place components next to each other, either horizontally or vertically. You can create an instance of **SimpleLayout** by using the **simplelayout** tag.

The **SimpleLayout** class adds three attributes, which are described in Table 4.2.

Name	Usage	Type	Default	Accessibility
axis	Tag and JS	string	y	read-write
	Description. The axis to lay out components. The value for this attribute is either "x" or "y".			
spacing	Tag and JS	number	0	read-write
	Description. The distance between two views in pixels.			
inset	Tag and JS	number	0	read-write
	Description. The distance between the container's border and the first view in pixels.			

Table 4.2: The attributes defined in the SimpleLayout class

You can use the **simplelayout** tag in a view to lay out components and child views added to the former. As an example, consider the code in Listing 4.2 that places three views horizontally.

Listing 4.2: Arranging views horizontally

```
<canvas height="60">
    <simplelayout axis="x" spacing="4"/>
    <view bgcolor="silver" width="20" height="20"/>
    <view bgcolor="gray" width="20" height="20"/>
    <view bgcolor="black" width="20" height="20"/>
</canvas>
```

To test this application, use this URL:

```
http://localhost:8080/lps-4.0.x/app04/simpleLayoutTest1.lzx
```

The generated output is shown in Figure 4.2.

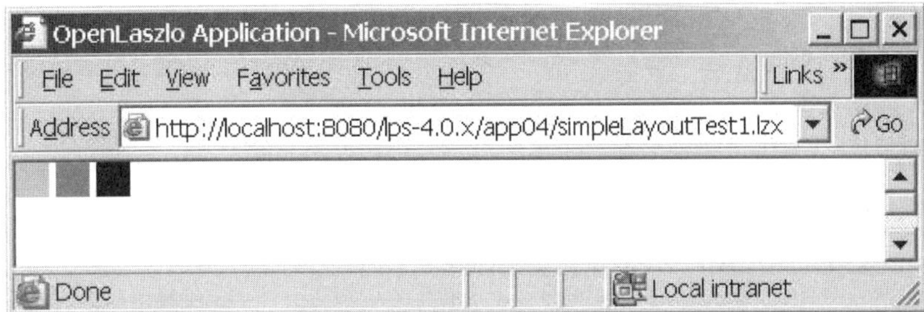

Figure 4.2: Laying out component horizontally using SimpleLayout

The code in Listing 4.3 lays out its components vertically.

Listing 4.3: Laying out views vertically

```
<canvas height="200">
    <view x="5" y="4">
        <simplelayout axis="y" spacing="6" inset="6"/>
        <view bgcolor="silver" width="20" height="20"/>
        <view bgcolor="gray" width="20" height="20"/>
        <view bgcolor="black" width="20" height="20"/>
    </view>
</canvas>
```

Note that the **simplelayout** is added to a view position at (5, 4) and the first view is positioned at pixel 6 (thanks to the **inset** attribute).

To test this application, direct your browser to the following URL:

```
http://localhost:8080/lps-4.0.x/app04/simpleLayoutTest2.lzx
```

Figure 4.4 shows the generated output.

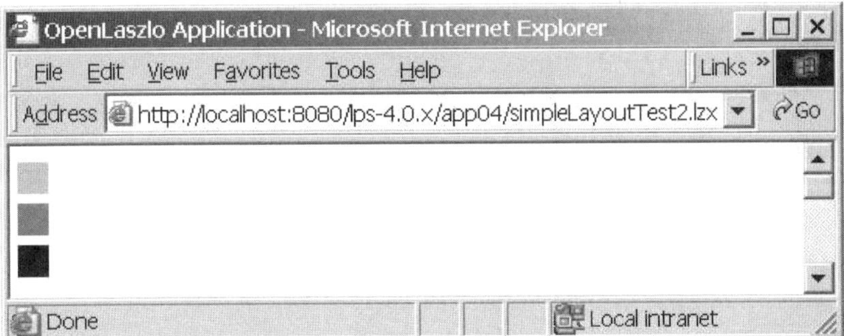

Figure 4.4: Laying out component vertically using SimpleLayout

Besides using a tag, you can also use the **layout** attribute of the **LzView** class to lay out the child views of a view. To this attribute, you assign the class name and the values for the layout manager's attributes.

For example, the LZX application in Listing 4.4 shows an **LzView** that uses the layout attribute.

Listing 4.4: Using the layout attribute

```
<canvas height="200">
    <view layout="class:simplelayout;axis:x;spacing:50">
        <button>OK</button>
        <button>Cancel</button>
    </view>
</canvas>
```

To test this application, direct your browser to the following URL:

```
http://localhost:8080/lps-4.0.x/app04/layoutAttributeTest1.lzx
```

The generated output is displayed in Figure 4.5.

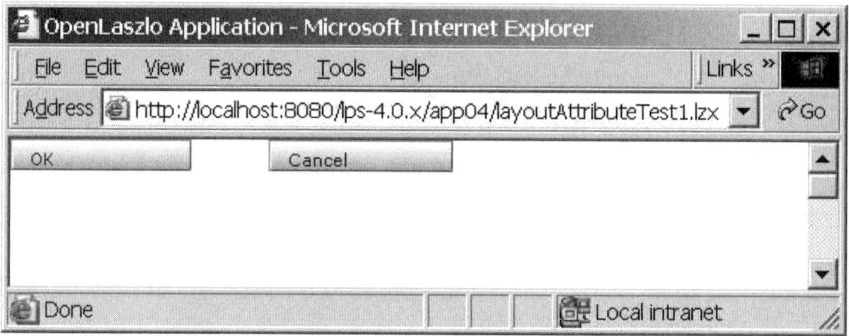

Figure 4.5: Using the layout attribute

ResizeLayout

ResizeLayout is similar to **SimpleLayout**, allowing you to position views horizontally or vertically. However, with **ResizeLayout** you can also resize the views being managed. You can construct a **ResizeLayout** object by using the **resizelayout** tag.

To resize a view, assign "releasetolayout" to the **options** attribute of the view you want to resize. This attribute causes the corresponding view to be resized to fill in the width or height of the container that is not taken by the fixed-length views. If more than one view have their **options** attribute assigned "releasetolayout", the available space is split evenly among those views.

The **ResizeLayout** class's attributes are given in Table 4.3.

Name	Usage	Type	Default	Accessibility
axis	Tag and JS	string	y	read-write
	Description. The axis to lay out components. The value for this attribute is either "x" or "y".			
spacing	Tag and JS	number	0	read-write
	Description. The distance between two views in pixels.			

Table 4.3: The attributes defined in the ResizeLayout class

The following are the methods defined in the **ResizeLayout** class.

`hold(subview)`
>   Prevents the specified subview from being resized when the parent view is resized.

`release(subview)`
>   Allows the specified subview to be resized after being held.

`setAxis(axis)`
>   Sets the **axis** attribute.

For example, the LZX application in Listing 4.5 demonstrates a canvas that uses **resizelayout**.

Listing 4.5: Using resizelayout

```
<canvas height="200">
    <resizelayout axis="y" spacing="5"/>
    <view width="20" height="20" bgcolor="silver"/>
    <view width="20" height="20" bgcolor="gray"/>
    <view width="20" height="20" bgcolor="black"
            options="releasetolayout"/>
</canvas>
```

To test the application in Listing 4.4, use this URL:

```
http://localhost:8080/lps-4.0.x/app04/resizeLayoutTest1.lzx
```

Figure 4.5 shows the result

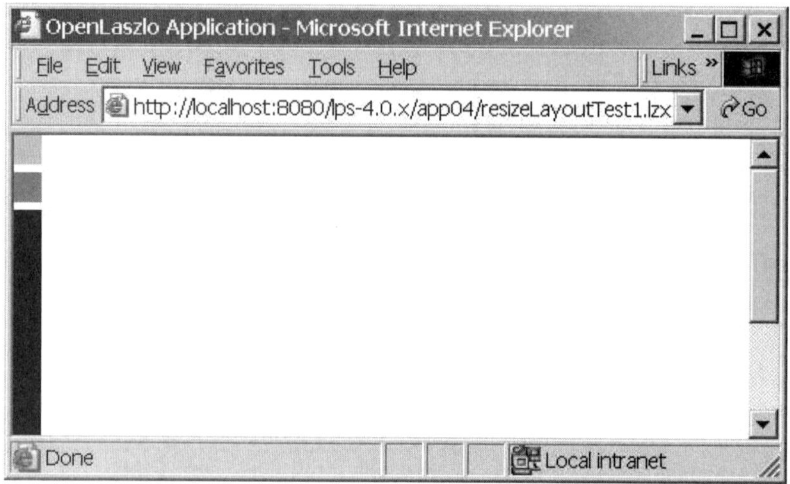

Figure 4.5: Using ResizeLayout

SimpleBoundsLayout

SimpleBoundsLayout is like **SimpleLayout**, positioning views horizontally or vertically. However, **SimpleBoundsLayout** makes sure that no views overlaps other views when a view is rotated.

Table 4.4 shows the attributes in **SimpleBoundsLayout**.

Name	Usage	Type	Default	Accessibility
axis	Tag and JS	string	y	read-write
	Description. The axis to lay out components. The value for this attribute is either "x" or "y".			
spacing	Tag and JS	number	0	read-write
	Description. The distance between two views in pixels.			

Table 4.4: The attributes defined in the SimpleBoundsLayout class

For example, the LZX application in Listing 4.6 uses **SimpleBoundsLayout**.

Listing 4.6: Using SimpleBoundsLayout

```
<canvas height="100">
```

```
    <include href="utils/layouts/simpleboundslayout.lzx"/>
    <simpleboundslayout axis="x"/>
    <view width="60" height="60" bgcolor="silver"/>
    <view width="60" height="60" bgcolor="gray" rotation="30"/>
    <view width="60" height="60" bgcolor="black"/>
</canvas>
```

Note that you must include the **simpleboundslayout.lzx** file under
utils/layouts to use this layout. To compile the application, invoke this URL:

```
http://localhost:8080/lps-4.0.x/app04/simpleBoundsLayoutTest1.lzx
```

The generated output is displayed in Figure 4.6.

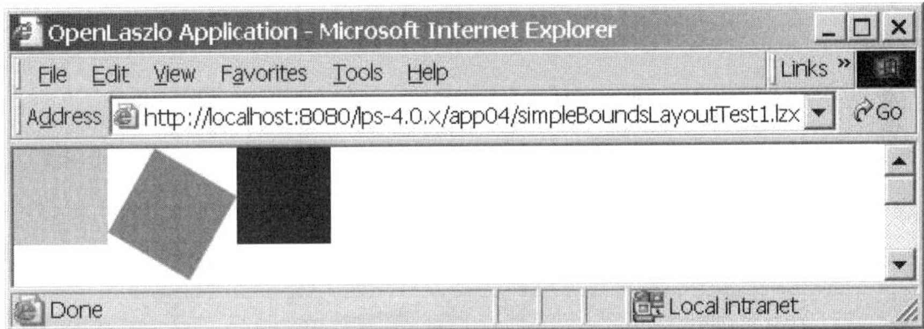

Figure 4.6: Using SimpleBoundsLayout

For comparison, Listing 4.7 shows similar code that uses **SimpleLayout**.

Listing 4.7: Views may overlap in SimpleLayout:

```
<canvas height="100">
    <simplelayout axis="x"/>
    <view width="60" height="60" bgcolor="silver"/>
    <view width="60" height="60" bgcolor="gray" rotation="30"/>
    <view width="60" height="60" bgcolor="black"/>
</canvas>
```

Use this URL to compile and run the code in Listing 4.7.

```
http://localhost:8080/lps-4.0.x/app04/simpleBoundsLayoutTest2.lzx
```

The result is shown in Figure 4.7:

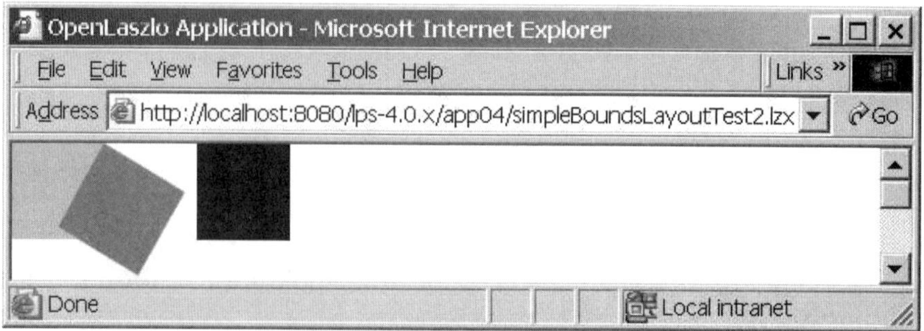

Figure 4.7: Using simplelayout with rotated views

ReverseLayout

ReverseLayout is similar to **SimpleLayout**, however views are laid out from the right to the left (for the x axis) or from the bottom to the top (for the y axis).

The attributes defined in **ReverseLayout** are listed in Table 4.5.

Name	Usage	Type	Default	Accessibility
axis	Tag and JS	string	y	read-write
	Description. The axis to lay out components. The value for this attribute is either "x" or "y".			
spacing	Tag and JS	number	0	read-write
	Description. The distance between two views in pixels.			
inset	Tag and JS	number	0	read-write
	Description. The distance between the container's border and the first view in pixels.			
end	Tag and JS	boolean	true	read-write
	Description. Indicates whether or not the layout will push the subviews to the right or bottom of the containing view.			

Table 4.5: The attributes defined in the ReverseLayout class

For example, listing 4.8 shows an LZX application that uses **ReverseLayout**.

Listing 4.8: Using reverselayout

```
<canvas height="100">
    <include href="utils/layouts/reverselayout.lzx"/>
    <reverselayout axis="x" end="false" spacing="10"/>
```

```
    <view width="60" height="60" bgcolor="silver"/>
    <view width="60" height="60" bgcolor="gray"/>
    <view width="60" height="60" bgcolor="black"/>
</canvas>
```

Note that you must include the **utils/layouts/reverselayout.lzx** file to use
ReverseLayout.

To compile the application, use this URL:

```
http://localhost:8080/lps-4.0.x/app04/reverseLayoutTest1.lzx
```

Figure 4.8 shows the result.

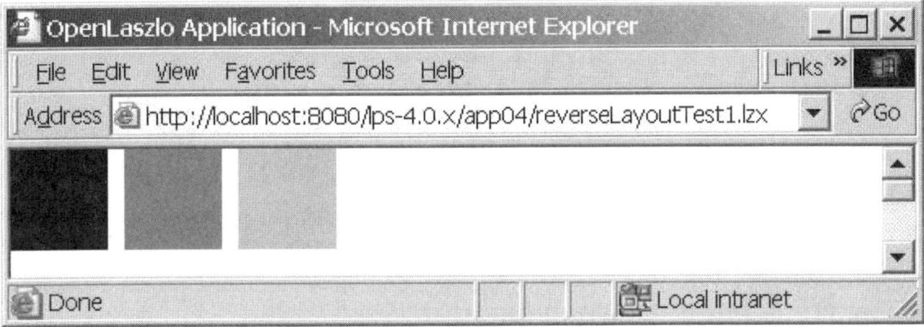

Figure 4.8: Using ReverseLayout

Note that the black view in Figure 4.8 is the leftmost view.

StableBorderLayout

StableBorderLayout is similar to **SimpleLayout**. However, there are two
differences between the two. No **spacing** attribute is allowed in
StableBorderLayout and it ignores all views but the last three. The second
last view will be stretched to fill the rest of the container's width/height.

Table 4.6 shows the attribute in **StableBorderLayout**.

Name	Usage	Type	Default	Accessibility
axis	Tag and JS	string	y	read-write
	Description. The axis to lay out components. The value for this attribute is either "x" or "y".			

Table 4.6: The attribute defined in the StableBorderLayout class

Listing 4.9 shows an LZX application that uses **StableBorderLayout**.

Listing 4.9: Using stableborderlayout

```
<canvas height="100">
    <stableborderlayout axis="x"/>
    <view width="60" height="60" bgcolor="red"/>
    <view width="30" height="60" bgcolor="silver"/>
    <view width="30" height="60" bgcolor="black"/>
    <view width="60" height="60" bgcolor="gray"/>
</canvas>
```

To compile the code, use this URL:

```
http://localhost:8080/lps-4.0.x/app04/stableLayoutTest1.lzx
```

The generated output is shown in Figure 4.9.

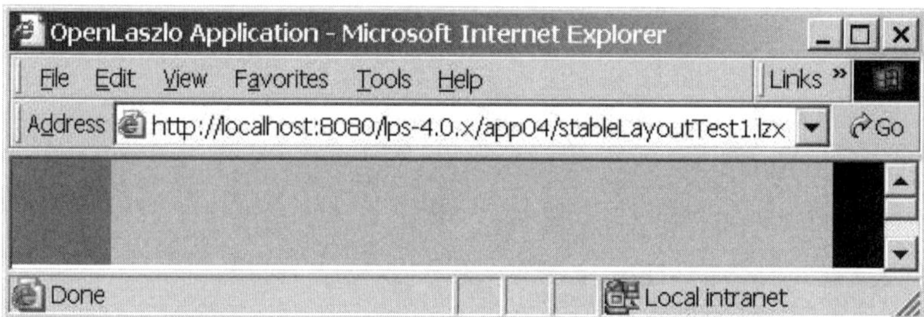

Figure 4.9: Using StableBorderLayout

Note that the red view is ignored. The gray view takes the first place and the silver view is stretched.

ConstantLayout

This layout places views on top of each other. As with **SimpleLayout**, you specify the **axis** attribute. The **value** attribute specifies the number of pixels the axis is shifted from. Any view managed by **ConstantLayout** may have its **xoffset** and **yoffset** attributes assigned a value. The **xoffset** attribute shifts the view to the right or to the left. The **yoffset** attribute causes the view to be shifted vertically.

Table 4.7 shows the attributes defined in the **ConstantLayout** class.

Name	Usage	Type	Default	Accessibility
axis	Tag and JS	string	y	read-write
	Description. The axis to lay out components along. The value for this attribute is either "x" or "y".			
value	Tag and JS	string		read-write
	Description. The number of pixels the axis is shifted from.			

Table 4.7: The attributes defined in the ConstantLayout class

For example, the code in Listing 4.10 shows how to use **ConstantLayout**.

Listing 4.10: Using ConstantLayout

```
<canvas height="80">
    <constantlayout axis-"x" value="10"/>
    <view width="80" height="80" bgcolor="silver" xoffset="-5"/>
    <view width="60" height="60" bgcolor="gray"/>
    <view width="40" height="40" bgcolor="black"/>
</canvas>
```

To compile this code, invoke the following URL:

```
http://localhost:8080/lps-4.0.x/app04/constantLayoutTest1.lzx
```

Upon successful compilation, you will see something similar to Figure 4.10 in your browser.

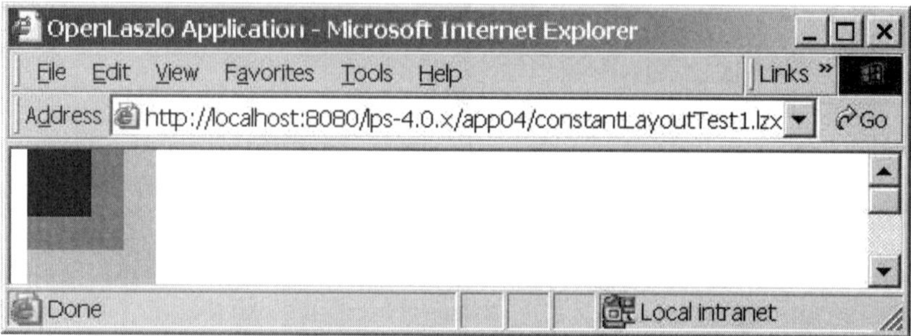

Figure 4.10: Using ConstantLayout

ConstantBoundsLayout

ConstantBoundsLayout is similar to **ConstantLayout**, but it ignores the **xoffset** attribute value of any view if the layout's **axis** attribute is assigned "x" and ignores the **yoffset** attribute value of any view if the value of the layout's **axis** attribute is "y".

Table 4.8 shows the attributes defined in the **ConstantBoundsLayout** class.

Name	Usage		Type	Default	Accessibility
axis	Tag and JS	string		y	read-write
	Description. The axis to lay out components along. The value for this attribute is either "x" or "y".				
value	Tag and JS	string			read-write
	Description. The number of pixels the axis is shifted from.				

Table 4.8: The attributes defined in the ConstantLayout class

For example, the code in Listing 4.11 shows how to use **ConstantBoundsLayout**.

Listing 4.11: Using ConstantBoundsLayout

```
<canvas height="80">
    <include href="utils/layouts/constantboundslayout.lzx"/>
    <constantboundslayout axis="x" value="10"/>
    <view width="80" height="80" bgcolor="silver" xoffset="-5"/>
    <view width="60" height="60" bgcolor="gray"/>
    <view width="40" height="40" bgcolor="black"/>
```

```
</canvas>
```

Note that you need to include the **constantboundslayout.lzx** file in the **utils/layouts** directory to use **ConstantBoundsLayout**.

To compile the code, use this URL:

```
http://localhost:8080/lps-4.0.x/app04/constantBoundsLayoutTest1.lzx
```

Figure 4.11 shows the generated output.

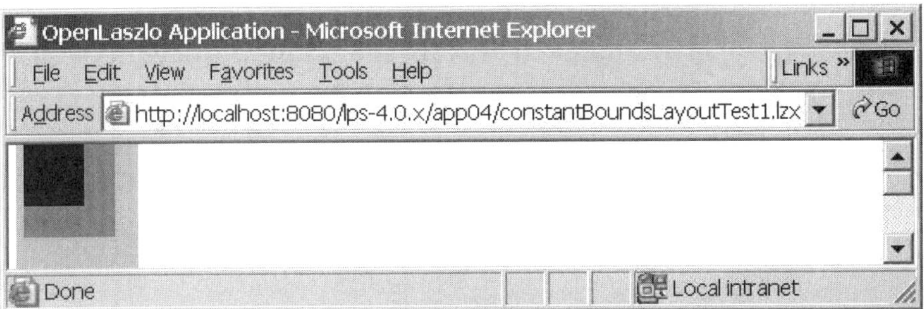

Figure 4.11: Using ConstantBoundsLayout

WrappingLayout

WrappingLayout is similar to **SimpleLayout**, but it will 'wrap' the views it manages by changing lines or columns. Table 4.9 shows the attributes defined in **WrappingLayout**.

Name	Usage	Type	Default	Accessibility
axis	Tag and JS	string	y	read-write
	Description. The axis to lay out components. The value for this attribute is either "x" or "y".			
spacing	Tag and JS	number	1	read-write
	Description. The distance between two views in both axes in pixels. By default, both **xspacing** and **yspacing** are assigned this value.			
xinset	Tag and JS	number	0	read-write
	Description. The distance between the container's border and the first view in x axis in pixels.			
yinset	Tag and JS	number	0	read-write

	Description. The distance between the container's border and the first view in y axis in pixels.			
xspacing	Tag and JS	number		read-write
	Description. The distance between two views in x axis in pixels.			
yspacing	Tag and JS	number		read-write
	Description. The distance between two views in y axis in pixels.			
duration	Tag and JS	number	0	read-write
	Description. The number of milliseconds to use to animate the laying out of the views.			

Table 4.9: The attributes defined in the WrappingLayout class

For example, Listing 4.12 presents an LZX application that employs **WrappingLayout**.

Listing 4.12: Using wrappinglayout

```
<canvas height="100" width="80">
    <wrappinglayout axis="x" spacing="5"/>
    <view width="30" height="40" bgcolor="silver"/>
    <view width="30" height="40" bgcolor="black"/>
    <view width="60" height="40" bgcolor="gray"/>
</canvas>
```

To compile the program, use the following URL:

```
http://localhost:8080/lps-4.0.x/app04/wrappingLayoutTest1.lzx
```

Figure 4.12 shows the result.

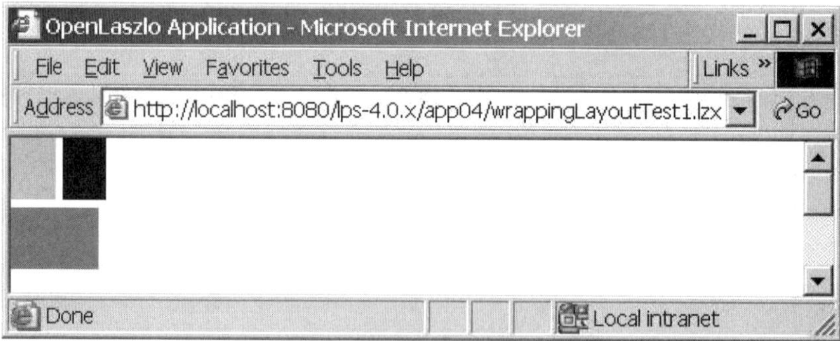

Figure 4.12: Using WrappingLayout

As you can see, the third view is displayed on the second line. Otherwise, using **SimpleLayout**, it would have been truncated.

Summary

In this chapter you have learned how to lay out views and components in a container using the **LzLayout** class and its subclasses.

Chapter 5
Event Handling

OpenLaszlo objects can raise events. Some events are raised as the response to the user's action, such as a mouse click or a keyboard input. Some are raised programmatically, for example as the response to data change. You can harness this feature to make your applications more interactive. If you have programmed JavaScript, you'll feel very much at home with OpenLaszlo event programming. All you need to do to respond to an event is write an event handler and link the handler to the event in question.

How do you write an event handler? In Chapter 1, "Starting OpenLaszlo" you've seen that you can use the **script** tag to write a JavaScript script that will be executed when the application loads. Event handlers are basically methods or functions. Therefore, you can write JavaScript functions within a **script** tag. However, since scripts can only appear directly within **<canvas>**, you use the **script** tag for global functions that will be called from multiple points in an application. If your function is local to an object, you should write a method under the tag that creates the object that raises the event.

This chapter shows you how to deal with events and event handlers. Most events are defined in the **LzNode** and **LzView** classes. Therefore, a list of events in these two classes will be given first.

Note
If you are not familiar with JavaScript, make sure you read Appendix B, "Introduction to JavaScript" before you read this chapter.

The handler Tag

You use the **handler** tag to write an event handler. This tag's attributes are summarized in Table 5.1.

Name	Usage	Type	Default	Accessibility
args	Tag only	string		final
	Description. The list of arguments for this event handler.			
method	Tag only	string		final
	Description. The name of the method that will be invoked by this handler.			
name	Tag only	reference	this	final
	Description. The name of the event this handler must respond to.			
reference	Tag only	string		final
	Description. The name of the variable that will be set to this object when the application started.			

Table 5.1: The handler tag's attributes

You will see examples of the **handler** tag in the sections to come.

Events Defined in the LzNode and LzView Classes

Since all OpenLaszlo classes are directly or indirectly derived from the **LzNode** class and all views and components are subclasses of **LzView**, the events defined in these two classes are inherited by the majority of objects ever created in LZX applications and therefore are worth discussing.

Event names in OpenLaszlo start with **on** followed by an action. For example, the event caused by the user click is **onclick**. The event raised when the mouse button is released is **onmouseup**.

The following are the events defined in the **LzNode** class.

`onconstruct`

This event is raised at the beginning of the instantiation process of this node.

`ondata`

This event is raised when the data referenced by this node's datapath changes.

`oninit`

This event is raised right before a node becomes active.

Of the three, the **oninit** event is used most often. You use this event to write initialization code that needs to be executed when an object is initialized.

For example, Listing 5.1 shows an LZX application that employs the **oninit** event of the **Alert** class to invoke the **open** method on an **Alert** object.

Listing 5.1: Using oninit on an Alert window

```
<canvas>
    <alert name="warning" button1="Yes" button2="No">
        Do you want to continue?
        <handler name="oninit">
            this.open();
        </handler>
    </alert>
</canvas>
```

You can test the code by using this URL:

```
http://localhost:8080/lps-4.0.x/app05/oninitTest1.lzx
```

Figure 5.1 shows the generated result.

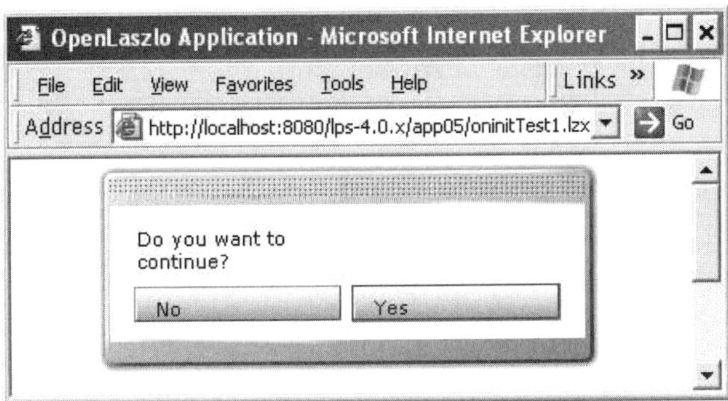

Figure 5.1: Using oninit on an Alert window

Without the event handler, the **Alert** window will not be displayed.

The **LzView** class has dozens of events, listed in Table 5.2.

Event	Description
onaddsubresource	Raised when a subview adds a resource.
onaddsubview	Raised when this view adds a subview.
onblur	Raised when a focusable view loses focus.
onclick	Raised when a clickable view is clicked.

ondblclick	If there is an event handler for this event, raised when a clickable view is double-clicked. If no event handler is registered, two consecutive onclick events will be sent instead.
onerror	Raised when there is an error when loading the view's associated resource. The event will send the error message to the event handler.
onfocus	Raised when a focusable view receives focus.
onheight	Raised upon the view's height change.
onlastframe	Raised when the view sets its frame to the last frame. This event can be used to send a notification when the view finishes playing its associated resource.
onload	Raised when the view loads its associated resource.
onmousedown	Raised when the mouse button is pressed on a clickable view.
onmousedragin	Raised when the mouse is clicked and its pointer is dragged into a clickable view.
onmousedragout	Raised when the mouse is clicked on a clickable view and dragged out.
onmouseout	Raised when the mouse pointer moves out of a clickable view.
onmouseover	Raised when the mouse rolls over a clickable view.
onmouseup	Raised when the mouse button is released on a clickable view.
onmouseupoutside	Raised when the mouse button that has been clicked upon a clickable view is released outside the view.
onopacity	Raised when the opacity of a view changes
onplay	Raised when a view begin playing its associated resource
onremovesubview	Raised when a subview is removed.
onstop	Raised when the associated resource stops playing.
ontimeout	Raised when the request to load media for the view times out.
onwidth	Raised when the width of a view changes.
onx	Raised when the view's x attribute changes.
onxscale	Raised when a view which is resizing in the x axis changes its width.
ony	Raised when the view's y attribute changes.
onyscale	Raised when a view which is resizing in the y axis changes its height.

Table 5.2: The events defined in LzView

As you can see, many of the **LzView** class's events are raised when the value of an attribute changes. For example, the **onwidth** event is raised when the view's width changes.

OpenLaszlo Event Programming

Event programming means you can respond to an event raised by an object. To do so, you wire the event with an event handler that contains code to be executed when the object raises the event. A handler is basically a function or a method. If you are a Java programmer, this wiring is the same as registering an event listener in the Java programming language.

There are several ways to wire an event with an event handler.

1. By assigning the name of the event handler to the event name in the tag declaration of the object. The event handler can be a method nested inside the object's tag declaration or a JavaScript function. For example, the following tag creates a **Window** object whose **onx** event is wired to the event handler **myHandler**.

```
<window name="win" onx="myHandler">
```

2. By writing a method nested in the tag declaration of an object, and then assign the event handler to the event attribute of the method. For example, the following snippet wires a button's **onclick** event to the event handler within its tags.

```
<button>
    <handler name="onclick">
        // code to be executed when the button is clicked here
    </handler>
</button>
```

For example, a button emits the **onclick** event when the user clicks the button. To wire this event to a handler, you specify the name of the method that is the event handler for the event. Listing 5.2 shows you how.

Listing 5.2: Wiring an event with an event handler

```
<canvas>
    <button>Click here
        <handler name="onclick">
            setAttribute("text", "Hello");
```

```
            setAttribute('width', 200);
        </handler>
    </button>
</canvas>
```

The button's **onclick** event is wired to handler defined within the **button** tag's body. There are two lines of code that will be executed when the button is clicked:

```
setAttribute("text", "Hello");
setAttribute('width', 200);
```

The first line changes the button's text to **Hello**. The second one changes the button's width to 200 pixels. Note that the **setAttribute** method is defined in the **LzNode** class:

```
setAttribute(name, value)
```

You use double quotes or single quotes around an attribute name.

Because the **handler** tag is written within the **button** tag, the **setAttribute** method is called on the **Button** object.

You can compile the code in Listing 5.2 by using this URL:

```
http://localhost:8080/lps-4.0.x/app05/onclickTest1.lzx
```

Figure 5.2 shows a button that will respond to a click.

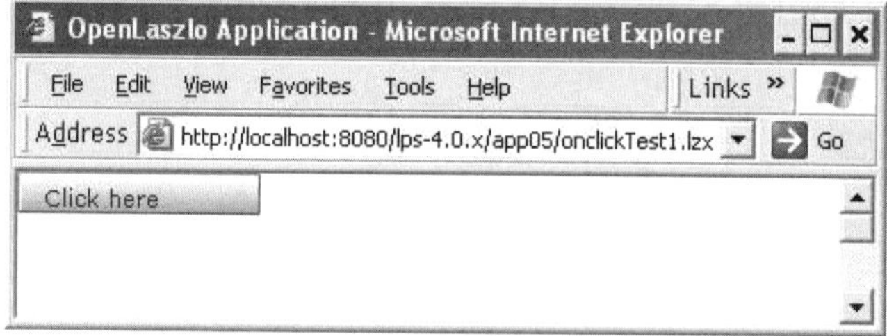

Figure 5.2: Handling the click event of a button

Alternatively, you can embed the method body in the tag that defines the object, as shown in Listing 5.3.

Listing 5.3: Embedding code in the tag

```
<canvas>
    <button onclick="setAttribute('text', 'Hello');
```

```
        setAttribute('width', 200);">
    Click here
  </button>
</canvas>
```

However, this is only suitable if the event handler consists of only one statement. If the handler is longer than that, This syntax is not recommended as it reduces code readability. If you must do this, make sure you do not use double quotes in your event handler because the occurrence of a double quote will indicate to the compiler that it is the end of your event handler.

Passing Arguments to a Handler

A method can also be used as an event handler, and using **<method>** instead of **<handler>** allows you to pass arguments from the object that raised the event . For example, the code in Listing 5.4 shows how to pass two arguments to the handler that responds to the **onclick** event.

Listing 5.4: Passing arguments to a handler

```
<canvas>
    <button onclick="myHandler('Welcome', 300)">Click here
        <method name="myHandler" args="text, componentWidth">
            setAttribute("text", text);
            setAttribute('width', componentWidth);
        </method>
    </button>
</canvas>
```

You can test the code in Listing 5.4 by using this URL:

```
http://localhost:8080/lps-4.0.x/app05/argumentPassingTest1.lzx
```

Functions as Event Handlers

A method is associated with a class. Therefore, it is normally only used with the instance of the class. If you want to have a global event handler that can be called from multiple objects, you cannot use a method. Instead, you use JavaScript functions.

For example, the code in Listing 5.5 defines the **myHandler** function that can be called from any point in the program.

Listing 5.5: Using functions as event handlers

```
<canvas>
    <button id="button1" onclick="myHandler()">
        Click here
    </button>
    <script>
    <![CDATA[
        function myHandler() {
            button1.setAttribute("text", "Hello");
            button1.setAttribute('width', 200);
        }
    ]]>
    </script>
</canvas>
```

Use this URL to compile and run the code in Listing 5.5.

```
http://localhost:8080/lps-4.0.x/app05/functionTest1.lzx
```

Passing an Object's Reference

In OpenLaszlo, you can pass a value as well as an object reference to a method. The example in Listing 5.6 shows how you can pass an object to a function.

Listing 5.6: Passing an object reference

```
<canvas>
    <simplelayout axis="x"/>
    <button id="button1" onclick="myHandler(this)">
        Click here
    </button>
    <button id="button2" onclick="myHandler(this)">
        Click here
    </button>
    <script>
    <![CDATA[
        function myHandler(b) {
            b.setAttribute("text", "Hello");
            b.setAttribute('width', 200);
        }
    ]]>
    </script>
</canvas>
```

There are two buttons in the LZX application in Listing 5.6, each of which is wired to the **myHandler** function. Each **onclick** calls **myHandler** by passing the button (by using the **this** keyword). This in effect causes a reference to the button to be passed to **myHandler**, as **b**. You can then use **b** to access the clicked button. Whichever button is clicked, its attributes will be changed.

You can test this application by using this URL:

```
http://localhost:8080/lps-4.0.x/app05/referencePassingTest1.lzx
```

Figure 5.3 shows the generated result.

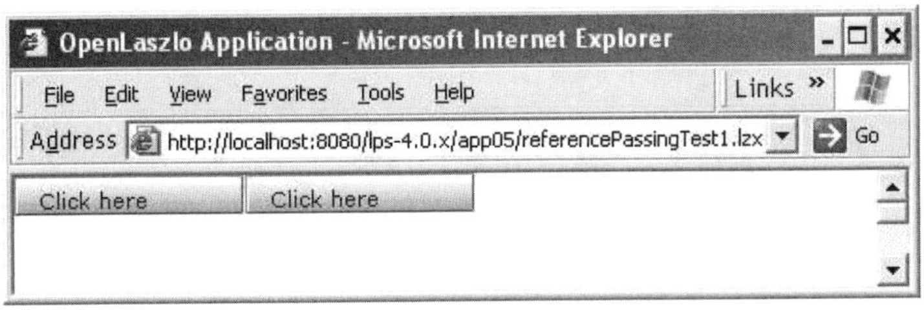

Figure 5.3: Passing an object reference to an event handler

Handling Mouse Events

So far you've seen examples that show how to handle the click event. There are dozens of other events that you might be interested in. One of them is the **onmouseover** event. Listing 5.7 shows such an example. It features a view that moves when the user moves the mouse over it.

Listing 5.7: Handling onmouseover

```
<canvas>
    <view width="280" bgcolor="silver">
        <view bgcolor="0x123456" height="50" width="50">
            <handler name="onmouseover">
                var newX = parent.getMouse("x") + 2;
                // if the newX would cause the view to be clipped
                // shift the moving view to left
                if ((newX + this.width) > parent.width) {
                    // shift to left
                    newX = parent.getMouse("x") - 2;
                }
                this.setX(newX);
            </handler>
```

```
        </view>
      </view>
</canvas>
```

As you can see, the second **view** tag nests a **handler** tag with its **name** attribute assigned "onmouseover". This makes the method get executed every time the user hovers over the view. Note also that the **getMouse** method returns the location of either the x or y position of the mouse pointer.

You can test this application by using this URL:

```
http://localhost:8080/lps-4.0.x/app05/onmouseoverTest1.lzx
```

Figure 5.4 shows the application.

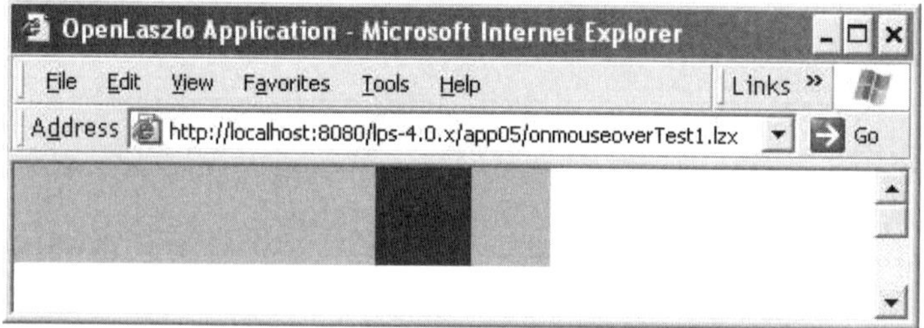

Figure 5.4: Handling onmouseover

Delegates

As you have seen, you can easily wire an event with an event handler by using the **handler** and **method** tags. This is not always the case, however. Some objects are created by using the **new** keyword, not by using its tag description. In such a case, the conventional way of wiring an event to an event handler cannot be used because there is no tag involved. OpenLaszlo however introduces the concept of delegates, which allows event wiring to occur dynamically.

A delegate, represented by the **LzDelegate** class in LZX, is an object used to bind an event with an event handler at runtime. The signature of the **LzDelegate** class's constructor is as follows:

```
LzDelegate(context, functionName, eventSender, eventName)
```

Here, *context* is the reference to the object to be called (the object that contains the event handler), *functionName* the name of the event handler, *eventSender* the object that raises the event, and *eventName* the event to register this delegate to. Both *eventSender* and *eventName* are optional, but the latter must be present if the former is present.

If an instance of **LzDelegate** is created without the *eventName* and *eventSender* arguments, the delegate can be registered to an event by using the delegate's **register** method.

Table 5.3 shows the attributes defined in **LzDelegate**.

Name	Usage	Type	Default	Accessibility
c	JS only	Object		read-only
	Description. The context in which to invoke the method.			
f	JS only	string		read-only
	Description. The method to call.			

Table 5.3: The attributes defined in the LzDelegate class

The **LzDelegate** class has the following methods:

```
disable()
```
Disables the delegate.

```
enable()
```
Enables the delegate.

```
execute(data)
```
Executes the name method in the given context with the specified data.

```
register(eventSender, eventName)
```
Registers the delegate for the specified event in the given context.

```
unregisterAll()
```
Deregisters the delegate for all of the events that have been registered.
unregisterFrom(*event*)
Deregisters the delegate for the specified event.

For example,

```
var del = new LzDelegate( this, "changeText", b, "onclick");
```

is the same as

```
var del = new LzDelegate( this, "changeText");
del.register(b, "onclick");
```

For instance, the code in Listing 5.8 is an LZX application that uses a delegate to bind an event with an event handler.

Listing 5.8: Using a delegate

```
<canvas height="60">
    <button id="b">Click Here</button>
    <method name="changeText">
        b.setAttribute("text", "Hello");
    </method>

    <handler name="oninit">
        var del = new LzDelegate( this, "changeText", b, "onclick");
    </handler>
</canvas>
```

In this case, the **oninit** event's handler is triggered when the canvas is initialized, creating a delegate object that binds the button's **onclick** event with the **changeText** method.

Admittedly, the code in Listing 5.8 is contrived, because it is easier to bind the button with the handler at compile time. However, the LZX application in the following section illustrates a real-life use of delegates.

A Simple Game

The example in Listing 5.9 features a spaceship that can move and shoot. Use the left and right arrow keys to move and the up arrow key to shoot. The application shows delegates in action and how to handle keyboard events.

Listing 5.9: The spaceship game

```
<canvas height="500">
    <resource name="spaceShip" src="spaceShip.jpg"/>
    <view>
        <simplelayout axis="x" spacing="4"/>
        <view bgcolor="silver" width="40" height="40">
            <text>1</text>
        </view>
        <view bgcolor="silver" width="40" height="40">
            <text>2</text>
        </view>
        <view bgcolor="silver" width="40" height="40">
            <text>3</text>
```

```
            </view>
            <view bgcolor="silver" width="40" height="40">
                <text>4</text>
            </view>
            <view bgcolor="silver" width="40" height="40">
                <text>5</text>
            </view>
        </view>
        <view y="400" bgcolor="black" width="${parent.width}">
            <view id="spaceShip" resource="spaceShip" clickable="true"
          focusable="true">
                <handler name="onkeydown" args="k">
                    <![CDATA[
                    if (k == 38) {
                        var bullet = new LzView(canvas,
                                {width: 2, height: 5,
                                 bgcolor: green, name: "bullet"});
                        bullet.setX(this.x + 18);
                        bullet.setY(400);
                        bullet.animate("y", -10, 1000, false);

                    } else if (k == 37 && this.x > 0) {
                        this.setX(this.x - 6);
                    } else if (k == 39 && this.x < parent.width) {
                        this.setX(this.x + 6);
                    }
                    ]]>
                </handler>
            </view>
        </view>
        <handler name="oninit">
            LzFocus.setFocus(spaceShip);
        </handler>
    </canvas>
```

To test this application, use the following URL:

```
http://localhost:8080/lps-4.0.x/app05/spaceShip.lzx
```

Figure 5.5 shows the application.

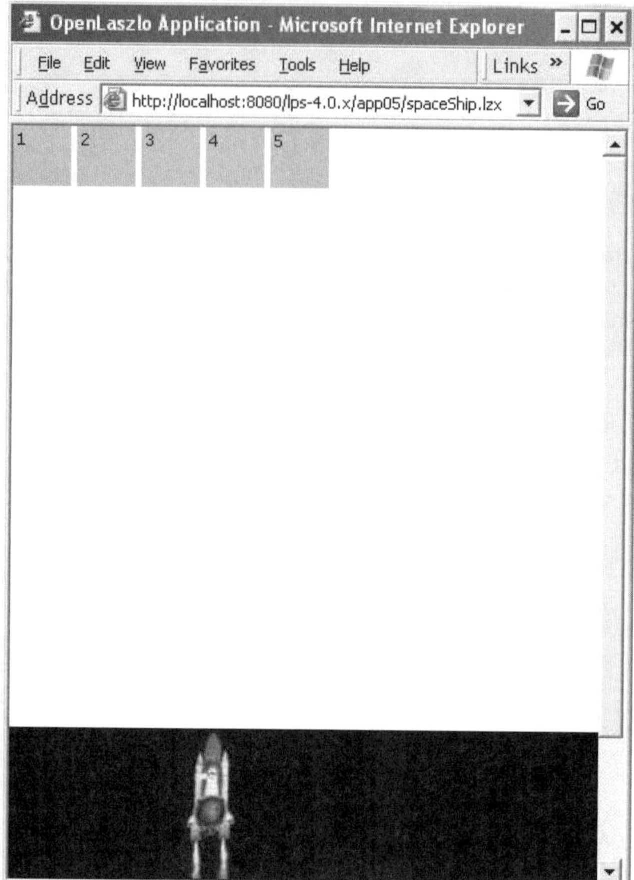

Figure 5.5: A simple game

The program in Listing 5.9 displays a view that uses the image **spaceship.jpg** as the resource. Its **clickable** and **focusable** attributes are both set to **true**, so that it can receive keyboard input. The view has its **onkeydown** wired to the following method:

```
<handler name="onkeydown" args="k">
    <![CDATA[
    if (k == 38) {
        var bullet = new LzView(canvas,
                {width: 2, height: 5,
                 bgcolor: green, name: "bullet"});
        bullet.setX(this.x + 18);
        bullet.setY(400);
```

```
        bullet.animate("y", -10, 1000, false);

    } else if (k == 37 && this.x > 0) {
        this.setX(this.x - 6);
    } else if (k == 39 && this.x < parent.width) {
        this.setX(this.x + 6);
    }
    ]]>
</handler>
```

The **onkeydown** event of an object occurs when the object has the focus and the user presses a keyboard key. It passes the key code as the argument (k). The event handler responds if the key pressed is the up, left, or right arrow. The left and right arrows move the spaceship. The up arrow creates another view on the fly and animates it (animation is discussed in Chapter 7).

Note also, you use the **setFocus** method of the **LzFocus** class to make sure that the spaceship view has the focus when the application loads.

```
<handler name="oninit">
    LzFocus.setFocus(spaceShip);
</handler>
```

Summary

LZX is an event-driven language and event programming is very easy. This chapter has shown how to wire an event to an event handler and introduced delegates.

Chapter 6
Constraints and States

A constraint is the return value of an expression and is often assigned to an attribute. You use a constraint if you want an attribute to have a dynamic value that changes according to some external state. States are conditional constraints. Both constraints and states are very useful features in OpenLaszlo.

This chapter discusses constraints and states and show how to use them.

Introduction to Constraints

A constraint can be assigned to a tag's attribute. Its syntax is as follows.

$when\{expression\}

Here, *expression* is a JavaScript expression and *when* is one of the following compiler directives: **immediately, once**, or **always**. $always\{*expression*\} can be written as $\{*expression*\}.

For example, the LZX application in Listing 6.1 uses a constraint as the value of the **text** attribute of a text component.

Listing 6.1: Using a constraint

```
<canvas>
    <text x="110" text="${win.x}"/>
    <window id="win" width="100" height="100"/>
</canvas>
```

The constraint in this case is:

```
${win.x}
```

win.x is an expression, representing the value of the **x** attribute of **win**, a **Window** component. You can compile this application by directing your browser here:

```
http://localhost:8080/lps-4.0.x/app06/constraintTest1.lzx
```

The text and the window are shown in Figure 6.1.

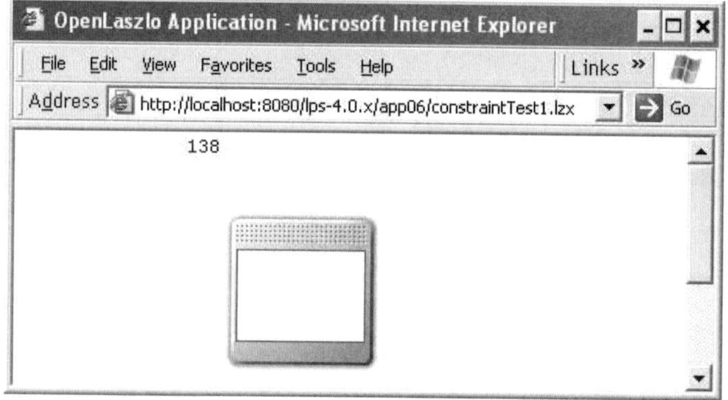

Figure 6.1: Using a constraint

Initially, the value of the **x** attribute is 0, however if you drag the window, the value of **x** will change and the change is reflected in the text.

As another example, consider the LZX application in Listing 6.2.

Listing 6.2: Using constraint to follow mouse move

```
<canvas>
    <view y="0" bgcolor="0xbbccdd" height="4"
          width="${parent.width}">
        <view width="4" height="4" bgcolor="red"
          x="${parent.parent.getMouse('x')}"/>
    </view>
</canvas>
```

You can use this URL to compile and run the example.

```
http://localhost:8080/lps-4.0.x/app06/constraintTest2.lzx
```

Figure 6.2 shows the application.

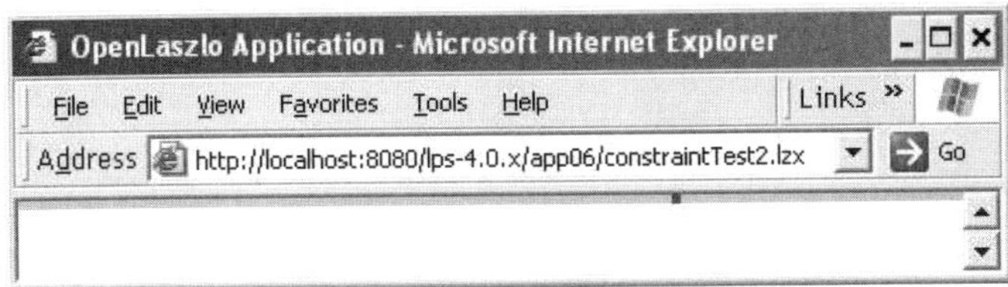

Figure 6.2: Following the mouse motion

The small red view in Figure 6.2 follows your mouse movement because its **x** attribute is assigned this constraint:

```
${parent.parent.getMouse('x')}
```

That is another constraint in action.

The code in Listing 6.3 shows another example of using a constraint. This time a slider is used to control the opacity of a view.

Listing 6.3: Controlling opacity

```
<canvas height="300" width="700">
    <view bgcolor="red" id="display" width="200" height="200"
            opacity="${parent.adjuster.value/100}"/>
    <slider x="0" y="200" name="adjuster" value="100"/>
</canvas>
```

We assign the following constraint to the **opacity** attribute of the view in Listing 6.3:

```
opacity="${parent.adjuster.value/100}"
```

The opacity value will then change according to the value of the slider. You can use this URL to compile and run the example:

```
http://localhost:8080/lps-4.0.x/app06/constraintTest3.lzx
```

Figure 6.3 shows the generated output. Drag the slider and witness how the view's opacity changes.

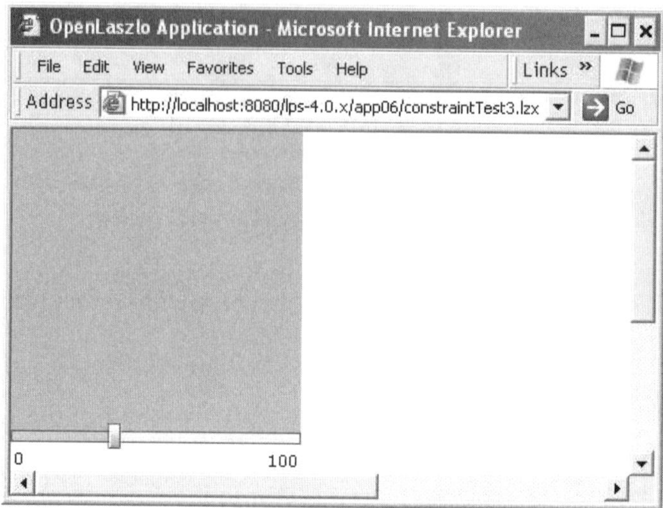

Figure 6.3: Controlling opacity

Constraints with once

A constraint is dynamically evaluated and this imposes some penalty on performance. Sometimes, you don't want or don't need a constraint to be evaluated continuously, but only when your object is initialized. For this, you can use the **once** keyword. For example, the constraint **${parent.width}** in the view in Listing 6.4 is probably only required to be initialized once, because the canvas width never changes throughout its lifetime.

Listing 6.4: A constraint that gets evaluated all the time

```
<canvas>
    <view y="0" bgcolor="0xbbccdd" height="4"
            width="${parent.width}">
</canvas>
```

In this case, you can use **once** for better performance, as shown in Listing 6.5:

Listing 6.5: A constraint that gets evaluated once

```
<canvas>
    <view y="0" bgcolor="0xbbccdd" height="4"
            width="$once{parent.width}">
</canvas>
```

If no keyword is present between **$** and **{**, the value of **always** is implied. Using **once** can help your application perform better.

Using the applyConstraint Method

Just as you can use delegates to wire event with an event handler at runtime, you can set a constraint to an object's attribute after the object is created. You may also want to do this if the expression in long and does not fit in a single line.

To achieve this, you use the **applyConstraint** method of the **LzNode** class. This method has the following signature.

```
applyConstraint(property, function, dependencies)
```

where *property* is the attribute to be assigned the constraint, *function* is the function that sets the attribute to the value, and *dependencies* is an array of reference/attribute pairs that the constraint depends on.

For example, revisit the LZX application in Listing 6.1, reprinted here for your reading convenience.

```
<canvas>
    <text x="110" text="${win.x}"/>
    <window id="win" width="100" height="100"/>
</canvas>
```

The code in Listing 6.6 rewrites the code in Listing 6.1 to apply a constraint at runtime.

Listing 6.6: Applying a constraint at runtime

```
<canvas>
    <text x="110">
        <method event="oninit">
            var f = function() {
                this.setAttribute("text", win.x)
            }
            var d = [win, "x"];
            this.applyConstraint("text", f, d);
        </method>
    </text>
    <window id="win" width="100" height="100"/>
```

```
</canvas>
```

Now the **text** tag does not have a constraint assigned to its **text** attribute. However, it now has a method that will be invoked when the **text** tag is initialized. The method defines a function called f:

```
var f = function() {
    this.setAttribute("text", win.x)
}
```

This sets the **text** attribute with the value of **win.x**, which is the **x** attribute of **win**.

The method also defines an array of dependencies (d):

```
var d = [win, "x"];
```

Lastly, the method calls the **applyConstraint** method of the text component:

```
this.applyConstraint("text", f, d);
```

This effectively sets a constraint to the text attribute of the **text** tag.

States

A state is a conditional constraint. With states, you can determine certain conditions under which the LZX constraints engine should work. Have a look at the constraint in Listing 6.3 which we reprint here.

```
<canvas height="300" width="700">
    <view bgcolor="red" id="display" width="200" height="200"
            opacity="${parent.adjuster.value/100}"/>
    <slider x="0" y="200" name="adjuster" value="100"/>
</canvas>
```

Here, the value of the **opacity** attribute of the view is a function of the value of the slider. As you can see, the view becomes invisible when its opacity is less than 18 or so. If you don't want the view color to become too pale, you can use a state to restrict the constraint so that it won't follow the slider if the slider moves to below, say, 50.

To use a state, you first identify the attribute you are currently applying a constraint to. Then, you write the **state** tag inside the object whose attribute is constrained. Rewriting the code above, we get the LZX application in Listing 6.7.

Listing 6.7: Using a state

```
<canvas height="300" width="700">
    <view bgcolor="red" id="display" width="200" height="200">
        <state apply="${adjuster.value > 50}">
            <attribute name="opacity"
      value="${adjuster.value/100}"/>
        </state>
    </view>
    <slider x="0" y="200" id="adjuster" value="100"/>
</canvas>
```

Now, the opacity only changes if the slider's value is between 50 and 100. You can test the program by using this URL:

```
http://localhost:8080/lps-4.0.x/app06/constraintTest7.lzx
```

State objects are represented by the **LzState** class, which is a direct descendant of the **LzNode** class. The attributes of the **LzState** class are given in Table 6.1.

Name	Usage	Type	Default	Accessibility
apply	Tag and JS	boolean		read-write
	Description. A condition that must be met for the associated constraint to take effect.			
isapplied	JS only	boolean		read-only
	Description. Indicates whether or not this state is currently applied.			
onapply	Tag only	script		event handler
	Description. The script that will be executed when the state is applied to its parent.			
onremove	Tag only	script		event handler
	Description. The script that will be executed when the state is removed from its parent.			
pooling	Tag and JS	boolean	false	read-write
	Description. A value of true indicates that the state will pool any views it has created. This means when the state is remove, the views will be hidden, instead of being destroyed.			

Table 6.1: The attributes of the LzState class

The **LzState** class adds the following methods:

```
apply()
```
Applies the state to its parent.

```
remove()
```
Removes the constraints and views created when the state was applied.

In addition, an **LzState** object can emit these events:

```
onapply
```
Occurs when the state is applied.

```
onremove
```
Occurs when the state is removed.

Summary

A constraint is the return value of a JavaScript expression and you can write constraints that get evaluated continuously or only once. A state is a conditional constraint. This chapter taught you how to use constraints and states.

Chapter 7
Animation

One of the features that make OpenLaszlo so appealing is animation. Animation is easy to achieve in OpenLaszlo. Basically, to animate an object you dynamically change the value of its attribute(s). A view whose **x** attribute gets incremented every second will move along the X axis. Keep changing the **rotation** attribute of a view, and you'll see it rotate.

There are two related tags you need to learn: **animator** and **animatorGroup**. You use the **animator** tag within an object to perform a movement. The **animatorGroup** tag is used to group multiple **animator** tags to perform more than one animation type. With the **animator** tag, you can also repeat a movement multiple times or even indefinitely. Another way to perform animation is by using the **animate** method of the **LzNode** class.

In addition, the **LzTimer** class can be used to invoke a method after a specified period of time elapses. Invoking an **LzTimer** object a few times will also simulate animation. We will look at the **LzTimer** class at the end of this chapter.

The LzAnimatorGroup and LzAnimator Classes

The **animator** tag should be nested within the tag of the object you want to animate. The **animator** tag creates an **LzAnimator** object. The **LzAnimator** class is a subclass of **LzAnimatorGroup**, which in turn is a subclass of **LzNode**. All attributes in **LzAnimator** are inherited from **LzAnimatorGroup** and are given in Table 7.1.

Name	Usage	Type	Default	Accessibility
attribute	Tag and JS	string		read-write
	Description. The attribute whose value will be changed to create animation.			
duration	Tag and JS	number		read-write
	Description. The duration of animation in milliseconds.			
ease	JS only			read-write
	Description. The motion for the animator.			
from	Tag and JS	number		read-write
	Description. A start value for the attribute that will be the base of the animation.			
motion	Tag and JS	string		read-write
	Description. The motion of the animation. The value is one of the following: "linear", "easein", "easeout", and "easeboth".			
onrepeat	JS only	script		read-only
	Description. The script that will be called at the beginning of each repeat.			
onstart	Tag only	script		event handler
	Description. The script that will be called when the animation starts.			
onstop	Tag only	script		event handler
	Description. The script that will be called when the animation finished.			
paused	Tag and JS	boolean	false	read-write
	Description. Indicates whether the animation is paused.			
process	Tag and JS	string	sequential	read-only
	Description. Indicates if the animation actions are to be performed sequentially or simultaneously. The valid value is either "sequential" or "simultaneous".			
relative	Tag and JS	boolean	false	read-write
	Description. Indicates if the value of the to attribute is relative to the initial value.			
repeat	Tag and JS	boolean		read-write
	Description. The number of times to repeat the animation. The value must be a positive integer or "Infinity" to indicate that the animation should be repeated indefinitely.			
start	Tag and JS	boolean	true	read-write
	Description. Indicates if the animation should be performed immediately after loading.			
started	JS only	boolean		read-only

	Description. Indicates if the animation has started.		
target	Tag and JS	reference	read-write
	Description. The object to animate.		
to	Tag and JS	number	read-write
	Description. The final value of the attribute to animate.		

Table 7.1: The attributes defined in the AnimatorGroup class

Here are the methods defined in the **LzAnimatorGroup** class.

`doStart()`
>   This method is invoked to set the starting flags and value, raise the **onstart** event, and register the animator that will process the main idle loop.

`pause(arg)`
>   Pauses the animation if *arg* is **true** and resumes animation if *arg* is **false**.

`setTarget(target)`
>   Sets the target of the animation. The *target* argument must be a reference to an object.

`stop()`
>   This method is invoked when the animation is complete or when the animator is destroyed.

The **Animator** class adds two methods:

`setMotion(motion)`
>   Sets the motion style for the animator. The motion argument can be one of these: "easein", "easeout", "linear", or "easeboth". The default is "easeboth".

`setTo(value)`
>   Assigns *value* to the destination value.

In addition, the **animator** and **animatorgroup** tags have the following events:

`onstart`
>   Triggered when the animation starts.

`onstop`
>   Raised when the animation stops.

`onrepeat`
>   Raised when the animation repeats.

There is also the **onfinish** event that has been deprecated and replaced by **onstop**.

As an example, the LZX application in Listing 7.1 shows a button that moves along a horizontal line.

Listing 7.1: A simple animation

```
<canvas height="400">
    <button width="70" text="Example">
        <animator attribute="x" from ="0" to="300" duration="1000"/>
    </button>
</canvas>
```

The button in Listing 7.1 cruises from x=0 to x=300. If the **from** attribute is missing, the current value of **x** is assumed as the start value.

To test this application, direct your browser to this URL:

```
http://localhost:8080/lps-4.0.x/app07/animationTest1.lzx
```

Figure 7.1 shows the application in Listing 7.1.

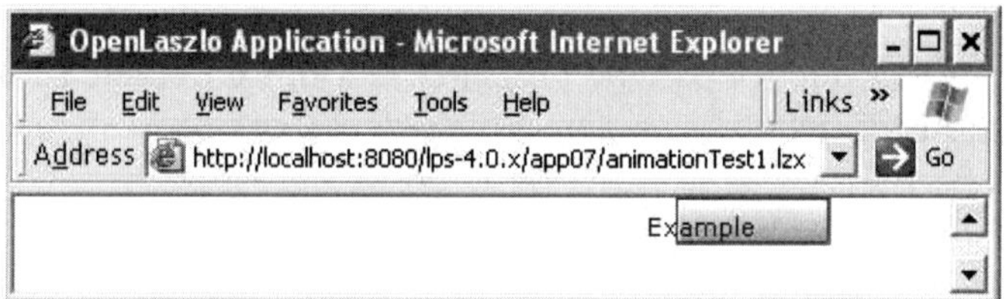

Figure 7.1: Animation in OpenLaszlo

Using Relative Values

If the **relative** attribute of the **animator** tag is set to **true**, the **to** attribute specifies a value that is relative to the current value. For example, the code in Listing 7.1 is rewritten in Listing 7.2

Listing 7.2: Using relative values

```
<canvas height="400">
    <button x="70" width="70" text="Example">
        <animator attribute="x" relative="true" to="70"
      duration="1000"/>
    </button>
```

```
</canvas>
```

Because the initial value of **x** is 70, after the animation, the button's **x** attribute will be 140. If the **relative** attribute is taken out from the **animator** tag in Listing 7.2, the button will not move at all.

You can test the code in Listing 7.2 using this URL:

```
http://localhost:8080/lps-4.0.x/app07/animationTest2.lzx
```

Multiple Animation Pieces

By employing more than one **animator** tag, you can move an object simultaneously in two or more directions. Consider the code in Listing 7.3. It will rotate as it moves along the X axis.

Listing 7:3: Using multiple animator tags

```
<canvas>
    <view y="100" x="100" width="70" height="50" bgcolor="gray">
        <animator attribute="x" to="200" duration="3000"/>
        <animator attribute="rotation" to="360" duration="3000"/>
    </view>
</canvas>
```

To test this application, use the following link:

```
http://localhost:8080/lps-4.0.x/app07/animationTest3.lzx
```

Figure 7.2 shows the result.

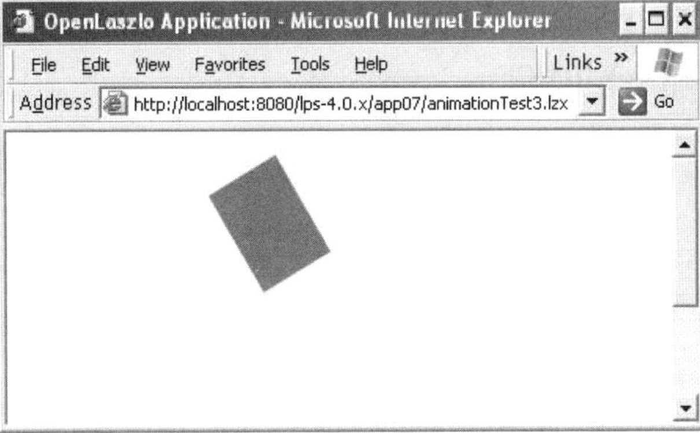

Figure 7.2: Multiple animator tags

Starting Manually

The animation in the previous examples starts to move as soon as the generated application loads. To make it start only when it is told to do so, set the **animator** tag's **start** attribute to **false**. Consider the code in Listing 7.4.

Listing 7.4: Starting animation manually

```
<canvas height="400">
    <button width="70" text="Click here" onclick="this.a.start()">
        <animator name="a" attribute="x" start="false"
                from ="0" to="300" duration="1000" motion="easein"/>
    </button>
</canvas>
```

This time, the button will be stationary, until it is clicked. The **onclick** event of the button is set to invoke the **start** method of the animator. If there is more than one **animator** tag, you must start all of them.

To compile and run the application in Listing 7.4, use this URL.

```
http://localhost:8080/lps-4.0.x/app07/animationTest4.lzx
```

Repeating Animation

The **duration** attribute of the **animator** tag can be set to determine how many times the animation repeats itself. Set it to "Infinity" to make the animation repeat for an indefinite number of times.

For example, the OpenLaszlo application in Listing 7.5 shows an animation that is repeated three times.

Listing 7.5: Repeating animation

```
<canvas width="200" height="200" bgcolor="silver" >
  <view bgcolor="black" x="100" y="100" width="40" height="40">
    <animator attribute="rotation" from ="0" to="360"
        duration="3000" repeat="3"/>
  </view>
</canvas>
```

To test the application, use this URL:

```
http://localhost:8080/lps-4.0.x/app07/animationTest5.lzx
```

As another example, the code in Listing 7.6 shows a view that circles another view.

Listing 7.6: Moving along a circle

```
<canvas height="400">
    <view bgcolor="red" x="98" y="98" width="4" height="4"/>
    <view width="20" height="20" bgcolor="silver"
            x="${ 100 + 30 * Math.cos(angle*Math.PI/180)}"
            y="${ 100 + 30 * Math.sin(angle*Math.PI/180)}">
        <attribute name="angle" value="0"/>
        <animator motion="linear" attribute="angle" from ="0"
                to="360" duration="2000" repeat="Infinity"/>
        <animator motion="linear" attribute="rotation" from ="0"
                to="360" duration="2000" repeat="Infinity"/>
    </view>
</canvas>
```

This URL can be used to compile and run the animation in Listing 7.6.

Figure 7.3 shows the result

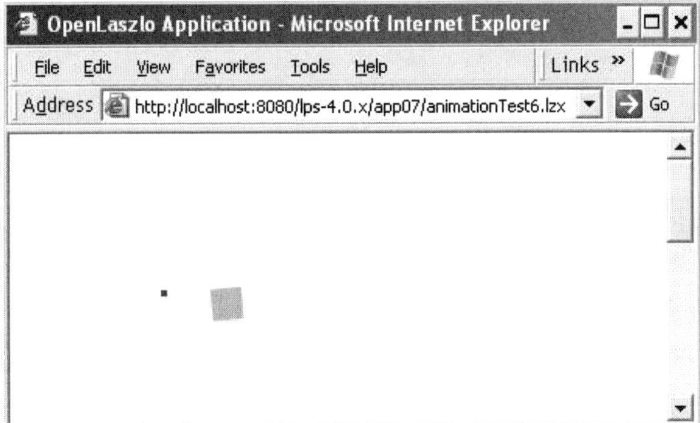

Figure 7.3: Moving along a circle

Using the animate Method

In the previous examples, we used the **animator** tag to create animation. The **animate** method of the **LzNode** class can also be used to achieve the same. This method has the following signature.

```
animate(property, to, duration, isRelative, args)
```

The parameters are as follows.

- *property*. Specifies the property to animate.
- *to*. The end value of the animation.
- *duration*. The duration of the animation in milliseconds.
- *isRelative*. Specifies if the value of the to argument is applied relative to the current value.
- *args*. A dictionary of attributes to pass to the **LzAnimator** constructor.

For example, the code in Listing 7.7 shows an LZX application that uses the **animate** method.

Listing 7.7: Using the animate method

```
<canvas height="300">
    <view width="200">
        <simplelayout axis="y"/>
        <button>Help
            <method event="onclick">
                if (parent.helpView.height==0) {
                    parent.helpView.animate("height",70, 300,
    false);
                } else {
                    parent.helpView.animate("height",0, 300, false);
                }
            </method>
        </button>
        <view name="helpView" bgcolor="#dddddd" height="0"
                width="${parent.width}" clip="true" >
            <text y="10" multiline="true" width="${parent.width}">
                You can use the animator and animatorgroup tags to
                create animation
            </text>
        </view>
    </view>
</canvas>
```

In the code in Listing 7.7, the button has an **onclick** event handler as follows:

```
<method event="onclick">
    if (parent.helpView.height==0) {
        parent.helpView.animate("height",70, 300, false);
    } else {
        parent.helpView.animate("height",0, 300, false);
    }
```

```
</method>
```

The **parent** keyword refers to the parent of the button, the view. The **animate** method checks the value of the **height** attribute of the **helpView** view and assigns 70 if it is 0, and 0 otherwise.

The **if** block can be replaced with a single line of code:

```
parent.helpView.animate("height",
        parent.helpView.height==0?70:0, 300, false);
```

You can use the following URL to compile and run the code in Listing 7.7.

```
http://localhost:8080/lps-4.0.x/app07/animationTest7.lzx
```

Figure 7.4 shows the result.

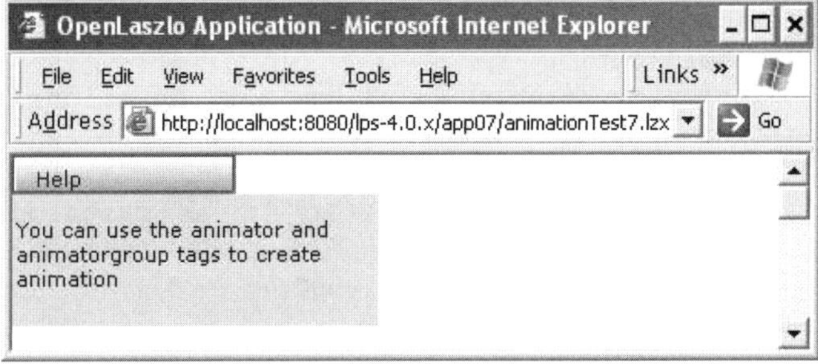

Figure 7.4: Using the animate method

Using animatorgroup

You can use the **animatorgroup** tag to group multiple **animator** tags. Each individual animation can then be run simultaneously (by setting the **process** attribute to **simultaneous**) or sequentially (by assigning **sequential** to the process attribute). By default, the **process** attribute in the **animatorgroup** is **sequential**.

For instance, the code in Listing 7.8 shows the use of **animatorGroup**.

Listing7.8: Using animatorGroup

```
<canvas height="400">
    <button width="70" text="Click here">
        <animatorgroup process="sequential">
            <animator attribute="x" from ="0" to="300"
```

```
                    duration="1000"/>
            <animator attribute="rotation" from ="0" to="90"
                    duration="1000"/>
        </animatorgroup>
    </button>
</canvas>
```

You can test the animation in Listing 7.8 by using this URL:

```
http://localhost:8080/lps-4.0.x/app07/animationTest8.lzx
```

You can also nest an **animatorgroup** tag within another **animatorgroup** tag. Listing 7.9 shows an example.

Listing 7.9: Nesting animatorgroup

```
<canvas height="400">
    <button width="70" text="Click here">
        <animatorgroup >
            <animator attribute="x" to="300" duration="1000"/>
            <animator attribute="rotation" to="90" duration="1000"/>
            <animatorgroup process="simultaneous">
                <animator attribute="x" to="0" duration="1000"/>
                <animator attribute="rotation" to="0"
                        duration="1000"/>
            </animatorgroup>
        </animatorgroup>
    </button>
</canvas>
```

Note that the **process** attribute of the nested **animatorgroup** has the value of **simultaneous**. You can use this URL to test the code in Listing 7.9:

```
http://localhost:8080/lps-4.0.x/app07/animationTest9.lzx
```

Scrolling Text

As another example of animation, the LZX application in Listing 7.10 shows a piece of text that scrolls.

Listing 7.10: Scrolling text

```
<canvas height="90">
    <view width="400" bgcolor="white">
        <text id="t1" height="30" width="${parent.width}"
                fgcolor="red">
```

```
            <font face="Verdana" size="18">AJAX and Flash
    Development</font>
        </text>
    </view>
    <view width="400" bgcolor="white">
        <text id="t2" height="30" width="${parent.width}"
                fgcolor="green">
        <font face="Verdana" size="18">with OpenLaszlo</font>
        </text>
        <animatorgroup process="sequential" repeat="Infinity">
            <animator attribute="width" from ="0" to="400"
                    duration="2000"/>
            <animator attribute="width" from ="400" to="400"
                    duration="1000"/>
            <animator attribute="width" from ="400" to="0"
                    duration="2000"/>
            <animator attribute="width" from ="0" to="0"
                    duration="1000"/>
        </animatorgroup>

    </view>
</canvas>
```

To try the application, direct your browser to this URL:

```
http://localhost:8080/lps-4.0.x/app07/animationTest10.lzx
```

Figure 7.5 shows the result.

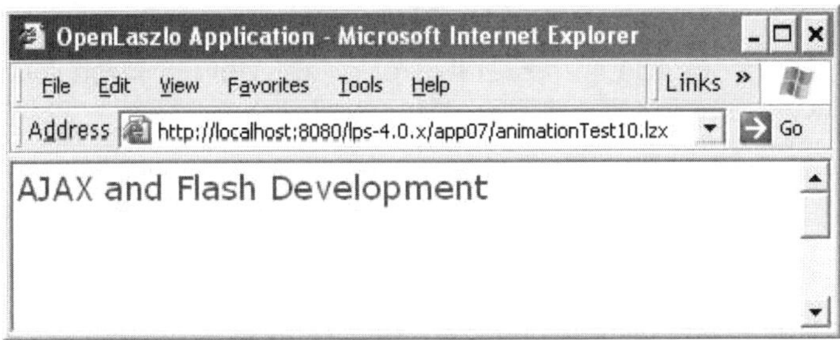

Figure 7.5: Scrolling text

Using Timer

A timer is an object that can be set to invoke a method after the specified period of time elapses. For example, you can display a message ten minutes after user inactivity. The **LzTimer** class encapsulate the behavior of all timer objects in **OpenLaszlo**.

Table 7.2 shows the attribute of the **LzTimer** class.

Name	Usage	Type	Default	Accessibility
timerList	JS only	array of LzTimer		read-only
	Description. The array of active timers.			

Table 7.2: The attribute of the LzTimer class

The following are the methods defined in the **LzTimer** class.

`addTimer(delegate, timeElapse)`
> Adds a timer that will invoked the specified delegate after the specified number of milliseconds elapses.

`removeTimer(delegate)`
> Removes the timer that is associated with the delegate. If more than one timer is linked to the specified delegate, the first timer will be removed.

`resetTimer(delegate, time)`
> Resets the timer for the specified delegate to the new amount of time.

For example, the code in Listing 7.11 displays an **Alert** box ten seconds after loading.

Listing 7.11: Using LzTimer

```
<canvas>
    <alert id="alertBox">Your session will expire in 10
      minutes</alert>
    <method event="oninit">
        var delegate = new LzDelegate(this, "showAlertBox");
        LzTimer.addTimer(delegate, 3000);
    </method>
    <method name="showAlertBox">
        alertBox.open();
    </method>
</canvas>
```

To test this application, direct your browser here:

```
http://localhost:8080/lps-4.0.x/app07/animationTest11.lzx
```

Figure 7.6 shows the generated result.

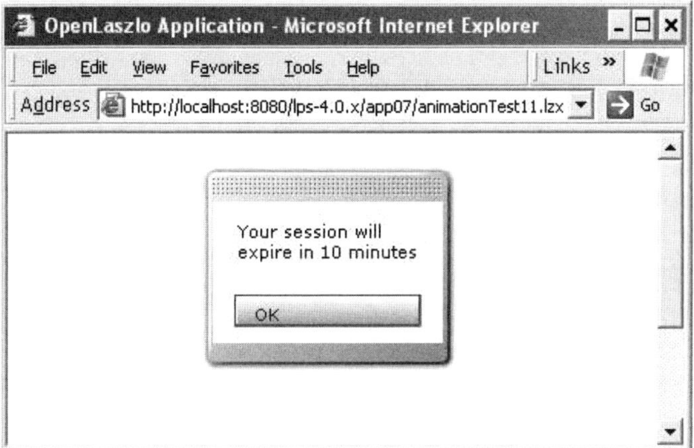

Figure 7.6: Using LzTimer

As another example, consider the application in Listing 7.12. It is a digital clock that relies on an **LzTimer** object.

Listing 7.12: Digital clock

```
<canvas fontsize="48">
    <text id="display" width="250" bgcolor="0x99DDEE"/>
    <method event="oninit">
        this.myDelegate = new LzDelegate (this, "updateClock");
        LzTimer.addTimer( myDelegate, 1000);
    </method>
    <method name="updateClock">
        LzTimer.addTimer(this.myDelegate, 1000);
        var now = new Date();
        var hour = now.getHours();
        var minute = format(now.getMinutes());
        var second = format(now.getSeconds());
        display.setText(hour + ":" + minute + ":" + second);
    </method>

    <method name="format" args="n">
    <![CDATA[
        if (n < 10) {
```

```
        return "0" + n;
    } else {
        return n;
    }
  ]]>
  </method>
</canvas>
```

To compile and run this program, use this URL:

```
http://localhost:8080/lps-4.0.x/app07/animationTest12.lzx
```

Figure 7.7 shows the digital clock.

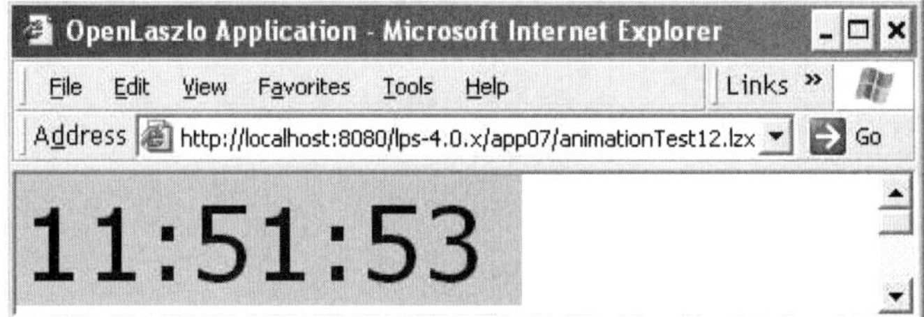

Figure 7.7: The digital clock

Summary

Animation is a powerful feature in OpenLaszlo. You can either use the **animator** tag or the **animate** method to perform animation. You've seen how to do both in this chapter. In addition, you've learned how to use the **LzTimer** class and created a digital clock as an example.

Chapter 8
Working with Data

OpenLaszlo is much more than animation. In fact, OpenLaszlo is close to a typical general programming platform. One of the OpenLaszlo features enables you to access and manipulate data using XPath. The first section of this chapter is an introduction to XPath. This is followed by sections that explain how to access and manipulate data in OpenLaszlo.

Introduction to XPath

XPath, short for XML Path language, is a language for retrieving information in an XML document. XPath finds information by navigating through elements and attributes in the document. You access an XML node by specifying an expression that refers to the node by its position (either relative or absolute), type, content, or other criteria.

Note

XPath is a standard from the World Wide Web Consortium (W3C), a body that develops specifications, guidelines, software, and tools for the Web. Currently at version 2.0, the XPath specification can be found at http://www.w3.org/TR/xpath20/.

Consider the XML document in Listing 8.1.

Listing 8.1: The library.xml document

```
<library>
    <book available="true">
        <isbn>1234567890</isbn>
        <title>In the Middle of the Night</title>
        <author>Jane Volvic</author>
        <pageCount>256</pageCount>
        <price>19.95</price>
```

```
    </book>
    <book available="false">
        <isbn>1234567893</isbn>
        <title>The Man who Never Grows Old</title>
        <author>Anthony Hophop</author>
        <pageCount>400</pageCount>
        <price>29.95</price>
    </book>
    <book available="true">
        <isbn>1234567894</isbn>
        <title>No Excuses</title>
        <author>Sherma Shaun</author>
        <pageCount>160</pageCount>
        <price>9.95</price>
    </book>
</library>
```

The root node of the XML document is **library**. It describes the book collection in a library. There are two books specified using the **book** element. Each book has the **isbn, title, author,** and **pageCount** subelements. In addition, the **available** attribute of the **book** element indicates whether or not the book is available in the library.

In XPath you use the forward slash / to access the root node. Therefore, **/library** references the root node in the **library.xml** document. To refer to the first **book** element under **<library>** you specify the name of the child node, followed by an index number. For example, the following expression refers to the first book child element of **<library>**.

```
/library/book[1]
```

To refer to all **book** elements under **<library>**, remove the index:

```
/library/book
```

The following expression references the first author of the first book in the XML document:

```
/library/book[1]/author[1]
```

To reach a node without qualifying the whole path, you can use the // characters, followed by the name of the element. For instance, this expression represents all **book** elements in the XML document, regardless where they are:

```
//book
```

In the case of the XML document in Listing 8,1, **//book** returns the same value as **/library/book**. However, this is not always the case. If **<book>** can be found in other places than directly under **<library>**, **//book** will include the **book** elements not directly under **<library>** too, while **/library/book** only returns the **book** elements directly under **<library>**.

In addition to specifying a node position, you can search for nodes by attribute, using the **@** character. For example, the following expression refers to all **book** elements whose **available** attribute is **true**.

```
//book[@available='true']
```

The following expression refers to all **book** elements with the **available** attribute, because the value of the attribute is not specified,.

```
//book[@available]
```

XPath also allows you to pass search criteria in your expression. For example, the following expression returns the titles of books under $20.

```
/library/book[price<20.00]/title
```

XPath has built-in functions that provides another way of retrieving information. Here are some of the functions:

```
first()
```
    Specifies the first element.

```
last()
```
    Specifies the last element.

```
position()
```
    Specifies the index number of an element.

For example, the following expression returns the first **book** element under **<library>**:

```
/library/book[first()]
```

And, this one returns the last **book** element under **<library>**:

```
/library/book[last()]
```

This one, on the other hand, refers to the second **book** element in the whole XML document.

```
//book[first() + 1]
```

The following expression specifies the first two **book** elements in the document:

```
//book[position() < 3]
```

The LzDataset Class

You access data by using an **LzDataset** object and bind the data with an object by using the **datapath** attribute that all LZX objects inherits from the **LzNode** class. This section explains the **LzDataSet** class and the next section explains the **datapath** attribute.

The **LzDataset** class hierarchy is shown in Figure 8.1.

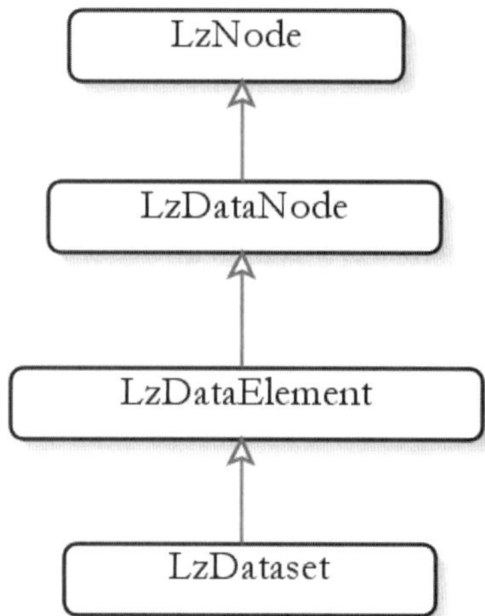

Figure 8.1: The class hierarchy of LzDataset

Table 8.1 lists the attributes defined in the **LzDataset** class.

Name	Usage	Type	Default	Accessibility
acceptencodings	Tag and JS	boolean		read-only
	Description. Indicates whether or not this LzDataset object accepts encoded responses.			
cacheable	Tag and JS	boolean	false	read-only
	Description. Indicates if the OpenLaszlo Server will attemp to cache response.			
getresponseheaders	Tag and JS	boolean	true	read-only

	Description. Indicates whether or not the server will encode and send the HTTP response headers along with the data. This attribute will not work in SOLO deployment			
ondata	Tag only	script		
	Description. Invoked when new data arrives.			
onerror	Tag only	script		
	Description. Invoked when an error occurs.			
ontimeout	Tag only	script		
	Description. Invoked when a request times out.			
querystring	Tag and JS	string		read-only
	Description. The query string of the request URL.			
querytype	Tag only	string		read-write
	Description. The method of the request. The value is either get or post.			
queuerequests	Tag and JS	boolean		read-write
	Description. Indicates whether or not the client should ensure each request is queued.			
request	Tag and JS	boolean	false	read-write
	Description. Indicates if the dataset will make a request right after initialization.			
secure	Tag and JS	boolean	false	read-write
	Description. Indicates if a secure connection should be used.			
timeout	Tag and JS	number		read-write
	Description. The nuber of seconds the dataset will wait for a response before it times out.			
trimwhitespace	Tag and JS	boolean	true	read-only
	Description. Indicates whether white spaces in XML data will be trimeed.			
type	Tag and JS	string		read-write
	Description. A value of 'http' will make the dataset load its content form the URL specified by the src attribute, rather than as a static XML file to inline.			

Table 8.1: The attributes defined in the LzDataset class

The following are the methods added to the **LzDataset** class.

```
abort()
```
  Aborts the request.

```
clearRequestHeaderParams()
```
  Clears all request headers.

`doRequest`
> Sends the request.

`getAllResponseHeaders()`
> Returns an **LzParam** object containing name/value pairs of the response headers.

`getErrorString()`
> Returns an error string, in any.

`getLoadTime()`
> Returns the number of milliseconds it took to load the last request.

`getParams()`
> Returns an **LzParam** object containing the request parameters.

`getPointer()`
> Returns a datapointer referencing the root of the dataset.

`getQueryString()`
> Returns the query string.

`getRequestHeaderParams()`
> Returns an **LzParam** object containing the request headers.

`getResponseHeaderParams()`
> Returns an **LzParam** object containing the response headers.

`getResponseHeader(headerName)`
> Returns the value of the specified header.

`getSrc()`
> Returns the **src** attribute of the dataset.

`setHeader(headerName, headerValue)`
> Sets the specified header.

`setProxyRequests(value)`
> Assigned the specified boolean that indicates whether or not the request will be proxied.

`setQueryParam(name, value)`
> Adds the specified query parameter.

`setQueryParams(object)`
> Adds the query parameters in the specified object.

`setQueryString(queryString)`
> Sets the query string.

```
setQueryType(type)
```
Sets the request method. The value of *type* must be either "post" or "get".

```
setRequest(value)
```
Indicates whether or not the dataset makes its request upon initialization.

```
setSrc(src)
```
Sets the **src** attribute.

The datapath Attribute

Now that you understand XPath basics, you are ready to apply your knowledge in OpenLaszlo. Various tags posses the **datapath** attribute that takes an XPath expression.

Let's see the **datapath** attribute in action. Consider the LZX application in Listing 8.2.

Listing 8.2: Binding XML data

```
<canvas height="200" width="500">
    <dataset name="myData">
        <library>
            <book available="true">
                <isbn>1234567890</isbn>
                <title>In the Middle of the Night</title>
                <author>Jane Volvic</author>
                <pageCount>256</pageCount>
                <price>19.95</price>
            </book>
            <book available="false">
                <isbn>1234567893</isbn>
                <title>The Man who Never Grows Old</title>
                <author>Anthony Hophop</author>
                <pageCount>400</pageCount>
                <price>29.95</price>
            </book>
            <book available="true">
                <isbn>1234567894</isbn>
                <title>No Excuses</title>
                <author>Sherma Shaun</author>
                <pageCount>160</pageCount>
```

```
            <price>9.95</price>
          </book>
        </library>
      </dataset>
      <view layout="axis:y">
        <text width="200"
      datapath="myData:/library/book[1]/title/text()"/>
        <text width="200"
      datapath="myData:/library/book[2]/title/text()"/>
        <text width="200"
      datapath="myData:/library/book[3]/title/text()"/>
      </view>
</canvas>
```

You use the **dataset** tag to embed XML data. To bind data, use the **datapath** attribute, passing an XPath expression. The format for the **datapath** attribute value is as follows:

dataset:xpathExpression

Here, *dataset* is the name of the **dataset** tag that contains the data. You also need to call the **text** function to print the returned value.

You can run the LZX application in Listing 8.2 by invoking this URL:

`http://localhost:8080/lps-4.0.x/app08/datasetTest1.lzx`

The result is shown in Figure 8.1.

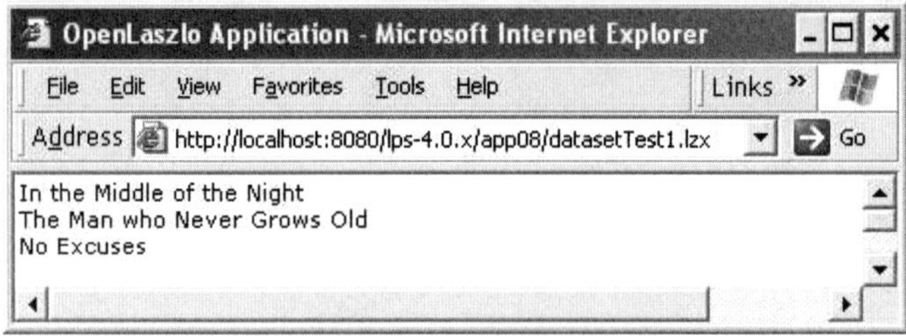

Figure 8.1: Data binding in OpenLaszlo

Before we go further exploring more of OpenLaszlo's data binding features, let's first discuss a relevant issue that you will need when working with data: the separation between data (XML documents) and business logic (LZX application).

Including XML documents

In Listings 8.1 and 8.2 you saw that you could embed the XML document containing data in your LZX application. While this is fine when the data is small, it is not always the best approach. Some data are big and complex and might obscure code if they are put together. Some data are dynamic and come from other servers and not known at compile time.

The **dataset** tag has the **src** attribute that lets you include XML data from an external source. There are two uses of this attribute, depending upon whether the data is static or dynamic.

Including static data

If the data is static, the only requirement is to store it in a file. You then store the file in a resource that the OpenLaszlo compiler can find at compile time. For example, the code in Listing 8.3 has the same effect as the application in Listing 8.2 that embeds the data.

Listing 8.3: Including static data

```
<canvas height="200" width="500">
    <dataset name="myData" src="library.xml"/>
    <view layout="axis:y">
        <text width="200"
                datapath="myData:/library/book[1]/title/text()"/>
        <text width="200"
                datapath="myData:/library/book[2]/title/text()"/>
        <text width="200"
                datapath="myData:/library/book[3]/title/text()"/>
    </view>
</canvas>
```

Including dynamic data

If the data is dynamic and comes from a Web server, you don't include it at compile time. Instead, you tell the application to download it at runtime. Listing 8.4 shows how to include dynamic data.

Listing 8.4: Including dynamic data

```
<canvas height="200" width="500">
    <dataset name="myData" request="true"
            src="http://localhost:8080/lps-4.0.x/test/library.xml"/>
    <view layout="axis:y">
        <text width="200"
                datapath="myData:/library/book[1]/title/text()"/>
        <text width="200"
                datapath="myData:/library/book[2]/title/text()"/>
        <text width="200"
                datapath="myData:/library/book[3]/title/text()"/>
    </view>
</canvas>
```

The **request="true"** part in the **dataset** tag tells the generated output to download the data as soon as the application loads.

> **Note**
>
> The **autorequest** attribute does the same thing as request, but **autorequest** is deprecated.

In Listing 8.4, the **src** attribute is assigned an absolute URL. You can also assign it a relative URL, as shown in Listing 8.5.

Listing 8.5: Using a relative URL

```
<canvas height="200" width="500">
    <dataset name="myData" request="true" type="http"
            src="http:library.xml"/>
    <view layout="axis:y">
        <text width="200"
                datapath="myData:/library/book[1]/title/text()"/>
        <text width="200"
                datapath="myData:/library/book[2]/title/text()"/>
        <text width="200"
                datapath="myData:/library/book[3]/title/text()"/>
    </view>
</canvas>
```

Note that the value of the **src** attribute starts with **http:**. In this case, the **library.xml** document is in the same directory as the compiled LZX file.

Displaying Data in Grids

It is a very common task to display data in a table-like grid. For this, you can use the **grid** tag. The **grid** tag is used to create a **Grid** object. The **Grid** class is a subclass of **BaseGrid**, which itself is derived form **BaseComponent**.

Table 8.2 shows the attributes defined in the **BaseGrid** class and Table 8.3 presents the attribute defined in the **Grid** class.

Name	Usage	Type	Default	Accessibility
bgcolor0	Tag and JS	color code		read-write
	Description. The background color for even-numbered rows.			
bgcolor1	Tag and JS	color code		read-write
	Description. The background color for odd-numbered rows.			
columns	Tag and JS	object		read-write
	Description. An array containing the basegridcolumns used by this grid.			
contentdatapath	Tag only	string	*	read-write
	Description. The datapath to use for the contents of the grid.			
hilite	Tag and JS	LzView		read-write
	Description. The view which is currently highlighted.			
multiselect	Tag and JS	Boolean	true	read-write
	Description. Indicates whether or not multi selection is allowed.			
rowheight	Tag and JS	number		read-write
	Description. The height of the rows in pixels.			
selectable	Tag and JS	boolean	true	read-write
	Description. Indicates whether or not the rows are selectable.			
showhlines	Tag and JS	boolean	false	read-write
	Description. Indicates whether or not the lines between two columns are displayed.			
shownitems	Tag and JS	number	-1	read-write
	Description. The number of rows visible at a time.			
showvlines	Tag and JS	boolean	false	read-write
	Description. Indicates whether or not the lines between two rows are displayed.			
sizetoheader	Tag and JS	boolean		read-write
	Description. Indicates if the grid will keep its width set to the size of the header.			
spacing	Tag and JS	number	0	read-only

	Description. The spacing between the rows.

Table 8.2: The attributes defined in the BaseGrid class

Name	Usage	Type	Default	Accessibility
showhscroll	Tag and JS	boolean	true	read-write
	Description. Indicates whether or not to display a horizontal scrollbar.			

Table 8.3: The attribute added to the Grid class

The code in Listing 8.6 shows how to display data in a grid.

Listing 8.6: Using grid

```
<canvas height="300" width="500">
    <dataset name="myData" src="library.xml"/>
    <grid datapath="myData:/library" contentdatapath="book">
        <gridcolumn width="100">
            ISBN
            <text datapath="isbn/text()"/>
        </gridcolumn>
        <gridcolumn width="200">
            Title
            <text datapath="title/text()"/>
        </gridcolumn>
        <gridcolumn width="100">
            Price
            <text datapath="price/text()"/>
        </gridcolumn>
        <gridcolumn width="100">
            Available
            <view >
                <checkbox align="center"
                        value="$path{'@available'}"/>
            </view>
        </gridcolumn>
    </grid>
</canvas>
```

Note that the check box is placed in a view so that it can be centered.

```
<view >
    <checkbox align="center"
        value="$path{'@available'}"/>
</view>
```

To test the application in Listing 8.6, direct your browser to this URL:

```
http://localhost:8080/lps-4.0.x/app08/gridTest1.lzx
```

Figure 8.2 shows the result.

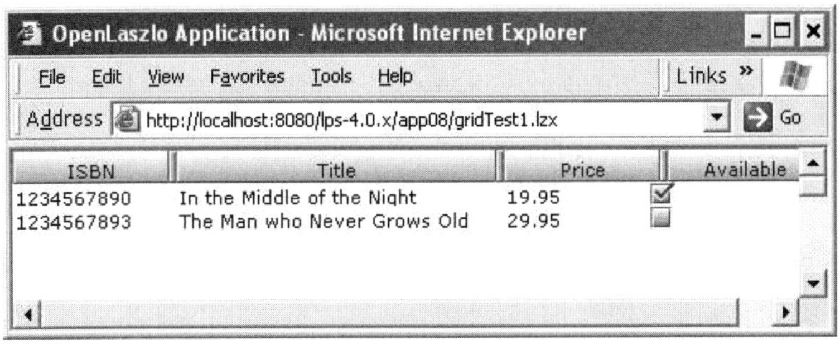

Figure 8.2: Displaying data in a grid

In addition, you can also use the **gridtext** tag, which is an extension of **gridcolumn**. The **gridtext** tag adds the **editable** attribute. A column whose **editable** attribute is true (the default) will be editable.

The application in Listing 8.7 shows how to use **gridtext**.

Listing 8.7: Using gridtext

```
<canvas height="300" width="500">
    <dataset name="myData" src="library.xml"/>
    <grid datapath="myData:/library" contentdatapath="book">
        <gridtext width="100" editable="false"
                datapath="isbn/text()">
            ISBN
        </gridtext>
        <gridtext width="200" datapath="title/text()">
            Title
        </gridtext>
        <gridtext width="100" datapath="price/text()">
            Price
        </gridtext>
        <gridcolumn width="100">
            Available
            <view >
                <checkbox align="center"
                        value="$path{'@available'}"/>
            </view>
        </gridcolumn>
```

```
    </grid>
</canvas>
```

Note that when using **gridtext**, you don't need to use the **text** tag. Instead, you can use the **datapath** attribute of the **gridtext** tag.

You can run the LZX application in Listing 8.7 by using this URL:

```
http://localhost:8080/lps-4.0.x/app08/gridTextTest1.lzx
```

The generated application is displayed in Figure 8.3. Note that the Title and Price columns are editable.

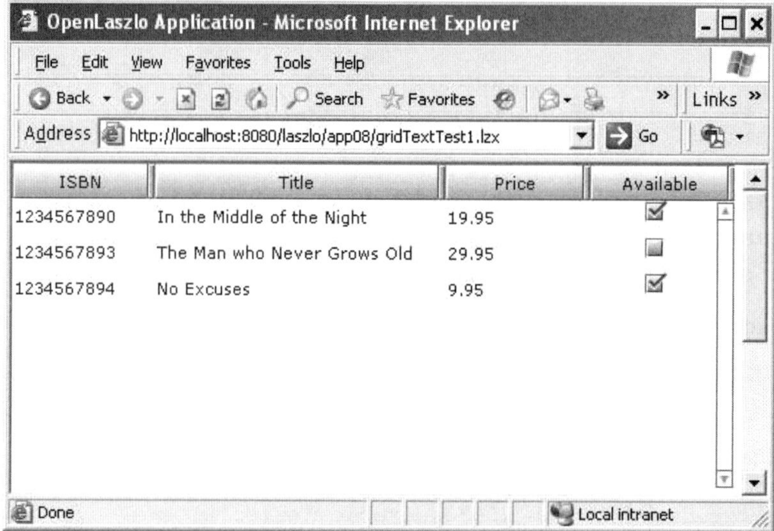

Figure 8.3: Using gridtext

Using Datapointer and Dataelement

A **Dataset** object internally employs a pointer to reference the current node of the XML data. This data pointer is represented by the **LzDataPointer** class, a direct child of **LzNode**. Table 8.4 shows the attributes defined in the **Datapointer** class.

Name	Usage	Type	Default	Accessibility
p	Tag and JS	string		read-write
	Description. The LzDataNode object the pointer is referencing.			
rerunxpath	Tag and JS	boolean		read-write
	Description. Indicates whether or not to reevaluate the XPath expression after the dataset is edited.			
spacing	Tag and JS	number	0	read-write
	Description. The spacing between elements in pixels.			

Table 8.4: The attributes in the LzDataPointer class

The **LzDataPointer** class defines the following methods:

`addNode(name, text, attributes)`
> Adds a new child node below the current context.

`addNodeFromPointer(pointer)`
> Copies the node pointed by the specified pointer to the current node.

`comparePointer(pointer)`
> Indicates whether or not the specified pointer references the same node as this pointer.

`deleteNode()`
> Deletes the node pointed by the pointer.

`deleteNodeAttribute(attribute)`
> Deletes the specified attribute from the current node.

`dupePointer()`
> Clones this pointer and returns the new pointer.

`getDataset()`
> Returns the data set associated with this pointer.

`getNodeAttribute(attribute)`
> Returns the value of the specified attribute in the current node.

`getNodeAttributes()`
> Returns an object containing all the attributes in the current node.

`getNodeCount()`
> Returns the number of element nodes that are children of the current node.

`getNodeName()`
> Returns the name of the current node.

```
getNodeText()
```
Returns the text of the current node.

```
isValid()
```
Tests if this pointer is referencing a valid node.

```
selectChild(howMany)
```
Moves down the data hierarchy by *howMany*.

```
selectNext(howMany)
```
Moves to the next sibling.

```
selectParent(howMany)
```
Moves up the data hierarchy by *howMany*.

```
selectPrev(howMany)
```
Moves to the previous sibling.

```
serialize()
```
Serializes the current node and its children as a string

```
setFromPointer(pointer)
```
Sets this data pointer to the location referenced by the specified pointer.

```
setNodeAttribute(name, value)
```
Sets the specified attribute in the current node.

```
setNodeName(name)
```
Changes the name of the current node.

```
setNodeText(text)
```
Changes the text of the current node.

```
setPointer(node)
```
Points this pointer to the specified node.

```
setXPath(path)
```
Sets the XPath of this pointer.

```
xpathQuery(path)
```
Returns the result of querying the path without changing the pointer.

As an example, the code in Listing 8.8 shows how to use data pointers.

Listing 8.8: Using data pointers

```
<canvas height="300">
    <simplelayout axis="y"/>
    <dataset name="myData">
        <phoneBook>
```

```
        <contact>
            <firstName>Linda</firstName>
            <lastName>Carter</lastName>
            <phone>999-789-8998</phone>
        </contact>
        <contact>
            <firstName>Amy</firstName>
            <lastName>Grant</lastName>
            <phone>992-123-1231</phone>
        </contact>
    </phoneBook>
</dataset>

<datapointer id="dataPointer" xpath="myData:/phoneBook"/>

<grid datapath="myData:/phoneBook" contentdatapath="contact">
    <gridtext width="100" editable="false"
  datapath="firstName/text()">
        First Name
    </gridtext>
    <gridtext width="100" datapath="lastName/text()">
        Last Name
    </gridtext>
    <gridtext width="100" datapath="phone/text()">
        Last Name
    </gridtext>
    <gridcolumn width="70">
        <view datapath="position()">
            <button text="delete">
                <method event="onclick">
                    parent.datapath.deleteNode();
                </method>
            </button>
        </view>
    </gridcolumn>
</grid>
<button>Add New Contact
    <method event="onclick">
        parent.addContactWindow.setVisible(true);
        LzFocus.setFocus(firstName);
    </method>
</button>
<window name="addContactWindow" title="Add Contact"
        width="180" visible="false">
    <simplelayout axis="y"/>
    <view>
```

```
            <simplelayout/>
            <text>First Name:</text>
            <edittext id="firstName" x="30"/>
        </view>
        <view>
            <simplelayout/>
            <text>Last Name:</text>
            <edittext id="lastName" x="30"/>
        </view>
        <view>
            <simplelayout/>
            <text>Phone:</text>
            <edittext id="phone" x="30"/>
        </view>
        <view>
            <button text="Add" x="85">
                <method event="onclick">
                    var newNode = new LzDataElement("contact");
                    dataPointer.p.insertBefore(newNode,
                            dataPointer.p.getFirstChild())
                    var childNode1 = new LzDataElement("firstName");
                    childNode1.appendChild(
                            new LzDataText(firstName.getText()));
                    var childNode2 = new LzDataElement("lastName");
                    childNode2.appendChild(
                            new LzDataText(lastName.getText()));
                    var childNode3 = new LzDataElement("phone");
                    childNode3.appendChild(
                            new LzDataText(phone.getText()));
                    newNode.appendChild(childNode1);
                    newNode.appendChild(childNode2);
                    newNode.appendChild(childNode3);
                    parent.parent.setVisible(false);
                    firstName.clearText();
                    lastName.clearText();
                    phone.clearText();
                </method>
            </button>
        </view>
    </window>
</canvas>
```

The example is an application that can take user input and use the input as values for the next node it will add to the current dataset.

To try this example, use this URL:

```
http://localhost:8080/lps-4.0.x/app08/gridPointerTest1.lzx
```

Figures 8.4 and 8.5 show the generated application.

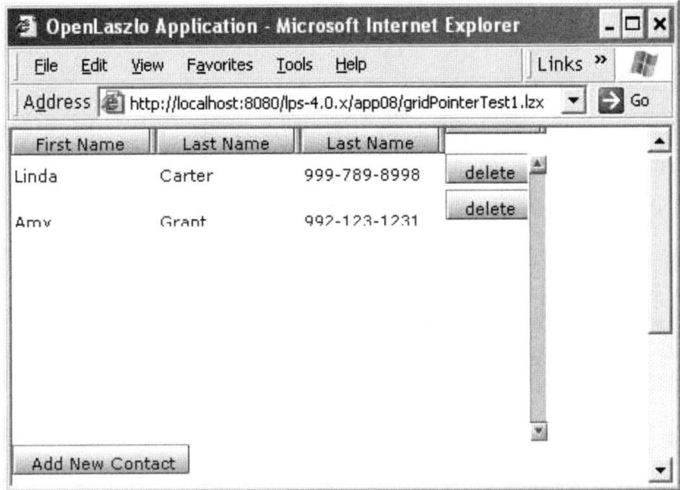

Figure 8.4: Using data pointers

If you click the Add New Contact button, you will see a window you can use to enter the details of a new contact. This window is shown in Figure 8.5.

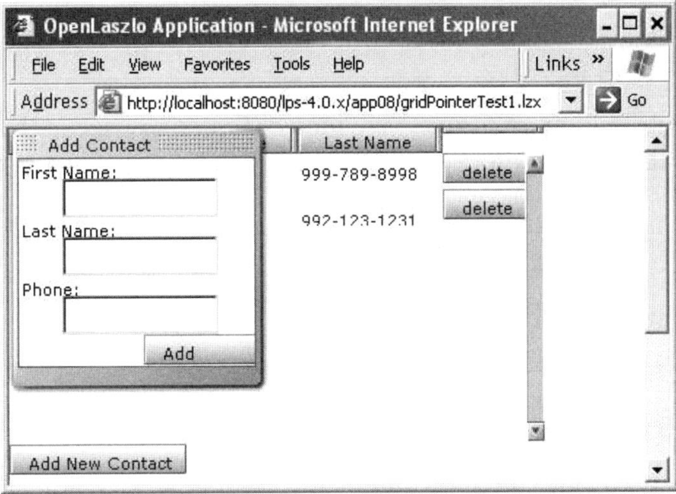

Figure 8.5: Adding a contact

Refreshing Data

As you have learned from the previous sections, you can use the **dataset** tag to retrieve XML data. But there is more. As you will witness shortly, **dataset** can also refresh the data.

Consider the LZX application in Listing 8.9. This application displays the server current time and you can click a button to force it to load new data.

Listing 8.9: Submitting user input

```
<canvas width="340">
    <simplelayout axis="y"/>
    <dataset name="myDataset"
            request="true" src="http://localhost:8080/lps-
       4.0.x/app08/getTime.jsp"/>
    <text width="340" datapath="myDataset:/serverTime/text()"/>
    <button onclick="myDataset.doRequest()">Update Time</button>
</canvas>
```

It uses the **dataset** tag to download data from the server. To be precise, it sends an HTTP request to this JSP page:

```
http://localhost:8080/lps-4.0.x/test/getTime.jsp
```

Note

If you're using a different version of OpenLaszlo, change the URL above accordingly.

To test the application, you must have the **getTime.jsp** page in the same directory as the application in Listing 8.9. The **getTime.jsp** page is presented in Listing 8.10.

Listing 8.10: The getTime.jsp page

```
<serverTime>
<%
    out.println(new java.util.Date());
%>
</serverTime>
```

The JSP page generates the following XML:

```
<serverTime>
    currentTime
```

```
</serverTime>
```

where *currentTime* is the current time on the server.

You can use this URL to test the LZX application in Listing 8.9.

```
http://localhost:8080/lps-4.0.x/app08/submitTest1.lzx
```

Figure 8.6 shows how the application looks like.

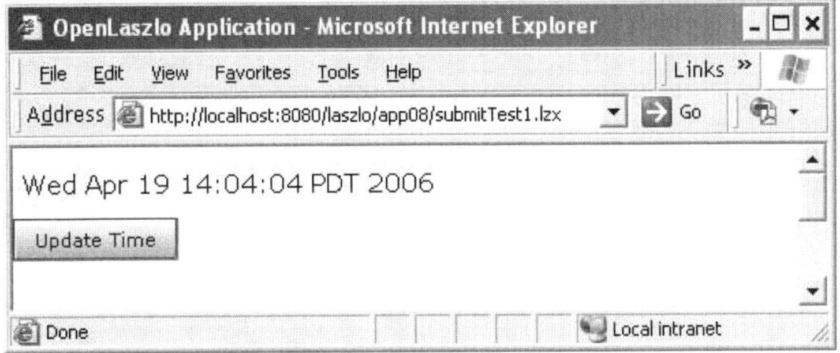

Figure 8.6: Refreshing data

In addition, you can also use the **ondata** event of the **dataset** tag to get notification when the data arrives. For example, you can display a splash screen that begs the user's patience and then hides it when the data arrives.

The LZX application in Listing 8.11 demonstrates the use of **ondata**.

Listing 8.11: Using the ondata event

```
<canvas width="340">
    <simplelayout axis="y"/>
    <dataset name="myDataset"
            request="true" src="http://localhost:8080/lps-
    4.0.x/app08/getTime.jsp"
            ondata="splash.setAttribute('visible', false)"
    />
    <text name="myText" width="340"
        datapath="myDataset:/serverTime/text()"/>
    <button onclick="splash.setAttribute('visible',
        true);myDataset.doRequest()">Update Time</button>
    <view width="100" height="20" name="splash" bgcolor="silver">
        <text>Loading</text>
    </view>
</canvas>
```

When the application loads, it will display the view that acts as a splash screen. When the data arrives, the splash screen disappears.

To test the application in Listing 8.11, use this URL.

```
http://localhost:8080/lps-4.0.x/app08/ondataTest1.lzx
```

Figure 8.7 shows the splash screen

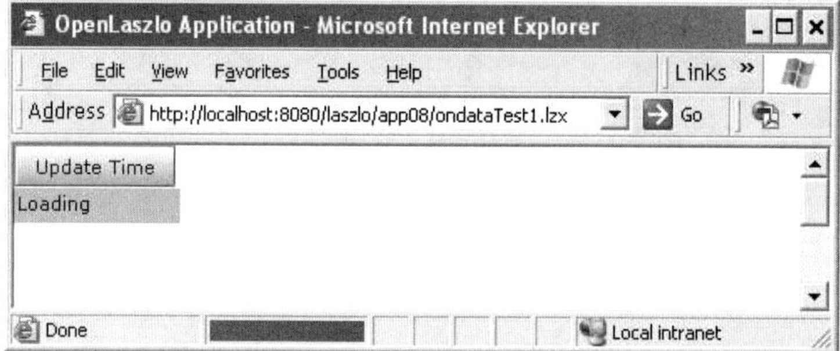

Figure 8.7: Splash screen

Communicating with the Server

You can even use the **dataset** tag to communicate with an HTTP server. For example, the application in Listing 8.12 is a page that accepts user registration. Upon the user registering, the application will consult the **checkUserName.jsp** (in Listing 8.13) to enquiry if the user name has been taken.

Listing 8.12: Registration page

```
<canvas width="280">
    <dataset name="myDataset"
        src="http://localhost:8080/lps-
      4.0.x/app08/checkUserName.jsp"
    >
    </dataset>
    <datapointer id="mydp" xpath="myDataset:/response[1]">
        <method event="ondata">
            if (mydp.getNodeText() == "OK") {
                screen1.setAttribute('visible', false);
                screen2.setAttribute('visible', true);
```

```
        } else {
            userNameErrorText.setAttribute('text',
                    'User name already taken.');
            userNameErrorView.setAttribute('visible', true);
        }
    </method>
</datapointer>

<view id="screen1" x="10" y="20">
    <simplelayout axis="y"/>
    <view>
        <text x="10">User Name:</text>
        <edittext id="userName" x="140"/>
    </view>
    <view visible="false" id="userNameErrorView">
        <text fgcolor="red" resize="true" id="userNameErrorText"
                x="10"/>
    </view>
    <view>
        <text x="10">Password:</text>
        <edittext id="password" password="true" x="140"/>
    </view>
    <view visible="false" id="passwordErrorView">
        <text fgcolor="red" resize="true" id="passwordErrorText"
                x="10"/>
    </view>
    <view align="right">
        <button onclick="validateUser()">Register
            <method name="validateUser">
                var validated = true;
                userNameErrorView.setAttribute('visible',
                        false);
                passwordErrorView.setAttribute('visible',
                        false);
                if (userName.text.length &lt; 4) {
                    userNameErrorText.setAttribute('text',
                    'User name must be at least 4 characters.');
                    userNameErrorView.setAttribute('visible',
                            true);
                    validated = false;
                }
                if (password.text.length &lt; 4) {
                    passwordErrorText.setAttribute('text',
                    'Password must be at least 4 characters.');
                    passwordErrorView.setAttribute('visible',
                            true);
```

```
                            validated = false;
                    }
                    if (validated) {
                        myDataset.setQueryString("userName=" +
                                userName.text);
                        myDataset.doRequest();
                    }
                </method>
            </button>
        </view>
    </view> <!-- end of screen1 -->
    <view id="screen2" visible="false" x="10" y="20">
        <text>Thank you for registering.</text>
    </view>
</canvas>
```

Listing 8.13: The checkUserName.jsp page

```
<response>
<%
    String userName = request.getParameter("userName");
    if (userName!=null && !userName.equals("pandora")) {
        out.println("OK");
    } else {
        out.print("Error");
    }
%>
</response>
```

The **checkUserName.jsp** page is not connected to the database. In fact, it hardcodes the user name **pandora** as the only user name that has been used. Therefore, you can register using any name but **pandora**.

To test the registration application, use the following URL:

```
http://localhost:8080/lps-4.0.x/app08/registration.lzx
```

Figure 8.8 shows the result.

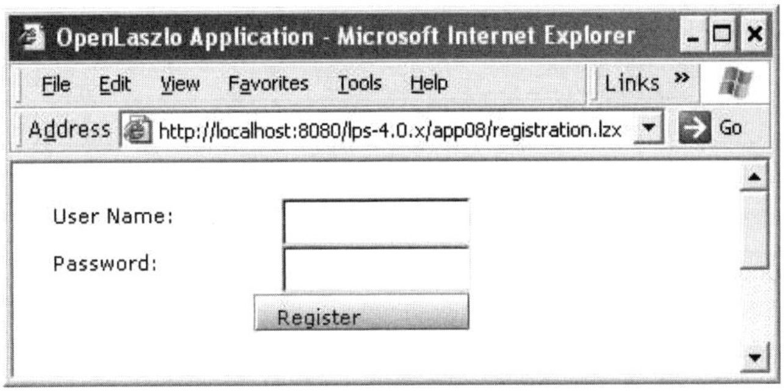

Figure 8.8: Registration page

Figure 8.9: A failed registration attempt

As another example, the code in Listing 8.14 offers a customer form that takes the user's name and email. Upon registration, a message will be displayed.

Listing 8.14: The customer form

```
<canvas height="600" width="500">
    <dataset name="myData" type="http"
            src="http:contact.jsp"/>
    <simplelayout axis="x"/>
    <form>
        <submit name="contact" data="${myData}"/>
        <text>Customer Name</text>
        <edittext name="customerName"/>
        <text>Email</text>
        <edittext name="email"/>
        <radiogroup name="customerType">
            <radiobutton>Individual</radiobutton>
```

```
        <radiobutton>Organization</radiobutton>
    </radiogroup>
    <button isdefault="true"
            onclick="parent.contact.submit()">Submit</button>
</form>

<view layout="axis:y">
    <text multiline="true" width="400"
            datapath="myData:/response/message/text()"/>
</view>
</canvas>
```

Listing 8.15: The contact.jsp page

```
<response>
    <message>
        <![CDATA[
Thank you <b><%=request.getParameter("customerName")%></b>.
Our &quot;<%=request.getParameter("customerType")%> Customer&quot;
    manager
will contact you at <%=request.getParameter("email")%>.
        ]]>
    </message>
</response>
```

You can use the following URL to test and run the application in Listing

```
http://localhost:8080/lps-4.0.x/app08/customerForm.lzx
```

Figure 8.10 shows the generated application.

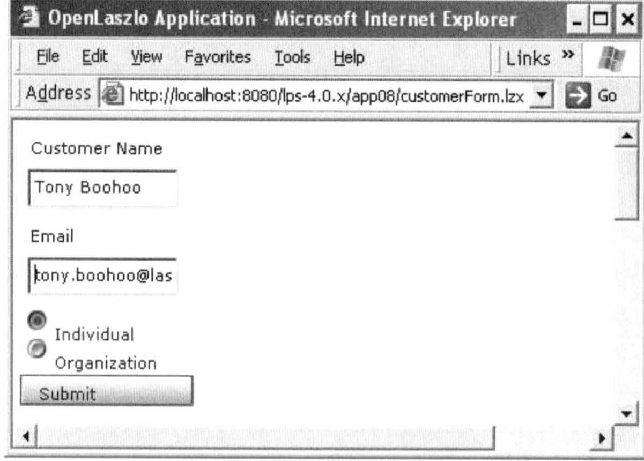

Figure 8.10: The first customer form

If you click the Submit button, you will see something similar to Figure 8.11.

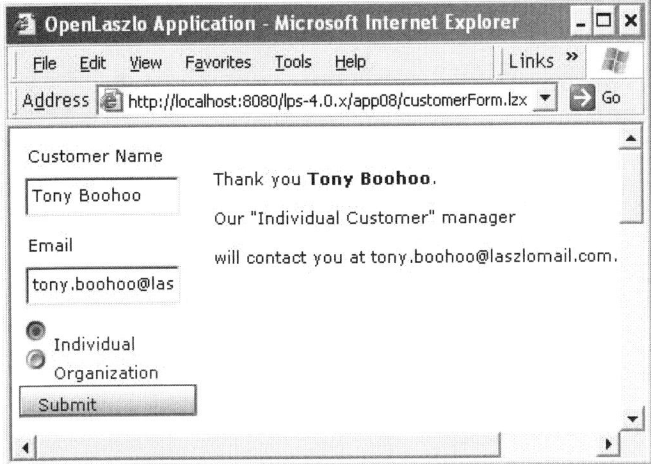

Figure 8.11: Registration confirmation

Summary

Working with XML data is one of the built-in features offered by OpenLaszlo. You will normally work with the **dataset** tag and the **datapath** attribute of the **LzNode** class. This chapter showed you how to read data and displays it in a table. In addition, for XML data manipulation, you can use a data pointer.

Chapter 9
Working with Menus

Rarely a serious UI application go by without menus. Menus are handy because they take only little space out of the screen real estate. Also, only a menu bar needs to appear at all times. Most menu items are in fact hidden and do not take space at all. To use menus, first add a menu bar to the container and add menus to the menu bar. Then, add menu items to a menu. To support hierarchical menus, you can add menu items to a menu item.

In OpenLaszlo, a menu bar is represented by the **Menubar** class, a menu by the **Menu** class, and a menu item by the **Menuitem** class. In this chapter you will learn about menus and how to use them.

The Menubar Class

The **Menubar** class is a direct descendant of **Basecomponent**. **MenuBar** does not add new attributes, but adds a method:

openMenu(*menuRef, open*)
> Opens or closes the specified menu. The *open* argument is a boolean. A value of true opens the menu, a value of false closes it.

To create a **Menubar** and add it to the application, you just need to nest the **menubar** tag within the **canvas** tag:

```
<canvas>
    <menubar>
        add menus here
    </menubar>
</canvas>
```

The Menu Class

The **Menu** class represents a menu and is a direct subclass of **Basecomponent**. Its attributes are given in Table 9.1.

Name	Usage	Type	Default	Accessibility
attach	Tag and JS	string	bottom	read-write
	Description. Specifies how a popup or floating menu attaches to a view. Valid values are "top", "bottom", "left", and "right".			
opened	Tag and JS	boolean	false	read-write
	Description. Indicates whether or not this menu is open.			

Table 9.1: The attributes of the Menu class

The following are the methods defined in the **Menu** class:

`close()`
> Closes this menu and all its children.

`createChildren(array)`
> Adds children specified in *array* to this menu.

`getTopMenu()`
> Returns the topmost menu in the hierarchy.

`open(open)`
> Shows this menu and other menus up in the hierarchy if *open* is **true** or hides them if *open* is **false**.

`setOpen(open)`
> Shows this menu, without affecting other menus in the hierarchy, if *open* is true or close it if *open* is **false**.

Most of the time, you don't need to do anything other than adding the **menu** tag to the **menubar** tag and inserting menu items. OpenLaszlo will take care of displaying the menu and menu items in the correct place.

The Menuitem Class

The **Menuitem** class is the template for creating menu items. Its hierarchy is depicted in Figure 9.1.

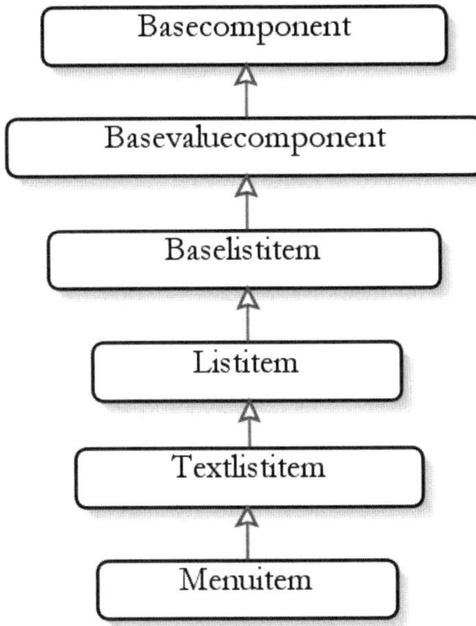

Figure 9.1: The Menuitem class hierarchy

The attribute of the **Baselistitem** class is given in Table 9.2, those of the **Textlistitem** class in Table 9.3, and that of the **Menuitem** class in Table 9.4. The **Listitem** class does not add new attributes. The **Basecomponent** and **Basevaluecomponent** classes are discussed in Chapter 2.

Name	Usage	Type	Default	Accessibility
onselected	Tag and JS	expression	null	read-write
	Description. The event that is raised when this item is selected.			

Table 9.2: The attribute of the Baselistitem class

Name	Usage	Type	Default	Accessibility
text_x	Tag and JS	number	4	read-write
	Description. The x position of the displayed text.			
text_y	Tag and JS	number		read-write
	Description. The y position of the text label.			

Table 9.3: The attributes of the Textlistitem class

Name	Usage	Type	Default	Accessibility
command	Tag and JS	expression	null	read-write
	Description. The command object to be executed when this menuitem is selected.			

Table 9.4: The attribute of the Menuitem class

You usually add an event handler to the selected event. This event handler is executed when the menu item is selected. You'll see how to achieve this in the next section.

Menuseparator

The **Menuseparator** class is a direct descendant of **Basecomponent**. It adds one attribute, which is described in Table 9.5.

Name	Usage	Type	Default	Accessibility
xinset	Tag and JS	number	3	read-write
	Description. The left margin in pixels.			

Table 9.5: The attributes of the Menuseparator class

A menu separator is like a menu item, you can add it to a menu. However, unlike a menu item, a menu separator does not have text and does not respond to user action.

A Simple Example

For starters, review the LZX application in Listing 9.1. It uses a menubar, several menus, and a separator.

Listing 9.1: Using menus

```
<canvas>
    <menubar>
        <menu text="File" width="100">
            <menuitem text="New"/>
            <menuitem text="Open"/>
            <menuitem text="Save"/>
```

```
            <menuseparator/>
            <menuitem text="Exit"/>
        </menu>
        <menu text="Help" width="100">
            <menuitem text="About"/>
        </menu>
    </menubar>
</canvas>
```

You can compile and test the code in Listing 9.1 by directing your browser to this URL:

```
http://localhost:8080/lps-4.0.x/app09/menuTest1.lzx
```

Figure 9.2 shows the application.

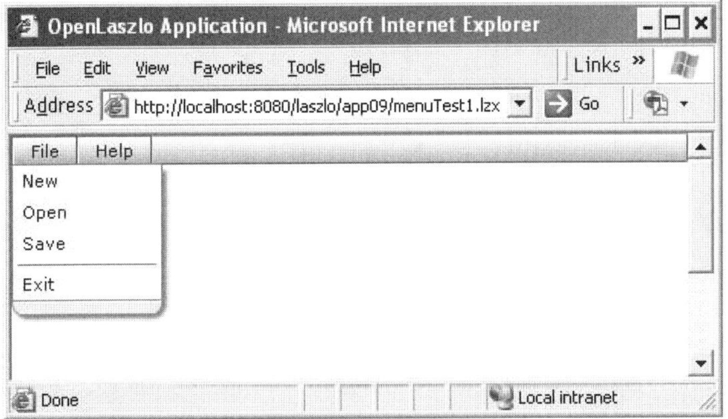

Figure 9.2: An LZX application that uses menus

Creating Submenus

You can create submenus by adding a menu to a menu item, and then add more menu items to the menu. The code in Listing 9.2 shows how you can create submenus.

Listing 9.2: Using submenus

```
<canvas>
    <menubar>
        <menu text="File" width="100">
```

```
            <menuitem text="New"/>
            <menuitem text="Open">
                <menu>
                    <menuitem text="From File"/>
                    <menuitem text="From the Internet"/>
                </menu>
            </menuitem>
            <menuitem text="Save"/>
            <menuseparator/>
            <menuitem text="Exit"/>
        </menu>
        <menu text="Help" width="100">
            <menuitem text="About"/>
        </menu>
    </menubar>
</canvas>
```

To test the application, use this URL:

```
http://localhost:8080/lps-4.0.x/app09/menuTest2.lzx
```

Figure 9.3 shows the result.

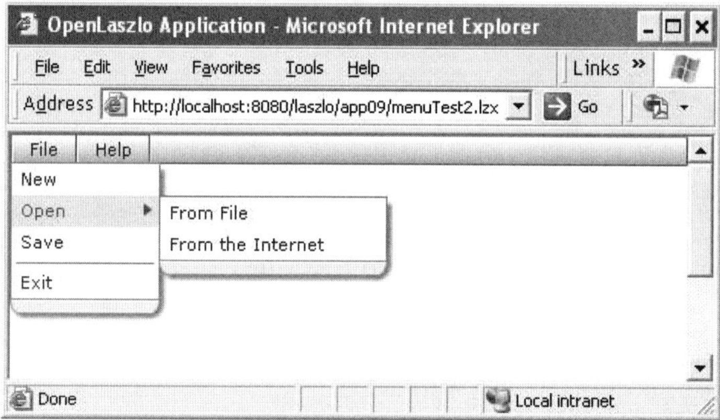

Figure 9.3: Using submenus

Creating Popup Menus

In addition to menus that reside inside a menu bar, there are also popup
menus that can appear anywhere in the application. Normally, these menus are

used as context-sensitive menus. Listing 9.3 shows code that creates a popup menu.

Listing 9.3: Creating Popup Menu

```
<canvas>
    <view name="main" width="$once{parent.width}"
            height="$once{parent.height}" clickable="true">
        <view name="dummy">
            <menu x="100" name="topmenu" attach="left">
                <menuitem text="Stop All Applications"/>
                <menuitem text="Icon Manager">
                    <menu>
                        <menuitem text="Arrange Icons"/>
                        <menuitem text="Default"/>
                    </menu>
                </menuitem>
            </menu>
        </view>
        <method event="onmousedown">
            this.dummy.x = this.getMouse("x");
            this.dummy.y = this.getMouse("y");
            this.dummy.topmenu.setOpen(true);
        </method>
    </view>
</canvas>
```

You cannot add a menu directly to the canvas, so we cover the canvas with an invisible view that has another view (named **dummy**) that is also invisible. Every time you click on the main view, the **onmousedown** event handler is invoked and it moves the dummy view to the click position and then open the menu.

Use this URL to compile and run the application:

```
http://localhost:8080/lps-4.0.x/app09/menuTest3.lzx
```

The application is shown in Figure 9.4. Click anywhere in the application to display the popup menu.

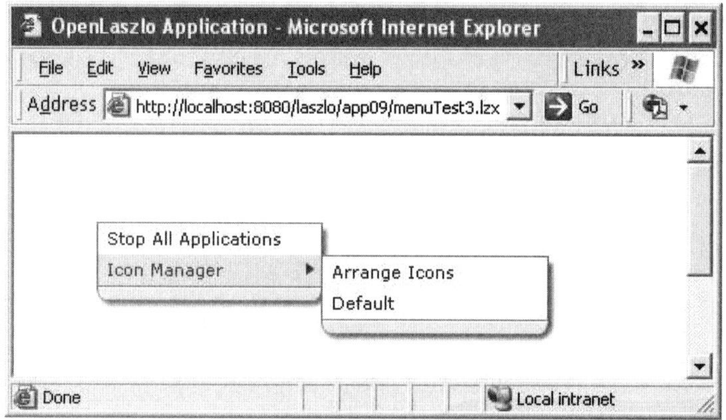

Figure 9.4: Popup menus

Adding Event Handlers

A menu item is only useful if it does something when selected. A menu item is just like other OpenLaszlo objects. All you need to do to make it react to an event is add an event handler to its **selected** event.

The code in Listing 9.4 shows an LZX application with menu items that resize a window when selected.

Listing 9.4: Responding to selection

```
<canvas>
    <window id="win" title="Demo" width="150" height="200"/>
    <menubar>
        <menu text="Action" width="100">
            <menuitem text="Minimize">
                <method event="onselect">
                    win.setWidth(50);
                    win.setHeight(50);
                </method>
            </menuitem>
            <menuitem text="Maximize">
                <method event="onselect">
                    win.setWidth(150);
                    win.setHeight(200);
                </method>
            </menuitem>
```

```
        </menu>
    </menubar>
</canvas>
```

Use this URL to compile the program in Listing 9.4.

```
http://localhost:8080/lps-4.0.x/app09/menuTest4.lzx
```

Figure 9.5 shows the result.

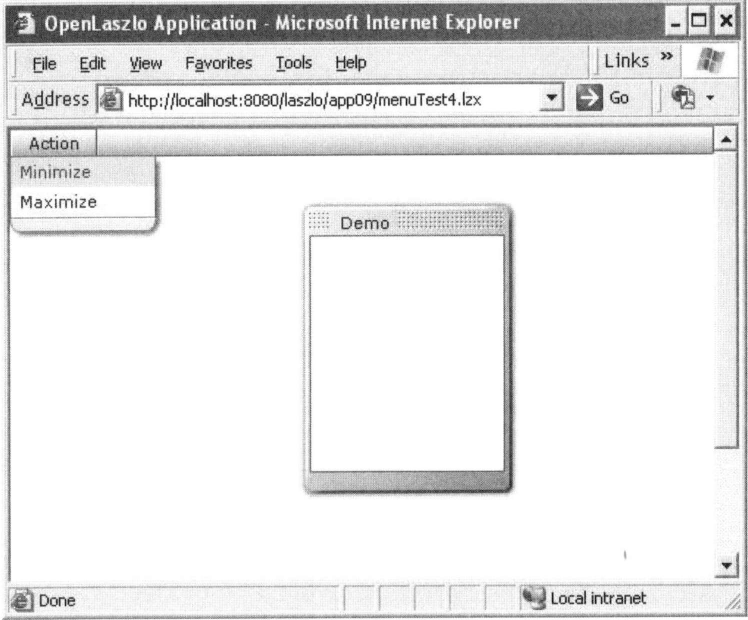

Figure 9.5: Menu items with event handlers

Summary

In this chapter you have learned to create menu and menu items. There are four classes that you can use: **Menubar, Menu, Menuitem**, and **Menuseparator**.

Chapter 10
Custom Drawing

OpenLaszlo comes with a vast collection of ready-to-use components that make development more rapid. However, there are times when you want to draw custom shapes. Custom drawing is possible in OpenLaszlo through the **LzDrawView** class. This chapter will show you how to use the **LzDrawView** class to draw lines, rectangles, ovals, arcs, and quadratic curves. You will also learn how to fill shapes with colors and create gradient colors.

The LzDrawView Class

An **LzDrawView** object represents a view on which you can draw various shapes. As you can guess, the **LzDrawView** class is a subclass of **LzView**. You can easily create an **LzDrawView** object by using the **drawview** tag. You can see the list of attributes of the **LzDrawView** class in Table 10.1.

Name	Usage	Type	Default	Accessibility
fillStyle	JS only	A color or an **LzCanvasGradient**		read-only
	Description. The color or style used to fill a shape.			
globalAlpha	JS only	Number	1.0	read-only
	Description. The alpha value applied to shapes and images before they are drawn onto the canvas. Valid values range from 0.0 to 1.0 (inclusive).			
lineWidth	JS only	Number		read-only
	Description. The line width.			
strokeStyle	JS only	A color		read-only
	Description. The color to use for the lines around shapes.			

Table 10.1: The attributes defined in the LzDrawView class

Here are the methods defined in the **LzDrawView** class.

`arc(x, y, radius, startAngle, endAngle, clockwise)`
> Draws an arc centered at (x, y) on this **LzDrawView**, starting from *startAngle* and ending at *endAngle*. The *radius* argument specifies the radius in pixels and the *clockwise* argument is a boolean that indicates whether or not the arc is drawn clockwise.

`beginPath()`
> Resets the list of subpaths and move to the coordinate $(0, 0)$.

`clear()`
> Clears the drawing area.

`closePath()`
> Draws a line from the current position to the first point in the last subpath and marks the subpath as closed if it has not been so. If there is only one point in the last path, this method does nothing.

`createLinearGradient(x0, y0, x1, y1)`
> Creates a gradient from $(x0, y0)$ to $(x1, y1)$ in the coordinate space and returns a linear **CanvasGradient** object initialized with that line.

`createRadialGradient(x0, y0, r0, x1, y1, r1)`
> Creates a radial gradient from $(x0, y0)$ and rotation $r0$ to $(x1, y1)$ and rotation $r1$. The return value is an **LzCanvasGradient** object.

`fill(m)`
> Fills each subpath of the current path using the current fillstyle and non-zero winding number rule. When an open subpath is filled, it also becomes closed.

`lineTo(x, y)`
> Draws a line from the current position to the specified coordinate (x, y) and adds (x, y) to the list of points of the subpath.

`moveTo(x, y)`
> Move the current position to the specified (x, y) coordinate.

`oval(x, y, radius, yRadius)`
> Draws an oval at the origin (x, y) with a radius *radius*. If the *yRadius* argument is not present, it is translated as the same as *xRadius*, and the result will be a circle.

`quadraticCurveTo(cpx, cpy, x, y)`
> Draws a quadratic curve with the control point (cpx, cpy) and sets the current position to (x, y).

```
rect(x, y, width, height, cornerRadius)
```
> Draws a rectangle with (*x*, *y*) as the top left corner with the width of *width* and height of *height*. The corner radius is specified by *cornerRadius*.

```
stroke()
```
> Strokes each subpath of the current path using the **strokeStyle** and **lineWidth** attributes.

Of special interest are the **moveTo** and **stroke** methods. An **LzDrawView** object employs an internal digital pen to draw. You use the **moveTo** method to move this pen to a position that will become the origin of the shape you are drawing. To actually draw a visible shape, you have to call the **stroke** method at the end of your drawing.

The next sections discuss how to use the methods in the **LzDrawView** class to draw various shapes.

Drawing Lines

You draw a line by using the **lineTo** method on an **LzDrawView** object. You start by moving the internal digital pen to the origin of the line. For example, to draw a line from coordinate (0, 100) to (80, 100), you will call the **moveTo**, **lineTo**, and **stroke** methods in this order:

```
moveTo(0, 100);
lineTo(80, 100);
stroke();
```

For example, the small program in Listing 10.1 shows you how to draw a few lines. Note that you must call the **stroke** methods to actually draw your shapes.

Listing 10.1: Drawing lines

```
<canvas height="200">
    <drawview height="200" width="200">
        <method event="oninit">
            this.moveTo(0, 100);
            this.lineTo(80, 100);
            this.lineTo(100, 140);
            this.lineTo(120, 100);
            this.lineTo(200, 100);
```

```
            this.stroke();
        </method>
    </drawview>
</canvas>
```

To test the program, direct your browser to this location:

```
http://localhost:8080/lps-4.0.x/app10/lineTest1.lzx
```

The generated OpenLaszlo application is shown in Figure 10.1.

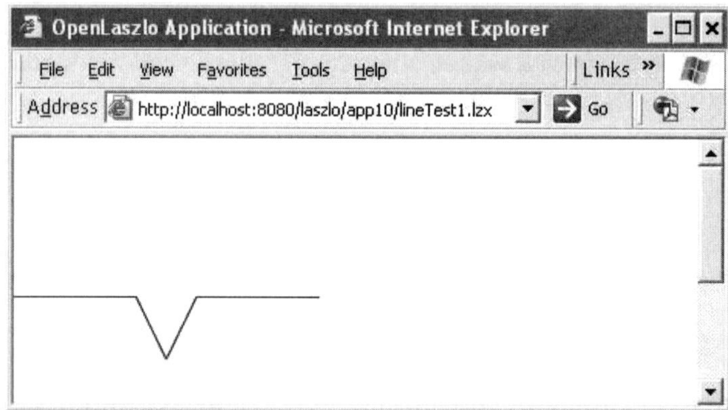

Figure 10.1: Drawing lines with OpenLaszlo

Drawing Rectangles

You use the **rect** method of the **LzDrawView** class to draw rectangles. The LZX application in Listing 10.2 draws three rectangles. The first rectangle's top-left corner is at (10, 10), the second's at (10, 50), and the third's at (10, 90). All rectangles have a width of 100 pixels and a height of 30 pixels. What differentiates them are the radii of the corners.

Listing 10.2: Drawing rectangles

```
<canvas height="200">
    <drawview height="200" width="200">
        <method event="oninit">
            this.rect(10, 10, 100, 30);
            this.rect(10, 50, 100, 30, 5);
            this.rect(10, 90, 100, 30, 15);
            this.stroke();
```

```
        </method>
    </drawview>
</canvas>
```

You can test and run the code in Listing 10.2 by using this URL:

```
http://localhost:8080/lps-4.0.x/app10/rectTest1.lzx
```

Figure 10.2 shows the rectangles.

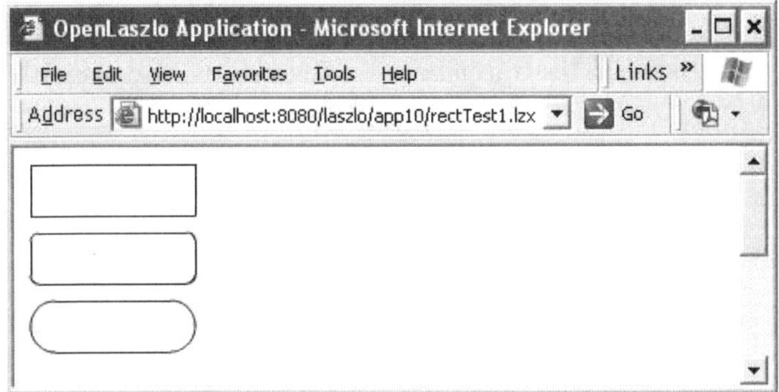

Figure 10.2: Drawing rectangles

Drawing Arcs

Drawing arcs is easy with the **arc** method defined in the **LzDrawView** class. All you need to do is pass the position of the arc center, the radius, the start and end angles, and whether OpenLaszlo should draw it clockwise or counterclockwise. Here is the signature of the **arc** method.

```
arc(x, y, radius, startAngle, endAngle, clockwise)
```
Draws an arc centered at (x, y) on this **LzDrawView**, starting from *startAngle* and ending at *endAngle*. The *radius* argument specifies the radius in pixels and the *clockwise* argument is a boolean that indicates whether or not the arc is drawn clockwise.

The LZX application in Listing 10.3 draws three arcs.

Listing 10.3: Drawing arcs

```
<canvas height="200">
    <drawview height="200" width="600">
```

```
<method event="oninit">
    this.arc(100, 100, 75, 0, 90, true);
    this.arc(200, 100, 75, 0, 90, false);
    this.arc(400, 100, 75, 0, 360, false);
    this.stroke();
</method>
    </drawview>
</canvas>
```

Note that the third arc spans 360 degrees to make a circle.

You can test and run the application in Listing 10.3 by using this URL:

```
http://localhost:8080/lps-4.0.x/app10/arcTest1.lzx
```

The generated application is displayed in Figure 10.3.

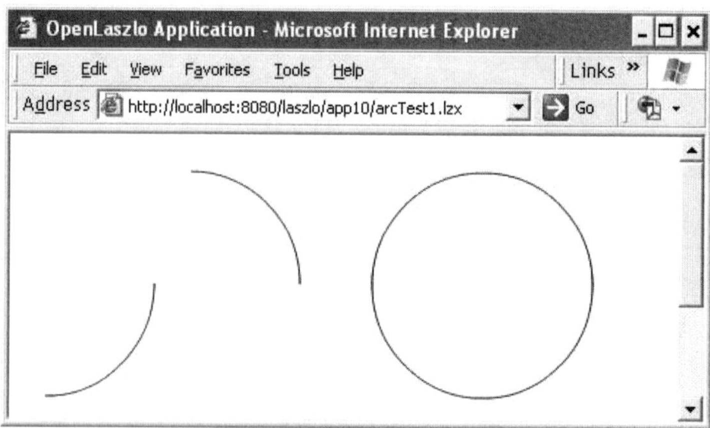

Figure 10.3: Drawing arcs

Drawing Ovals

You use the **oval** method to draw an oval. The signature of this method is as follows.

```
oval(x, y, radius, yRadius)
```

Draws an oval at the origin (x, y) with a radius *radius*. If the yRadius is not present, it is translated as the same as the x radius, and the result is a circle.

For instance, the code in Listing 10.4 shows two ovals.

Listing 10.4: Drawing ovals

```
<canvas height="200">
    <drawview height="200" width="600">
        <method event="oninit">
            this.oval(100, 100, 75, 30);
            this.oval(300, 100, 75);
            this.stroke();
        </method>
    </drawview>
</canvas>
```

You can use this URL to test and run the application.

```
http://localhost:8080/lps-4.0.x/app10/ovalTest1.lzx
```

Figure 10.4 shows the ovals drawn.

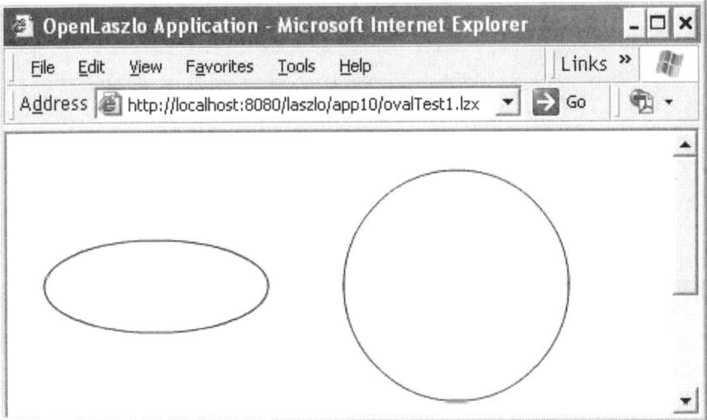

Figure 10.4: Drawing ovals

Drawing Quadratic Curves

You draw quadratic curves by using the **quadraticCurveTo** method defined in the **LzDrawView** class. The code in Listing 10.5 shows how to achieve this.

Listing 10.5: Drawing quadratic curves

```
<canvas height="200">
```

```
<drawview height="200" width="600">
    <method event="oninit">
        this.moveTo(200,100);
        this.quadraticCurveTo(40, 200, 100, 50);
        this.moveTo(400, 100);
        this.quadraticCurveTo(40, 200, 300, 50);
        this.stroke()
    </method>
</drawview>
</canvas>
```

To test the code in Listing 10.5, use this URL:

```
http://localhost:8080/lps-4.0.x/app10/quadTest1.lzx
```

Figure 10.5 shows the curves.

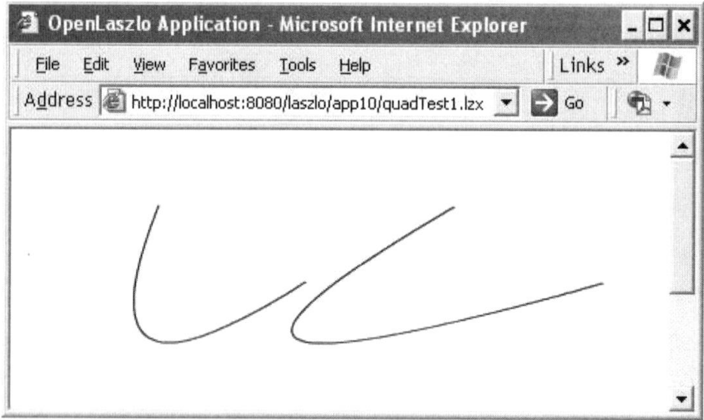

Figure 10.5: Drawing quadratic curves

Using Different Stroke Styles and Line Widths

As shown in the preceding examples, you use a digital pen to draw your shapes. What I have not mentioned is that you can configure this digital pen by changing the value of the **strokeStyle** and **lineWidth** attributes of the **LzDrawView** object.

For example, the code in Listing 10.6 shows how you can draw ovals by using nonstandard pen.

Listing 10.6: Configuring the LzDrawView pen

```
<canvas height="200">
    <drawview height="200" width="600">
        <method event="oninit">
            this.lineWidth = 5;
            this.strokeStyle = 0xff00ff;
            this.oval(100, 100, 75, 30);
            this.stroke();

            this.beginPath();
            this.lineWidth = 10;
            this.strokeStyle = 0xff0000;
            this.oval(300, 100, 75);
            this.stroke();

        </method>
    </drawview>
</canvas>
```

You need to call the **beginPath** method so that the subsequent **lineWidth**
and **strokeStyle** does not affect the previous one. To test this application,
direct your browser to this URL:

```
http://localhost:8080/lps-4.0.x/app10/strokeStyleTest1.lzx
```

Figure 10.6 shows the generated application

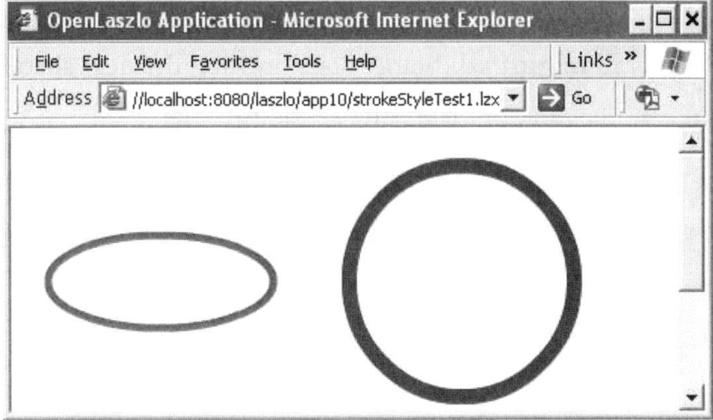

Figure 10.6: Configuring LzDrawView pen

Using Fills

To make your drawing more appealing, fill your shapes with colors. The LZX application in Listing 10.7 displays a rectangle and an oval that are filled with different colors.

Listing 10.7: Using fills

```
<canvas height="200">
    <drawview height="200" width="600">
        <method event="oninit">
            this.rect(10, 10, 100, 30);
            this.stroke();
            this.moveTo(60, 20);
            this.fillStyle = 0x00ee00;
            this.fill();

            this.beginPath();
            this.oval(350, 100, 75, 10);
            this.stroke();
            this.moveTo(150, 100);
            this.fillStyle = 0x330000;
            this.fill();
        </method>
    </drawview>
</canvas>
```

Note that you need to move the brush to a coordinate inside the shape before calling fill. Also, call **beginPath** before start drawing the next shape.

To test the application in Listing 10.7, use this URL.

```
http://localhost:8080/lps-4.0.x/app10/fillTest1.lzx
```

Figure 10.7 shows the colorful shapes

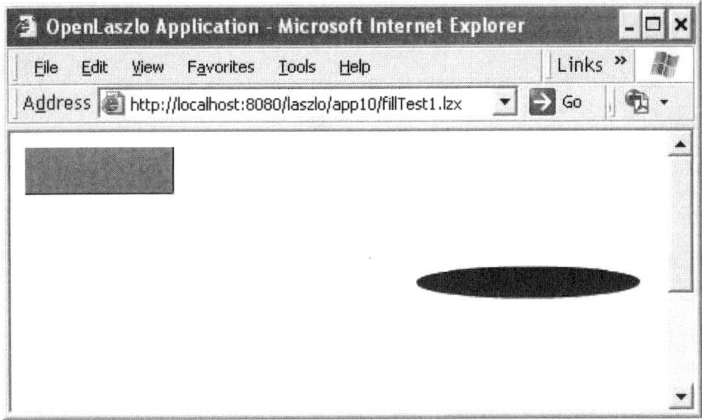

Figure 10.7: Filling shapes with different colors

Setting Opacity

What's amazing with the OpenLaszlo drawing kit is the fact that it supports advanced and complex features. One of these features is the ability to change the opacity of a shape. You do this by changing the value of the **globalAlpha** attribute.

Consider the code in Listing 10.8 that uses different opacities for different shapes.

Listing 10.8: Changing opacity

```
<canvas height="200">
    <drawview height="200" width="600">
        <method event="oninit">
            this.rect(10, 10, 100, 80);
            this.stroke();
            this.moveTo(60, 20);
            this.fillStyle = 0x00ee00;
            this.fill();

            this.beginPath();
            this.globalAlpha = 1;
            this.oval(100, 100, 75, 60);
            this.stroke();
            this.moveTo(150, 100);
            this.fillStyle = 0x330000;
```

```
            this.fill();

            this.beginPath();
            this.rect(310, 10, 100, 80);
            this.stroke();
            this.moveTo(60, 20);
            this.fillStyle = 0x00ee00;
            this.fill();

            this.beginPath();
            this.globalAlpha = 0.2;
            this.oval(300, 100, 75, 60);
            this.stroke();
            this.moveTo(150, 100);
            this.fillStyle = 0x330000;
            this.fill();
        </method>
    </drawview>
</canvas>
```

The first rectangle and the first oval are drawn with an opacity of 1. This is the most opaque. The second rectangle and the second oval are drawn with an opacity of 0.2. You can test the application by directing your browser to the following location:

```
http://localhost:8080/lps-4.0.x/app10/opacityTest1.lzx
```

Figure 10.8 shows two shapes with different opacities. Can you see the difference?

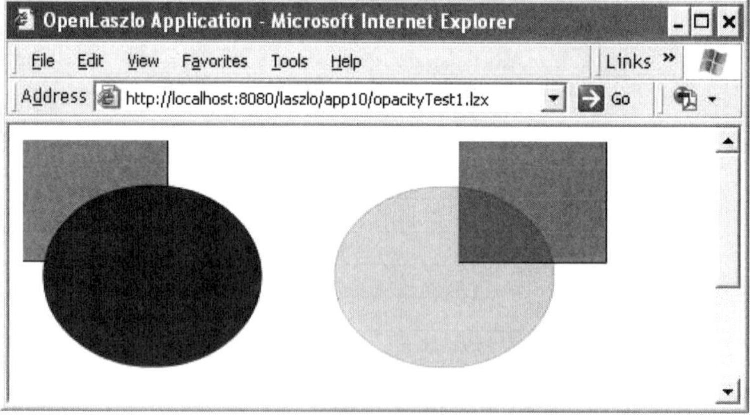

Figure 10.8: Playing with opacity

Using Gradients

So far, you've been using monochromatic colors to fill your shapes. The fact is OpenLaszlo drawing toolkit is more than that. It allows you to produce gradient colors by using the **createLinearGradient** and **createRadialGradient** methods.

The code in Listing 10.9 is an **LzDrawView** object in action. It draws a few shapes and fill them with gradient colors.

Listing 10.9: Using gradient colors

```
<canvas height="200">
    <drawview>
        <method event="oninit">
            // draw a rectangle;
            this.rect(5, 5, 145, 150);
            this.stroke();
            // create a gradient
            // that starts at the (5, 100) and ends at (150, 100)
            var g = this.createLinearGradient(5, 5, 150, 5);
            // set black as the starting color
            g.addColorStop(0, 0x000000);
            // set white as the ending color
            g.addColorStop(1, 0xffffff);
            this.fillStyle = g;
            this.fill();
        </method>
    </drawview>
</canvas>
```

To test and run the application in Listing 10.9, use the following URL.

```
http://localhost:8080/lps-4.0.x/app10/gradientTest1.lzx
```

Figure 10.9 shows the gradient colors.

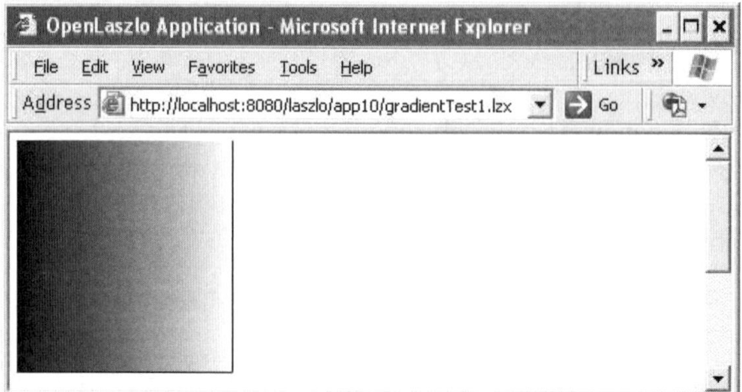

Figure 10.9: Using gradient colors

For comparison, take a look at the code in Listing 10.10. It draws the same rectangle as the one in Listing 10.9 but with a slightly different gradient. The gradient used in the code in Listing 10.10 starts from the top-left corner of the gradient and ends at its bottom-right corner.

Listing 10.10: Another radial gradient

```
<canvas height="200">
    <drawview>
        <method event="oninit">
            // draw a rectangle;
            this.rect(5, 5, 145, 150);
            this.stroke();
            // create a gradient
            // that starts at the (5, 100) and ends at (150, 100)
            var g = this.createLinearGradient(5, 5, 150, 55);
            // set black as the starting color
            g.addColorStop(0, 0x000000);
            // set white as the ending color
            g.addColorStop(1, 0xffffff);
            this.fillStyle = g;
            this.fill();
        </method>
    </drawview>
</canvas>
```

Test the application by directing your browser here.

```
http://localhost:8080/lps-4.0.x/app10/gradientTest2.lzx
```

Figure 10.10 shows a different linear gradient.

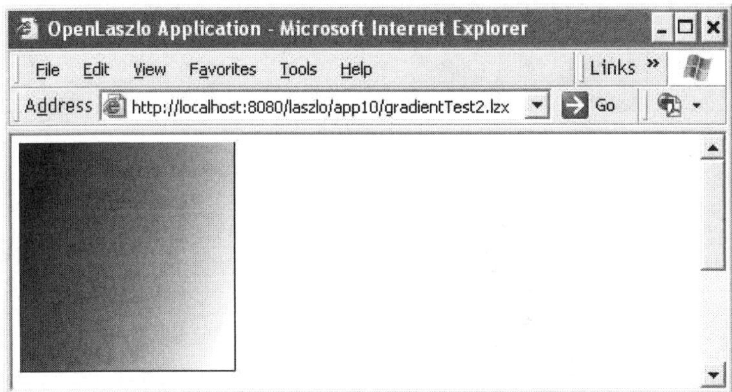

Figure 10.10: Another linear gradient

In addition to linear gradients, you can also use radial gradients. An example is given in Listing 10.11.

Listing 10.11: Using radial gradients

```
<canvas height="200">
    <drawview>
        <method event="oninit">
            // draw a rectangle;
            this.oval(100, 100, 75);
            this.stroke();
            // create a gradient
            // that starts at the (5, 100) and ends at (150, 100)
            var g =
                this.createRadialGradient(0, 0, .2, 300, 250, 1);
            // set black as the starting color
            g.addColorStop(0, 0x000000);
            // set white as the ending color
            g.addColorStop(1, 0xffffff);
            this.fillStyle = g;
            this.fill();
        </method>
    </drawview>
</canvas>
```

You can test and run the application in Listing 10.11 by using this URL:

```
http://localhost:8080/lps-4.0.x/app10/gradientTest3.lzx
```

Figure 10.11 shows the generated LZX application

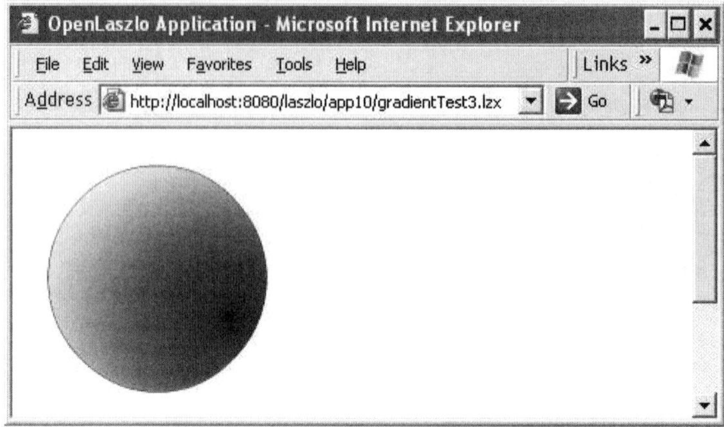

Figure 10.11: Radial gradients

Summary

OpenLaszlo comes equipped with a drawing toolkit that you can use to draw various shapes and fill them with monochromatic and gradient colors. You've seen how to achieve this in the examples in this chapter.

Chapter 11
Rich Components

In Chapter 2 you learned about some basic components in OpenLaszlo. There is much more. This chapter presents the more complex components that are readily useable from any LZX applications.

Slider

The **Slider** is a component that allows the selection of a value by dragging a button. Figure 11.1 shows a slider.

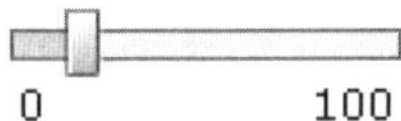

Figure 11.1: The slider

The **Slider** class is the template for all sliders. It is a direct child class of **Baseslider**. The **Baseslider** class in turn extends the **Basevaluecomponent** class, a direct descendant of **Basecomponent**. Figure 11.2 shows the class hierarchy for the **Slider** class.

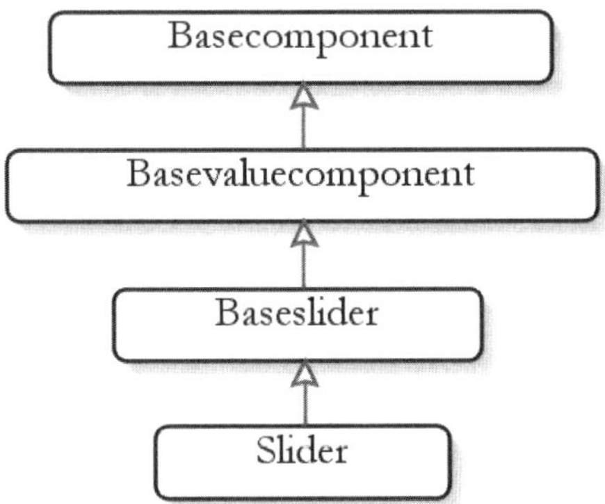

Figure 11.2: The Slider class hieararchy

The **Basevaluecomponent** class is an abstract class that represents a value. It defines a new attribute, **value**, and a new method, **getValue**. The attribute of the **Basevaluecomponent** class is given in Table 11.1.

Name	Usage	Type	Default	Accessibility
value	Tag and JS	string	null	read-write
	Description. The value contained in the Basevaluecomponent.			

Table 11.1: The attribute of the Basevaluecomponent class

The **getValue** method has the following signature.

```
getValue()
```
Returns the value of the **value** attribute.

The **Baseslider** class defines many of the attributes in a slider. These attributes are given in Table 11.2.

Name	Usage	Type	Default	Accessibility
bordersize	Tag and JS	number	1	read-write
	Description. The border size in pixels.			
keystep	Tag and JS	number	2	read-write
	Description. The number of units to increment or decrement the value every time the slider slides.			
maxvalue	Tag and JS	number	100	read-write
	Description. The maximum allowable value.			
minvalue	Tag and JS	number	0	read-write
	Description. The minimum allowable value.			
showfill	Tag and JS	boolean	true	read-write
	Description. Indicates whether or not the slider's fill area should be shown.			
showrange	Tag and JS	boolean	true	read-write
	Description. Indicates whether or not the range text should be displayed when the slider is being dragged.			
showvalue	Tag and JS	boolean	true	read-write
	Description. Indicates whether or not the value text is shown when the slider is being dragged.			
thumbheight	Tag and JS	number	18	read-write
	Description. The height of the thumb in pixels.			
thumbwidth	Tag and JS	number	10	read-write

	Description. The width of the thumb in pixels.				
trackheight	Tag and JS	number	8		read-write
	Description. The height of the track in pixels.				

Table 11.2: The attributes of the Baseslider class

The **Baseslider** class adds several methods to access some of its attributes:

```
getMaxValue()
```
Returns the maximum value.

```
getMinValue()
```
Returns the minimum value.

```
getPercentage()
```
Returns the percentage of the range selected by the value.

```
setMaxValue(value)
```
Sets the maximum value.

```
setMinValue(value)
```
Sets the minimum value.

```
setPercentage(percentage)
```
Sets the percentage of range from the minimum value to the maximum value.

The **Slider** class is a visual implementation of **Baseslider** and does not add new attributes or methods.

For example, the code in Listing 11.1 uses the slider to control the opacity of a view.

Listing 11.1: Using the slider

```
<canvas width="500" height="250">
    <simplelayout axis="y"/>
    <view width="100" height="100" bgcolor="black"
        opacity="${parent.s.value/100}"/>
    <slider name="s" width="100" value="50"/>
</canvas>
```

You can use this URL to test and run the application.

```
http://localhost:8080/lps-4.0.x/app11/sliderTest1.lzx
```

The generated application looks like the picture in Figure 11.3.

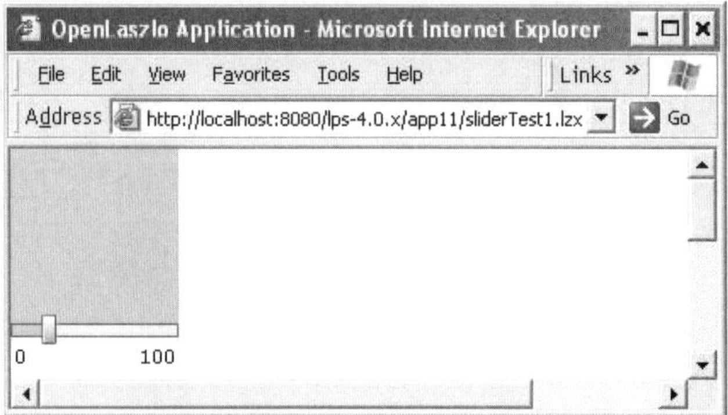

Figure 11.3: Using the slider

Date Picker

As the name implies, the date picker component allows you to easily select a date. This component is represented by the **Datepicker** class, which is a direct descendant of the **Basedatepicker** class. **Basedatepicker** is an abstract class and is a subclass of **Basecomponent**.

The **Basedatepicker** class adds eleven attributes and the **Datepicker** class adds one. The attributes defined in the **Basedatepicker** class are listed in Table 11.3.

Name	Usage	Type	Default	Accessibility
dayclass	Tag and JS	string		read-write
	Description. The dayclass to use in this date picker.			
earliestdate	Tag and JS	Date		read-write
	Description. The earliest selectable date.			
latestdate	Tag and JS	Date		read-write
	Description. The latest selectable date.			
selecteddate	Tag and JS	Date		read-write
	Description. The currently selected date.			
selecteddatepickerday	Tag and JS	Date	null	read-write
	Description. The selected datepickerday.			
showingdate	Tag and JS	Date		read-write
	Description. The Date object representing the month to be displayed.			
showingmonth	Tag and JS	number		read-write

	Description. The month currently showing.			
showingyear	Tag and JS	number		read-write
	Description. The year currently showing.			
weekclass	Tag and JS	string		read-write
	Description. The weekclasss to use in this date picker.			
xinset	Tag and JS	number		read-write
	Description. The left margin of the day portion in pixels.			
yinset	Tag and JS	number		read-write
	Description. The top margin of the day portion in pixels.			

Table 11.3: Attributes defined in the Basedatepicker class

Name	Usage	Type	Default	Accessibility
startAsIcon	Tag and JS	Boolean		read-write
	Description. Indicates whether or not to show the date picker as an icon.			

Table 11.4: The Datepicker class's attribute

Both the **Basedatepicker** and **Datepicker** classes add new methods. Here are the methods defined in the **Basedatepicker** class.

`focusOnDay(`*`week, day`*`)`
> Sets the focus on the specified day. The value of the week argument must be 0 to 5 (inclusive) and for the day argument 0 to 6 (inclusive).

`focusOnFirstDayInMonth()`
> Sends a notification to the first day of the month that it has received focus.

`focusOnLasDayInMonth()`
> Sends a notification to the last day of the month that it has received focus.

`getNumberOfDaysInMonth(`*`month, year`*`)`
> Returns the number of days in the specified month and year.

`handleKeyDown(`*`key`*`)`
> This method is invoked when a key goes down when the date picker has focus. The key is passed as the argument to this method.

`handleKeyUp(`*`key`*`)`
> This method is invoked when a key goes up when the date picker has focus. The key is passed as the argument to this method.

`isDayDisabled(`*`week, day`*`)`

Specifies if the given day and week is selected.

```
isLastWeekInMonth(week)
```
Specifies if the tiven week is the last week in the month.

```
removeFocusFromDay(week, day)
```
Removes the focus from a day.

```
selectFocusDay()
```
Returns the day that has the focus.

```
setMonthToShow(month, year)
```
Sets the month to show in the date picker.

```
setStartingDay(day, max)
```
Sets the day number that the first day of the month should have, and all subsequent days.

```
showNextMonth()
```
Shows the next month.

```
showPreviousMonth()
```
Shows the previous month.

The **Datepicker** class overrides several methods in its parent class, but it does not add new methods.

For example, the code in Listing 11.2 allows the user to select a date and displays the selected date in a **text** tag.

Listing 11.2: Using the date picker

```
<canvas height="200">
    <script>
        var today = new Date();
        var lastYear = new Date(today.getFullYear() - 1,
                today.getMonth(), today.getDate());
        var nextYear = new Date(today.getFullYear() + 1,
                today.getMonth(), today.getDate());

    </script>
    <simplelayout axis="y" spacing="5"/>
    <datepicker earliestdate="$once{lastYear}"
        selecteddate="$once{today}"
        latestdate="$once{lastYear}">
        <method event="onselecteddate">
            if( this.selecteddate != null ) {
                display.year.setText(
```

```
                this.selecteddate.getFullYear() );
            display.month.datapath.setXPath(
            "datepicker_strings_en:/months/month[@index='" +
                    this.selecteddate.getMonth() + "']/@full" );
            display.date.setText( this.selecteddate.getDate() );
        }
    </method>
  </datepicker>

  <view id="display">
      <text name="month" resize="true" datapath="."/>
      <text name="date" resize="true"/>
      <text name="year" resize="true"/>
      <simplelayout axis="x" spacing="2"/>
  </view>
</canvas>
```

To test the code, direct your browser to this link.

```
http://localhost:8080/lps-4.0.x/app11/datePickerTest1.lzx
```

Figure 11.4 shows the generated application.

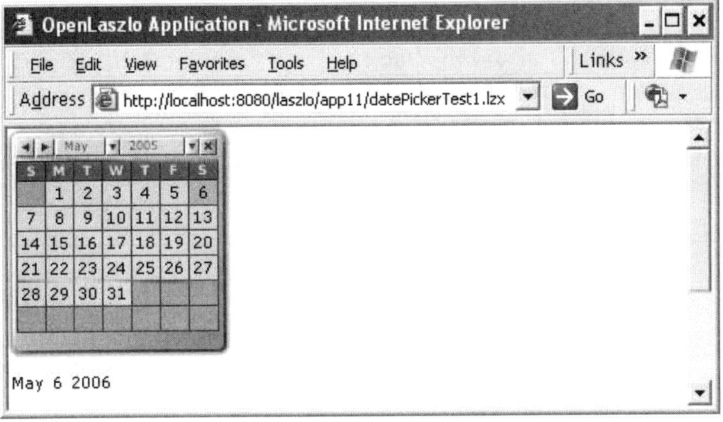

Figure 11.4: Datepicker in action

ScrollBar

The scrollbar component is represented by the **Scrollbar** class. It is a subclass of **Basescrollbar**, which is a direct subclass of **Basecomponent**. The members of both **Scrollbar** and **Basescrollbar** are discussed here.

Table 11.5 shows the attributes of the **Basescrollbar** class and Table 11.6 presents the **Scrollbar** class's attribute.

Name	Usage	Type	Default	Accessibility
axis	Tag only	string	y	final
	Description. The orientation of the scrollbar. Valid values are "x" and "y".			
focusview	Tag and JS	string		read-write
	Description. The view the scrollbar must listen to for mousewheel activation events. If this attribute is not present, it will be set to the scrolltarget or the immediateparent of the scrollbar.			
mousewheelactive	Tag and JS	boolean	false	read-only
	Description. Indicates whether or not the mousewheel is active for the focusview attribute.			
mousewheelevent_off	Tag and JS	string	onblur	read-write
	Description. The event that deactivates the mousewhen when sent from the focusview.			
mousewheelevent_on	Tag and JS	string	onfocus	read-write
	Description. The event that activates the mousewhen sent from the focusview.			
pagesize	Tag only	number		final
	Description. The maximum distance to scroll. The default value is the height or width of the scrollbar.			
scrollable	Tag and JS	Boolean	true	read-only
	Description. Indicates whether or not the scroll target is bigger than the containing view. A value of true means that the scrollbar is active.			
scrollattr	TAg only	string		final
	Description. The attribute of the scrolltarget that is modified by the scrollbar. By default, it is the axis attribute.			
scrollmax	Tag only	number		final

	Description. The maximum distance to scroll. The default value is the same as the height of the scroll target (for a vertical scrollbar) and the width of the scroll target (for a horizontal scrollbar).			
scrolltarget	Tag only	reference		final
	Description. Theview that is controlled by the scrollbar.			
stepsize	Tag and JS	number	10	read-write
	Description. The amount that the scrolltarget is moved when the user clicks on the scrolltrack or when the step metho is called.			
usemousewheel	Tag and JS	boolean	true	read-write
	Description. Indicates whether or not the scrollbar listens for mousewheel events.			

Table 11.5: The attributes of the Basescrollbar class

Name	Usage	Type	Default	Accessibility
disabledbgcolor	Tag and JS	number		read-write
	Description. The scrollbar's background color when it is disabled. If this attribute is not defined, the immediate parent's background color is used.			

Table 11.6: The attribute of the Scrollbar class

The **Basescrollbar** class adds two new methods:

```
page(n)
```
    Page ahead (by passing 1) or back (by passing –1).

```
step(n)
```
    Move ahead (by passing 1) or back (by passing –1).

The Scrollbar class does not define new methods.

The code in Listing 11.3 shows an LZX application that uses one vertical scrollbar and one horizontal scrollbar.

Listing 11.3: Using scrollbars

```
<canvas height="100">
    <view name="main" width="100" height="100" clip="true">
        <text multiline="true">
            The OpenLaszlo Server is a Java servlet/JSP <br/>
            application. This server makes LZX application <br/>
            development process supereasy.<br/>
            You can compile your code by directing your Web<br/>
```

```
            browser to the OpenLaszlo server. The server <br/>
            examines the URL and compiles the appropriate <br/>
            source code (LZX file). <br/>
            It then sends the generated Flash file to the <br/>
            browser so that you can view your application. <br/>
            If the compilation fails, the server sends a <br/>
            compile error, telling you which line or lines <br/>
            of code are causing the error. <br/>
            If there is an error but compilation can continue, <br/>
            the server generates the Flash file and sends
            warning messages.
        </text>
        <scrollbar axis="y"/>
        <scrollbar axis="x"/>
    </view>
</canvas>
```

You can test the code in Listing 11.3 by going to this URL.

```
http://localhost:8080/lps-4.0.x/app11/scrollbarTest1.lzx
```

Figure 11.5 shows what you will see if you run the code in Listing 11.3.

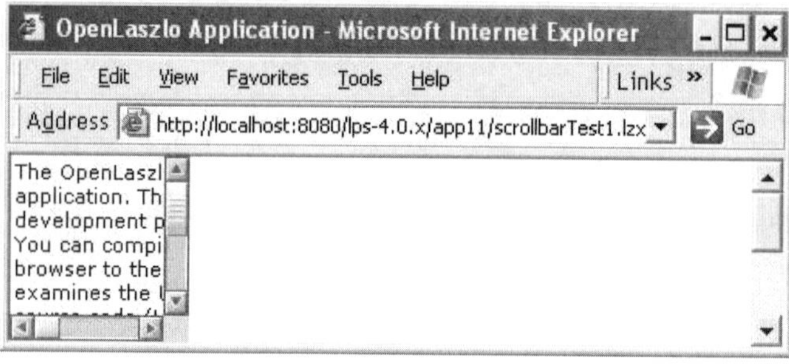

Figure 11.5: The scrollabar

Tabs and Tabpane

A tab is a view that can contain tab panes. Each tab pane has a title and can store other components. The tab and tab panes are a good way to arrange components in a small area.

This section discusses the two classes, **Tabs** and **Tabpane**, and provides an example.

The Tabs Class

The tabs component contains one or more tabpanes. The size of the tabs will be resize to the largest tabpane, unless you specifically set the height and or width attributes of the tabs. The **Tabs** class represents tabs and is derived from the **Basetabs** class. **Basetab** is a subclass of **Basecomponent**. It is therefore appropriate to list the attributes and methods of both **Tabs** and **Basetabs**.

Table 11.7 lists the attributes of the **Basetabs** class.

Name	Usage	Type	Default	Accessibility
bar	Tag and JS	string	null	read-only
	Description. A reference to its basetabsbar.			
barclass	Tag only	string	basetabsbar	final
	Description. The concrete implementation of barclass.			
bordersize	Tag and JS	number	0	read-write
	Description. The width of the border in pixels.			
content	Tag and JS	string	null	read-only
	Description. A reference to the basetab's content area.			
contentclass	Tag only	string	basetabscontent	final
	Description. The concrete implementation of the content area to instantiate.			
inset_bottom	Tag and JS	number	8	read-write
	Description. The bottom inset (margin) of the content.			
inset_left	Tag and JS	number	8	read-write
	Description. The left inset (margin) of the content.			
inset_right	Tag and JS	number	8	read-write
	Description. The right inset (margin) of the content.			
inset_top	Tag and JS	number	8	read-write
	Description. The top inset (margin) of the content.			
tabclass	Tag only	string	basetab	final
	Description. The concrete implementation for the tab.			

Table 11.7: The attributes of the Basetabs class

The **Tabs** class adds two attributes, listed in Table 11.8.

Name	Usage	Type	Default	Accessibility
tabalign	Tag and JS	string	left	read-write
	Description. The tab alignment. Valid values are "left", "center", and "right".			
tabspacing	Tag and JS	number	-15	final
	Description. The spacing between tab panes in pixels. The default is –15 so panes overlap by default.			

Table 11.8: The attributes of the Tabs class

Both the **Basetabs** and **Tabs** classes do not add new methods or events.

The Tabpane Class

The **Tabpane** class represents a tab pane that can be added to a tab. This class is a subclass of **Basetabpane**, a direct subclass of **Basecomponent**. Table 11.9 shows the attributes of **Basetabpane**.

Name	Usage	Type	Default	Accessibility
datacontrolsvisibility	Tag and JS	boolean	false	read-write
	Description. Indicates if the data control is visible.			
inset_bottom	Tag and JS	number		read-write
	Description. The bottom inset (margin) of the tabpane.			
inset_left	Tag and JS	number		read-write
	Description. The left inset (margin) of the tabpane			
inset_right	Tag and JS	number		read-write
	Description. The right inset (margin) of the tabpane.			
inset_top	Tag and JS	number		read-write
	Description. The top inset (margin) of the tabpane.			
selected	Tag and JS	boolean	false	read-write
	Description. Indicates if this tabpane is selected.			
tab	Tag and JS	string	null	read-only

	Description. A reference to the container tab.			
tabclass	Tag only	string		final
	Description. The class to use for the containing tab.			

Table 11.9: The attributes of the Basetabpane class

Name	Usage	Type	Default	Accessibility
tabwidth	Tag and JS	number	-1	read-write
	Description. The width of the tab pane. A value of −1 means the tab pane will resize to fit its components.			

Table 11.10: The attribute of the Tabpane class

Using Tabs and Tabpane

Now that you are familiar with both the **Tabs** and **Tabpane** classes, let's look at the example in Listing 11.4.

Listing 11.4: Using Tabs and Tabpane

```
<canvas height="600" width="500">
    <form inset_top="10">
        <tabs tabalign="right">
            <tabpane text="Name" tabwidth="80">
                <simplelayout axis="y"/>
                <text>Customer Name</text>
                <edittext name="customerName"/>
                <text>Email</text>
                <edittext name="email"/>
                <radiogroup name="customerType">
                    <radiobutton>Individual</radiobutton>
                    <radiobutton>Organization</radiobutton>
                </radiogroup>
                <button>Submit</button>
            </tabpane>
            <tabpane text="Address" tabwidth="80">
                <simplelayout axis="y"/>
                <text>Address</text>
                <edittext name="address"/>
                <text>City</text>
                <edittext name="city"/>
                <text>State</text>
                <edittext name="state"/>
                <text>Zip Code</text>
                <edittext name="zipcode"/>
```

```
        </tabpane>
      </tabs>
    </form>
</canvas>
```

You can test and run the code in Listing 11.5 by invoking the OpenLaszlo compiler using this URL.

```
http://localhost:8080/lps-4.0.x/app11/tabTest1.lzx
```

If you run the code in Listing 11.5, you will see a tab with two tab panes, just like the one in Figure 11.6.

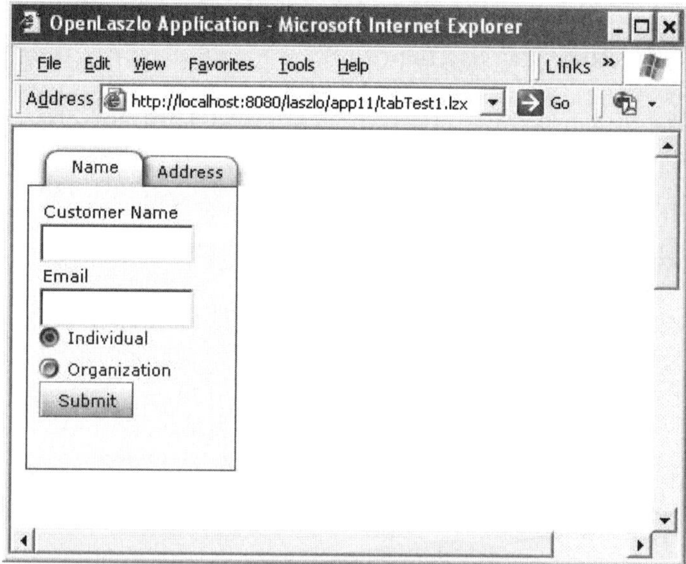

Figure 11.6: Using Tabs and Tabpane

Tree

A tree is an OpenLaszlo component to display hierarchical data, such as XML. The **Tree** class represents a tree and is a subclass of **Basetree**. **Basetree** itself is a child class of **Basecomponent**. This section discusses both **Basetree** and **Tree** and provides examples.

Table 11.11 lists the attributes defined in the **Basetree** class and Table 11.12 features the Tree class's attributes.

Name	Usage	Type	Default	Accessibility
autoscroll	Tag and JS	Boolean	false	read-write
	Description. Specifies whether or not autoscrolling is enabled.			
closechildren	Tag and JS	Boolean	false	read-write
	Description. Indicates if all immediate children should be closed if this tree is closed.			
closesiblings	Tag and JS	Boolean	false	read-write
	Description. Indicates if all siblings should be closed when this tree is opened.			
focused	Tag and JS	boolean	false	read-only
	Description. Indicates if this tree is focused.			
focusoverlay	Tag and JS	boolean	false	read-write
	Description. This attribute only takes effect if the tree is the root and its focusselect attribute is false. Specifies whether a visual bracket overlay over the focused tree is displayed.			
focusselect	Tag only	Boolean	false	read-write
	Description. This attribute only takes effect if the tree is the root. Flag to select a tree on focus.			
isleaf	Tag and JS	Boolean	false	read-write
	Description. Indicates if this is a leaf node.			
multiselect	Tag only	Boolean	false	final
	Description. Takes effect only if this tree is the root. Indicates if selecting multiple items is allowed.			
onfocused	Tag and JS	expression	null	read-write
	Description. This event is raised whenever this tree is focused.			
onopen	Tag only	expression	null	read-write
	Description. This event is raised when the tree is open.			
onselected	Tag and JS	expression	null	read-write
	Description. This event is raised when the tree is selected..			

open	Tag amd JS	boolean	false	read-write
	Description. Indicates if this tree is open.			
recurse	Tag only	boolean	true	final
	Description. This attribute is meaningful only with data replication. A value of true indicates it wil recursively followi the datapath's children.			
showroot	Tag only	boolean	true	final
	Description. Indicates if the root item is visible and its children are displayed. This attribute only takes effect if this tree is the root.			
toggleselected	Tag only	boolean	true	final
	Description. It takes effect only if this tree is the root. Indicates whether or not to toggle selected nodes.			
xindent	Tag and JS	number	10	read-write
	Description. The number of pixels to indent on the x axis.			
yindent	Tag and JS	number	20	read-write
	Description. The number of pixels to indent on the y axis.			

Table 11.11: The attributes of the Basetree class

Name	Usage	Type	Default	Accessibility
expander	Tag only	string	lztree_arrow_rsc	final
	Description. The resource to be displayed as the expanding icon. The resource should have three frames, the first for when the node is closed, the second for when it's open, and the third for when it is a leaf.			
icon	Tag only	string	lztree_folder_rsc	final
	Description. The resource for the item icon. The resource should have three frames, the first for when the node is closed, the second for when it's open, and the third for when it is a leaf.			
onactivate	Tag and JS	expression	null	read-write
	Description. This event is raised when the icon or the text is double-clicked.			

Table 11.12: The attributes of the Tree class

The following are the methods defined in the **Basetree** class.

```
changeFocus(focusedTree)
```
> Change the focus to the specified tree.

```
getChildClass()
```
> Returns the class used to instantiate replicated tree children. If this tree is a leaf, returns null.

```
getChildIndex(child)
```
> Returns the index of the specified child.

```
getRoot()
```
> Returns the root of this tree.

```
getSelection()
```
> Returns the current selected tree.

```
isRoot()
```
> Returns true if this tree is the root. Returns false, otherwise.

```
keySelect()
```
> This method is called when the tree is selected using the keyboard.

The Tree class adds one method:

```
toggleOpenAndFocus()
```
> Sets the tree on focus and toggle open, if this tree is not a leaf and is not being part of a multiselection.

As an example, the code in Listing 11.6 shows how to construct and use a tree.

Listing 11.6: A simple tree

```
<canvas width="450" height="250">
    <include href="../lps/components/lz/tree.lzx"/>
    <view width="200" height="200">
        <tree open="true" text="OpenLaszlo Tutorial">
            <tree text="Chapter 1: Get Started" isleaf="true"/>
            <tree open="true" text="Chapter 2: First Projects" >
                <tree text="Section 1: Animation" isleaf="true"/>
                <tree text="Section 2: Games" isleaf="true"/>
            </tree>
        </tree>
    </view>
</canvas>
```

Invoke this URL to compile and view your LZX application.

```
http://localhost:8080/lps-4.0.x/app11/treeTest1.lzx
```

Running the LZX application gives you the tree in Figure 11.7. Note that the root has two trees. The second child root in turn has two leaves.

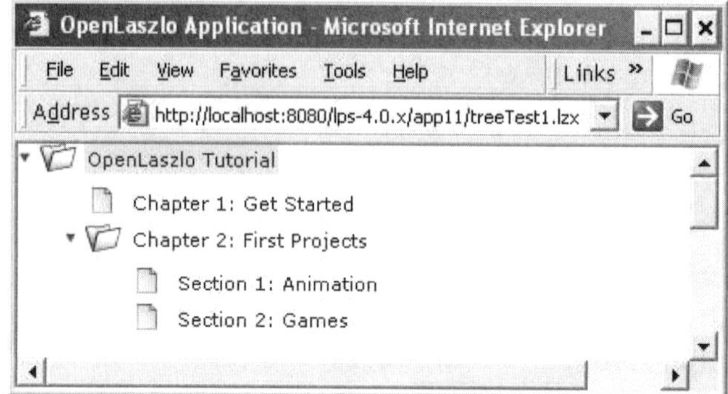

Figure 11.7: Using the Tree component

By default, the **Tree** component uses a folder icon for nodes with children. Open and closed nodes are represented by different icons. Trees with no children are called leaves and they are represented by a document icon.

You can change the icon of a tree by assigning a resource to the icon attribute. For example:

```
<resource name="r">
    <frame src="myIcon1.gif"/>
    <frame src="myIcon2.gif"/>
</resource>
<tree icon="r">
```

And you guessed right. Because the tree can represent hierarchical data, it can also be mapped to a dataset.

As another example, Listing 11.7 presents code that maps a tree with a dataset.

Listing 11.7: Mapping a tree to a dataset

```
<canvas width="450" height="450">
    <include href="../lps/components/lz/tree.lzx"/>
    <dataset name="phoneBook">
        <phoneBook text="Phone Book">
            <contact text="Contact">
                <firstName text="Linda" leaf="true"/>
                <lastName text="Carter" leaf="true"/>
```

```
                <phone text="999-0789-8998" leaf="true"/>
            </contact>
            <contact text="Contact">
                <firstName text="Amy" leaf="true"/>
                <lastName text="Grant" leaf="true"/>
                <phone text="992-907-1234" leaf="true"/>
            </contact>
        </phoneBook>
    </dataset>

    <view width="200" height="400">
        <tree datapath="phoneBook:/" icon="null" showroot="false">
            <tree datapath="*" text="$path{'@text'}" open="true"
              icon="null" isleaf="$path{'@leaf'}"/>
        </tree>
    </view>
</canvas>
```

To test the application in Listing 11.7, use this URL.

```
http://localhost:8080/lps-4.0.x/app11/treeTest2.lzx
```

If your code compiles, you'll see a result similar to Figure 11.8 in your browser.

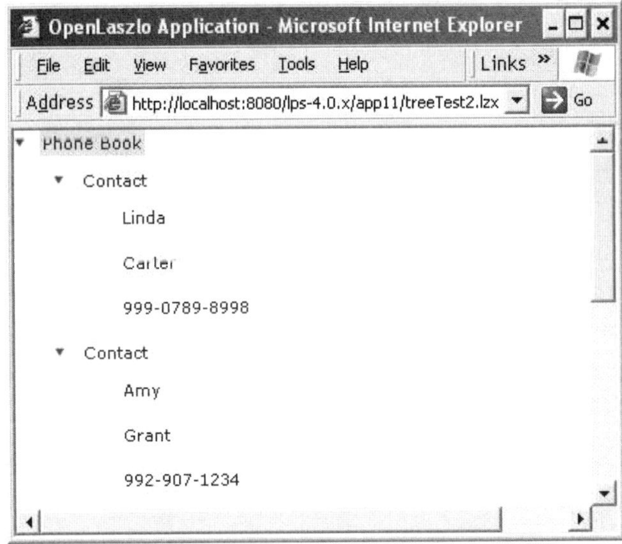

Figure 11.8: Mapping a tree to a dataset

Summary

As a framework for developing rapid Flash and AJAX applications, OpenLaszlo provides ready-to-use components. Chapter 2 discussed basic components and this chapter presents more complex OpenLaszlo components.

Chapter 12
Extending Classes

OpenLaszlo comes with hundreds of classes that make up the framework. You can use them to rapidly build your applications. However, sometimes—lots of times—there are circumstances whereby you need to add more functions to an existing class or change the behavior of a class. You can do this by creating a new class that encapsulates the functionality you want. In object-oriented programming, the process of creating a new class that is based on another class is called inheritance.

This chapter will take a look at how the LZX language supports inheritance. It also teaches you how to write new components you can use in your project or other projects.

An Overview of Inheritance

You extend a class by creating a new class. The former and the latter will then have a parent-child relationship. The original class is the parent class or the base class or the superclass. The new class is called a child class or a subclass or a derived class of the parent class. The process of extending a class in object-oriented programming is called inheritance. In a subclass you can add new methods and new fields as well as override existing methods in the parent class to change their behaviors.

Note that LZX does not support method overloading, a feature in Java, C#, and many other OOP languages. Method overloading allows you to have multiple methods with the same name in the same class.

Figure 12.1 shows the UML class diagram that depicts a parent-child relationship between a class and its child class.

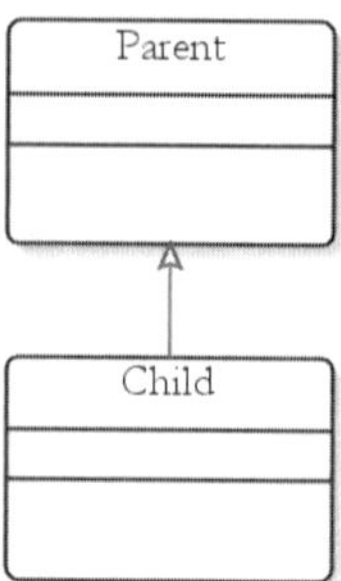

Figure 12.1: The UML class diagram for a parent class and a child class

Note that a line with an arrow like that in Figure 12.1 is used to depict generalization, e.g. the parent-child relationship.

The benefits of inheritance are obvious. Inheritance gives you the opportunity to add some functionality that does not exist in the original class. It also gives you the chance to change the behaviors of the existing class to better suit your needs.

The class Tag

In OpenLaszlo, you create a class by using the **class** tag. By default, any class you define implicitly extends the **LzView** class.

Note

You can write your class in the same LZX file that contains code that will use the new class. In this case, you can write your **class** tag directly below the **canvas** tag. Alternatively, you can isolate your new class in a separate file so that you can distribute it easily and the class can be used by different applications. In the latter cases, the **class** tag should be enclosed by the **library** tag.

For example, the LZX application in Listing 12.1 defines a new class called **square**. A square is like a view but by default its width is always equal to its height.

Listing 12.1: The square class

```
<canvas width="500" height="80">
    <class name="square" width="80" height="${this.width}">
```

```
    </class>

    <square bgcolor="#336699"/>
</canvas>
```

In Listing 12.1 you defined a class by using the **class** tag:

```
<class name="square" width="80" height="${this.width}">
</class>
```

Because you did not specify the parent class of your custom class, it will inherit the **LzView** class. Needless to say, the **square** class inherits all the attributes, methods, and events from the **LzView** class. To instantiate the class, you use the **square** tag:

```
<square bgcolor="#336699"/>
```

With the **square** class, you override the **height** attribute so that it always defaults to the square's width.

Note that you must not define the **id** attribute in the **class** tag when declaring a custom class.

To test the application in Listing 12.1, use this URL.

```
http://localhost:8080/lps-4.0.x/app12/customClassTest1.lzx
```

Figure 12.2 shows the result.

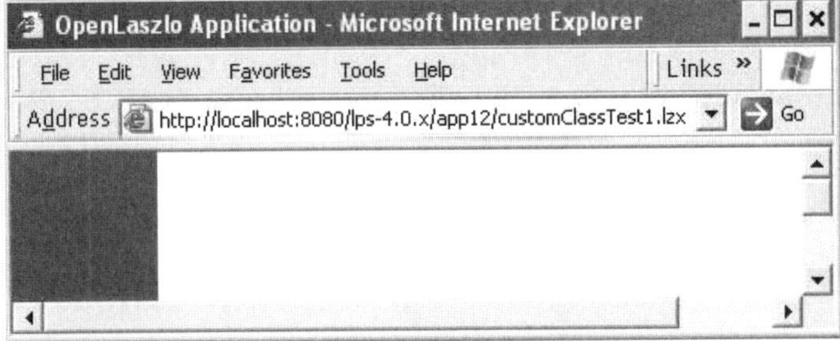

Figure 12.2: An instance of the square class

If you do not want your new class to extend **LzView**, you can use the **extends** attribute in your **class** tag to extend a different class. For example, the following class extends **drawview**.

```
<class name="roundwindow" extends="drawview">
```

You can only extend one class. However, your custom class can in turn be the parent class of other classes.

As another example, the **borderedview** class in Listing 12.2 adds a new behavior to **drawview**. As the class name implies, instances of **borderedview** have borders. Note that the **borderedview** class is written in a separate class. This way, it can be used by other applications easily. The **class** tag is located within the **library** tag and is saved as **borderedview.lzx** file.

Listing 12.2: The borderedview class

```
<library>
    <class name="borderedview" extends="drawview">
        <method name="init">
            super.init();
            this.rect(0, 0, this.width, this.height);
            this.stroke();
        </method>
    </class>
</library>
```

The code in Listing 12.3 shows how you can use the **borderedview** class.

Listing 12.3: Using borderedview

```
<canvas height="200">
    <include href="borderedview.lzx"/>
    <borderedview bgcolor="silver" x="40" y="40" width="50"
            height="50"/>
</canvas>
```

To compile the code in Listing 12.3, direct your browser to the following URL.

```
http://localhost:8080/lps-4.0.x/app12/borderedviewTest1.lzx
```

Figure 12.3 shows the result.

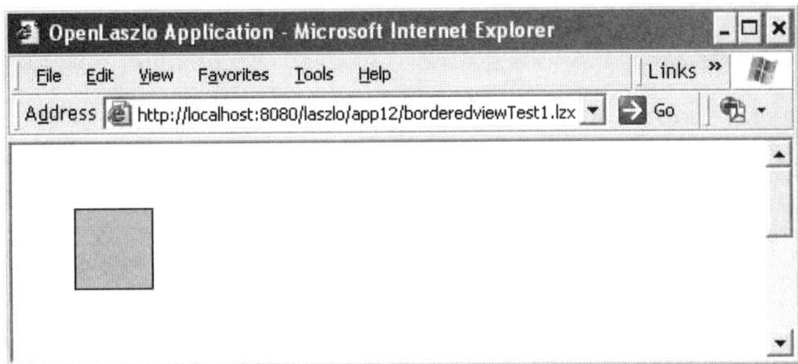

Figure 12.3: Using borderedview

Using the super Keyword

When overriding a parent class's method in a subclass, calls to the method in an instance of the subclass will invoke the implementation defined in the subclass. The **super** keyword enables you to call the method implementation defined in the superclass from a subclass.

For example, consider the code in Listing 12.4 that shows the **thickborderedview** class. This class extends the **borderedview** class given in Listing 12.2.

Listing 12.4: Using the super keyword

```
<library>
    <class name="thickborderedview" extends="borderedview">
        <method name="init">
            super.init();
            this.lineWidth = 10;
            this.stroke();
        </method>
    </class>
</library>
```

An instance of **thickborderedview** draws a thicker border than instances of its parent class. As you can see in Listing 12.4, the **thickborderedview** class overrides the **init** method in **borderedview**. It first calls **super.init()** to execute the **init** method in the parent class. It then sets the value of **lineWidth**

to 10 and calls the **stroke** method. By calling **super.init**, the
thickborderedview class does not need to draw a rectangle.

Listing 12.5 shows an example that uses **thickborderedview** class.

Listing 12.5: Using thickborderedview

```
<canvas height="200">
    <include href="borderedview.lzx"/>
    <include href="thickborderedview.lzx"/>
    <thickborderedview x="40" y="40" width="50"
            height="50"/>
</canvas>
```

You can compile the code in Listing 12.5 by using this URL:

```
http://localhost:8080/lps-4.0.x/app12/thickborderedviewTest1.lzx
```

Figure 12.4 shows the instance of **thickborderedview**.

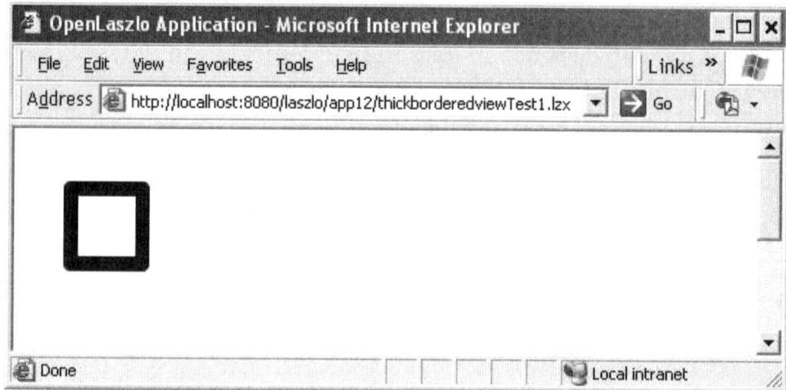

Figure 12.4: An instance of thickborderedview

Using the classroot property

The **classroot** property of the **View** class refers to the root node of a class
instance. It is often used from a deeply nested view or method to reference a
view near the root of the class. For example, consider the code in Listing 12.6.

Listing 12.6: Using the classroot keyword

```
<canvas>
```

```
<class name="root">
    <simplelayout axis="x"/>
    <view height="100" width="100">
        <button x="20" y="20" text="Red">
            <handler name="onclick">
                classroot.setAttribute("bgcolor", "0xff0000");
            </handler>
        </button>
    </view>
    <view height="100" width="100">
        <button x="20" y="20" text="Blue">
            <handler name="onclick">
                classroot.setAttribute("bgcolor", "0x0000ff");
            </handler>
        </button>
    </view>

</class>

    <root bgcolor="#cecece" height="400" width="400"/>
</canvas>
```

You can use the following URL to compile the code in Listing 12.6.

```
http://localhost:8080/lps-4.0.x/app12/classrootTest1.lzx
```

The result is shown in Figure 12.5.

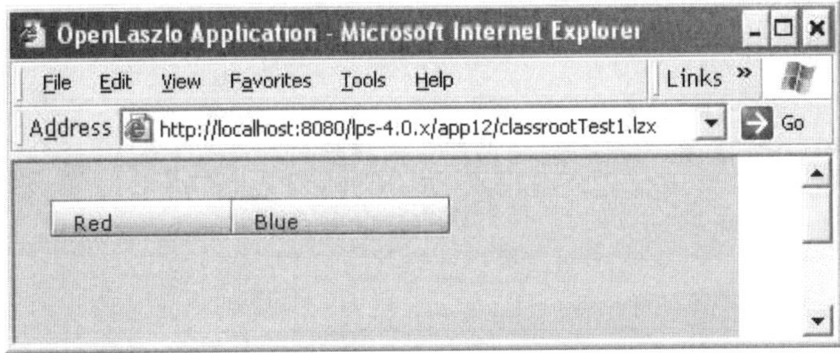

Figure 12.5: Using classroot

The buttons can be used to change the background color of the **root** instance. Clicking the Red button changes it to red and clicking the Blue button changes it to blue.

Overriding Event Handlers

Unlike methods, event handler cannot be overridden. However, you can use this trick to achieve a similar result.

If you suspect people might want to change the behavior of an event handler in your custom class, don't put code under the event handler. Instead, use the method attribute of the handler tag to reference a method:

```
<handler name="oninit" method="handleInit">
```

People who want to change **oninit** can then override **handleInit** to change the behavior of **oninit**.

Working with Custom Attributes

You can use an attribute in your LZX application. The attribute will act as a global variable that can be accessed from anywhere in the code. For example, the code in Listing 12.7 shows the use of the attribute inside the **canvas** tag.

Listing 12.7: Using custom attributes

```
<canvas width="200">
    <reverselayout axis="x"/>
    <attribute name="counter" type="number" value="1"/>
    <button text="Increment">
        <method event="onclick">
            var oldValue = parent.getAttribute("counter");
            parent.setAttribute("counter", oldValue + 1);
        </method>
    </button>
    <text name="my" text="${parent.counter}"/>
</canvas>
```

Note from Listing 12.7 that to read an attribute, you use the **getAttribute** method. To assign a value, use the **setAttribute** method.

An attribute can have a type. In the code in Listing 12.7 the **type** attribute of the **attribute** tag is used to define the attribute type. The following are attribute types in OpenLaszlo.

- string

- number
- text
- html

Normally, your custom attributes have the number or string type. However, if the attribute is named **text**, you may use the text or html type for it.

The text and html types are special because it allows you to assign an attribute value by passing the value as an element's value, in addition to the normal way of setting an attribute value. For example, the **text** attribute of the **text** tag is of type html. As such, you can set the value of the **text** tag's **text** attribute this way:

```
<text name="id1">This is a description</text>
```

which has the same effect as

```
<text name="id1" text="This is a description"/>
```

The advantage of using the text type is you can assign a long string conveniently. You do not even need to escape strings that contain double quotes.

For example, to assign the string **John "The Great" O'Connor** to a text attribute of the **myclass** tag, you can write

```
<myclass>John "The Great" O'Connor</myclass>
```

If you are to assign it the normal way, you would have to change the double quotes in the string to its entity code (").

```
<myclass text="John &quot;The Great&quot; O'Connor"/>
```

Summary

Inheritance is a powerful feature in object-oriented programming. The LZX language supports inheritance too. As shown in this chapter, you can extend a class by creating your own class using the **class** tag.

Chapter 13
Communicating with the browser

This chapter is for you if you decided to deploy your OpenLaszlo application as Flash. AJAX applications blend with the browser naturally because of the J in AJAX.

Flash files generated by OpenLaszlo are embedded in wrapper HTML pages. They can interact with each other using one of the following techniques.

1. Flash applications can receive parameter values from the browser.
2. JavaScript scripts can invoke the methods in and set the attributes of a Flash application.
3. Flash can run JavaScript methods and access JavaScript variables.

This chapter will discuss these types of communication, including how to use the **LzBrowser** class that represents the browser. First, however, we will talk about how to create a wrapper.

Creating the Wrapper

For the interaction between Flash and its wrapper to happen, the first thing to do is create an HTML page that will embed the generated Flash. You can generate the wrapper by adding the **lzt=html** query parameter when invoking the application. For example:

```
http://localhost:8080/lps-4.0.x/app13/test1.lzx?lzt=html
```

Listing 13.1 shows the generated wrapper.

Listing 13.1: The wrapper for passing values to the LZX application

```
<!DOCTYPE html
```

```
   PUBLIC "-//W3C//DTD HTML 4.01 Transitional//EN"
       "http://www.w3.org/TR/html4/loose.dtd">
<html>
   <head>
      <meta http-equiv="Content-Type" content="text/html;
       charset=utf-8">

      <link rel="SHORTCUT ICON"
        href="http://www.laszlosystems.com/favicon.ico">
      <title>Laszlo Application</title>
      <style type="text/css">
         html, body { margin: 0; padding: 0; height: 100%; }
         body { background-color: #ffffff; }
      </style>
      <script language="JavaScript1.1"
         src="/laszlo/lps/includes/vbembed.js"
         type="text/javascript">
      </script>
      <script src="/laszlo/lps/includes/embed.js"
         type="text/javascript">
      </script>
   </head>
   <body>
      <script type="text/javascript">
         lzLPSRoot = '/laszlo';
         lzCanvasRuntimeVersion = 7 * 1;
         if (lzCanvasRuntimeVersion == 6) {
           lzCanvasRuntimeVersion = 6.65;
         }
         if (isIE && isWin || detectFlash() >=
           lzCanvasRuntimeVersion) {
           lzEmbed({url: 'test.lzx?
           lzt=swf&__lzhistconn='+top.connuid+'&__lzhisturl=' +
      escape('/laszlo/lps/includes/h.html?h='), bgcolor: '#ffffcc',
      width: '280', height: '100%', id: 'lzapp'},
      lzCanvasRuntimeVersion);
           lzHistEmbed(lzLPSRoot);
         } else {
           document.write('This application requires Flash player '
      + lzCanvasRuntimeVersion + '. <a
      href="http://www.macromedia.com/go/getflashplayer"
      target="fpupgrade">Click here</a> to upgrade.');
         }
      </script>
      <noscript>
       Please enable JavaScript in order to use this application.
```

```
      </noscript>
    </body>
</html>
```

When the wrapper HTML page loads, it will run the **lzEmbed** function in either the **embed.js** or **vbembed.js** file, located in the **lps/includes** directory under the OpenLaszlo installation directory. This JavaScript file contains important functions for embedding Flash. The **embed.js** file is given in Listing 13.2.

Listing 13.2: The embed.js File

```javascript
// A_LZ_COPYRIGHT_BEGIN

/*
 * JavaScript library for embedding Laszlo applications
 *
 * Usage:
 * In the <html><head> of an HTML document that embeds a Laszlo
 * application, add this line:
 *    <script src="{$lps}/embed.js" language="JavaScript"
 *      type="text/javascript"/>
 * At the location within the <html><body> where the application is
 * to be embedded, add this line:
 *    <script language="JavaScript" type="text/javascript">
 *      lzEmbed({url: 'myapp.lzx?lzt=swf', bgcolor: '#000000', width:
 *      '800', height: '600'});
 *    </script>
 * where the url matches the URI that the application is served
 * from, and the other properties match the attributes of the
 * application's canvas.
 */

if (typeof(lzCanvasRuntimeVersion) == "undefined") {
    lzCanvasRuntimeVersion = 7;
}


/* Write a tag start.  This code assumes that the attribute values
 * don't require inner quotes; for instance, {x: '100'} works, but
 * {url: 'a>b'} or {url: 'a"b'} won't. */
function lzWriteElement(name, attrs, closep, escapeme) {
    var lt = escapeme ? '&lt;' : '<';
    var o = lt + name;
    for (var p in attrs)
```

```
        o += ' ' + p + '="' + attrs[p] + '"';
    if (closep)
        o += '/';
    o += '>';
    return o;
}


function containskey (arr, key) {
    return (arr[key] != null);
}


/* Update each property of a with the value of the same-named
 * property on b. For example, lzUpdate({a:1, b:2}, {b:3, c:4})
 * mutates the first argument into {a:1, b:3}.
 */
function lzUpdate(a, b) {
    for (var p in a)
        if (containskey(b,p)) {
            a[p] = b[p];
        }
}



__lzwroteiediv = false;
/* Write an <object> and <embed> tag into the document at the
 * location where this function is called.  Properties is an Object
 * whose properties override the attributes and <param> children of
 * the <object> tag, and the attributes of the <embed> tag.
 */
function lzEmbed(properties, ieupgradeversion, escapeme) {
    // don't upgrade IE activex control unless asked
    if (ieupgradeversion == null) ieupgradeversion = 6;

    var url = properties.url;

    // strip query string and use FlashVars instead
    var sp = properties.url.split('?');
    url = sp[0];
    if (sp.length == 1) sp[1] = ''
    var flashvars = new Query(sp[1]);

    var query = '?'
    for (var i in flashvars.d) {
        // add lps vars to query string
        if (i == 'lzr' || i == 'lzt'
            || i == 'krank' || i == 'debug' || i == 'profile'
```

```
            || i == 'lzdebug' || i == 'lzkrank' || i == 'lzprofile'
            || i == 'fb' || i == 'sourcelocators') {
            query += i + '=' + flashvars.d[i] + '&';
        }
    }
}
query = query.substr(0, query.length - 1);
url += query;

var width = properties.width;
var height = properties.height;
var id = properties.id;
var o = '';
var lt = escapeme ? '&lt;' : '<';

var wmode = properties.wmode;
objectAttributes = {
    type: 'application/x-shockwave-flash',
    data: url,
    width: 0, height: 0, name: 'lzapp', id: 'lzapp'
};
lzUpdate(objectAttributes, properties);
if (objectAttributes.name != objectAttributes.id)
   objectAttributes.name = objectAttributes.id;
if (wmode) objectAttributes['wmode'] = wmode;

objectParams = {
    movie: url,
    scale: 'noscale',
    quality: 'high',
    menu: lzCanvasRuntimeVersion > 6,
    salign: 'lt',
    // The properties parameter should override these.
    width: 0, height: 0, bgcolor: 0};
lzUpdate(objectParams, properties);
// only add wmode if it's specified
if (wmode) objectParams['wmode'] = wmode;

embedAttributes = {
    type: 'application/x-shockwave-flash',
    pluginspage: "http://www.macromedia.com/go/getflashplayer",
    scale: 'noscale',
    src: url,
    quality: 'high',
    salign: 'lt',
    menu: lzCanvasRuntimeVersion > 6,
    // The properties parameter should override these.
```

```
      width: 0, height: 0, bgcolor: 0, name: 'lzapp', id:
    'lzapp'};
  lzUpdate(embedAttributes, properties);
  if (embedAttributes.name != embedAttributes.id)
    embedAttributes.name = embedAttributes.id;
  // only add wmode if it's specified
  if (wmode) embedAttributes['wmode'] = wmode;

  // Prehistoric netscape (not Mozilla)
  var ns = (document.layers)? true:false;
  // Some windows browser
  var win = navigator.appVersion.indexOf('Win') != -1;
  // !&@#(&!@# safari requires an embed tag to use flash vars - go
    figure...
  var safari = navigator.appVersion.indexOf('Safari') != -1;
  var opera = navigator.userAgent.indexOf('Opera') != -1;
  var macie52 = navigator.userAgent.indexOf('MSIE 5.2') != -1 && !
    win;
  var isie = navigator.userAgent.indexOf('MSIE') != -1;
  //alert('win: ' + win + ', ns ' + ns + ', safari ' + safari)

  if (flashvars) {
      objectParams.FlashVars = flashvars.toString();
      embedAttributes.FlashVars = flashvars.toString();
  }

  if (ns || macie52 || (win && isie)) {
    o = lzWriteElement('embed', embedAttributes, true,
    escapeme);
    if (win && isie && __lzwroteiediv != true &&
    (window.lzLPSRoot || top.lzLPSRoot)) {
        // write out a hidden div with an object tag to force an
    upgrade in IE only
        o += '<div
    style="position:absolute;left:0px;top:0px;display:none"><obje
    ct
    ><param name="movie" value="' + lzLPSRoot +
    '/lps/includes/h.swf"></object></div>'
        __lzwroteiediv = true;
    }
  } else {
    o = lzWriteElement('object', objectAttributes, false,
    escapeme);
    for (var p in objectParams)
    o += lt + 'param name="' +
            p + '" value="' +
```

```
                    objectParams[p] + '" />\n';
            // More invalid XHTML, used only by windows
            // required by safari
            // must be omitted for opera
            if (win && ! opera || safari)  {
                o += lzWriteElement('embed', embedAttributes, true,
        escapeme);
            }
            o += lt + '/object>\n';
        }
        //alert(o);
        document.write(o);
        return o;
}


// Based on moock fpi, cleaned up and simplified by Max Carlson
// Javascript 1.1 / VBScript block must run/be included before this
        is called
//
// moock fpi [f.lash p.layer i.nspector]
// version: 1.3.6
// written by colin moock
// code maintained at:
        http://www.moock.org/webdesign/flash/detection/moockfpi/
// terms of use posted at: http://www.moock.org/terms/


function detectFlash() {
    var actualVersion = 0;
    var isIE  = navigator.appVersion.indexOf("MSIE") != -1;    //
        true if we're on ie
    if (navigator.plugins &&
        (navigator.plugins["Shockwave Flash 2.0"] ||
        navigator.plugins["Shockwave Flash"]) ) {

        // Some version of Flash was found. Time to figure out
        which.
        // Set convenient references to flash 2 and the plugin
        description.
        var isVersion2 = navigator.plugins["Shockwave Flash 2.0"] ?
        " 2.0" : "";
        var flashDescription = navigator.plugins["Shockwave Flash" +
        isVersion2].description;

        var flashVersion = parseInt(flashDescription.substring(16));
```

```
            var minorVersion =
            flashDescription.substring(flashDescription.indexOf('r') +
            1);
        } else if (! isIE) {
            var flashVersion = 0;
            var minorVersion = 0;
        } else {
            var vbver =  eval('VBFlashVer');
            if (vbver) {
                vbver = vbver.substring(vbver.indexOf(' ') +
            1).split(',');
                var flashVersion = vbver[0];
                var minorVersion = vbver[2];
            }
        }

        actualVersion = parseFloat(flashVersion + '.' + minorVersion)

        // If we're on msntv (formerly webtv), the version supported is
           4 (as of
        // January 1, 2004). Note that we don't bother sniffing
           varieties
        // of msntv. You could if you were sadistic...
        if (navigator.userAgent.indexOf("WebTV") != -1) actualVersion =
           4;

        return actualVersion;
    }

Query = function(s) {
    this.parse(s);
}

Query.prototype.parse = function(s) {
    if (s.indexOf('=') == -1) return;
    var p = s.split('&');
    this.d = {};
    for (i in p) {
        var nv = p[i].split('=');
        var n = nv[0];
        var v = nv[1];
        this.d[n] = v;
    }
}

Query.prototype.toString = function(del) {
```

```
    var o = '';
    if (!del) del = '';
    for (i in this.d) {
        o += del + i + '=' + this.d[i] + '&';
    }
    return o.substr(0, o.length - 1);
}

function getQuery(win) {
    if (win == null) win = top;
    var s = win.location.search;
    if (s.indexOf('=') > -1) {
        s = s.substr(1, s.length);
    }
    return s;
}

if (this != top) {
    top.Query = Query;
    top.getQuery = getQuery;
}

function lzHistEmbed(wr) {
    top.webapproot = wr;
    //alert(top.webapproot + ', ' + window.webapproot);
    document.write("<div
        style='position:absolute;left:0px;top:0px;'><iframe
        src='"+top.webapproot+"/lps/includes/h.html' name='_lzhist'
        frameborder='0' scrolling='no' width='22'
        height='0'></iframe></div>");
    document.write('<div id="_lzevent"
        style="position:absolute;top:0px;left:0px;"></div>');
}


// string name
// string value
// bool add history event
function lzSetCanvasAttribute(name, value, addhist) {
    var id = '_lzevent';
    var fv = 'n='+ escape(name) + '&v=' + escape(value)
        +'&__lzevent=1&__lzhistconn='+top.connuid;
    var src= top.webapproot+'/lps/includes/h.swf'
    var o = '<object
        >' +
'<param name="movie" value="'+ src +'" />' +
```

```
'<param name="FlashVars" value="'+ fv +'"/>' +
'<param name="quality" value="high" />' +
'<param name="bgcolor" value="#FFFFFF" />' +
'<embed src="'+ src +'" type="application/x-shockwave-flash"
        flashvars="'+ fv +'" quality="high" bgcolor="#FFFFFF"
        width="1" height="1"
        pluginspage="http://www.macromedia.com/go/getflashplayer"></e
        mbed>' +
'</object>';
    //alert(o);
    if (addhist) {
        var newurl = top.webapproot+'/lps/includes/h.html?n='+
        escape(name) + '&v=' + escape(value) +'&__lzevent=1';
        top.frames['_lzhist'].location = newurl;
    } else {
        if (document.getElementById) {
            var el = document.getElementById(id);
            // fix bug in IE Mac 5.1 and greater that causes the div
        to grow
            el.innerHTML = '';
            el.innerHTML = o;
        } else if (document.all) {
            document.all[id].innerHTML = o;
        } else if (document.layers) {
            var oLayer = document.layers[id].document;
            oLayer.open();
            oLayer.write(o);
            oLayer.close();
        }
    }
}

top.connuid = Math.floor(Math.random() * 10000);
```

The LzBrowser Class

The **LzBrowser** object provides services that allow you access to the browser
and the Flash player environment. For example, you can launch a URL, check
the version of the Flash player and so on, by invoking methods on the
LzBrowser object.

The **LzBrowser** class has the following methods:

```
getInitArg(queryParameter)
```

Returns the value of the specified query parameter.

`getLoadURL()`

Returns the URL used to request the application.

`getLoadURLAsLzURL()`

Returns the return value of the **getLoadURL** method as a new **LzURL** object.

`getVersion()`

Returns the version of the user's Flash player.

`loadJS(`*jsUrl, target*`)`

Runs the JavaScript script specified by the *jsUrl* in the target. If target is not specified, the JavaScript script runs on the current browser frame.

`loadURL(`*url, target*`)`

Loads the content of the specified URL. If target is not present the new page will be run on the current browser frame.

`urlEscape(`*string*`)`

Applies URL encoding to the specified string.

`urlUnescape(`*string*`)`

Unescapes the specified string to which URL encoding has been applied.

`xmlEscape(`*string*`)`

Escapes XML special characters, such as '<' and '>', so that they can be shown properly in the browser.

For instance, the LZX application in Listing 13.3 tells the user the version of their Flash player.

Listing 13.3: Enquiring the Flash player version

```
<canvas>
    <text width="300">
        <handler name="oninit">
            this.setText("You are using Flash version " +
                    LzBrowser.getVersion());
        </handler>
    </text>
</canvas>
```

Passing Values to A Flash Application

It is a useful feature to be able to pass values to a Flash application. For example, you can pass the value of the background color of the application, the default size of the window, initialize the states of components, etc, thus enabling you to cater to individual needs of your users. One way to accomplish this is by using the **getInitArg** method of the **LzBrowser** object.

For example, the code in Listing 13.4 prints the value of the **firstName** query parameter.

Listing 13.4: Retrieving query parameters.

```
<canvas debug="true">
    <script>
        Debug.write(LzBrowser.getInitArg("firstName"));
    </script>
</canvas>
```

To test the code, use the following URL to request the code:

```
http://localhost:8080/lps-4.0.x/app13/browserTest1.lzx?firstName=Ron
```

You will see the value of query parameter **firstName** printed in the Debugger window.

When working with URLs, you often work with the **LzUrl** class. Here are the methods:

```
parseURL(url)
```
Parses the specified string and returns a new LzURL object. You can then call the host, port, path, file, and query properties of the LzURL object.

```
toString()
```
Returns a string representation of this LzURL object.

For example, the LZX program in Listing 13.5 shows you how to work with the **LzUrl** class.

Listing 13.5: Working with LzUrl

```
<canvas debug="true">
    <script>
        var url = LzBrowser.getLoadURLAsLzURL();
```

```
        Debug.write("protocol:" + url.protocol);
        Debug.write("host:" + url.host);
        Debug.write("port:" + url.port);
        Debug.write("path:" + url.path);
        Debug.write("file:" + url.file);
        Debug.write("query:" + url.query);
    </script>
</canvas>
```

To test the code, use the following URL to request the code:

```
http://localhost:8080/lps-4.0.x/app13/lzUrlTest1.lzx
```

If you run the program, you will see something like the following in the
Debugger window.

```
protocol:http
host:localhost
port:8080
path:/lps-4.0.x/app13/
file:lzUrlTest1.lzx
query:lzt=swf
```

Another use of the **LzUrl** class is to prevent piracy. For example, the code in
Listing 13.6 always redirects the user to an error page (or any other page) if the
Flash is loaded from any host other than localhost.

Listing 13.6: Preventing piracy using LzUrl

```
<canvas debug="true">
    <script>
        var url = LzBrowser.getLoadURLAsLzURL();
        if (url.host != "myHost.com") {
            LzBrowser.loadURL("http://www.mydomain.com/error.html");
        }
        Debug.write("protocol:" + url.protocol);
        Debug.write("host:" + url.host);
        Debug.write("port:" + url.port);
        Debug.write("path:" + url.path);
        Debug.write("file:" + url.file);
        Debug.write("query:" + url.query);
    </script>
</canvas>
```

Summary

Browser integration is an important feature that allows your application communicates with the browser. This chapter showed you how OpenLaszlo facilitates the communication between applications deployed as Flash and the browser.

Chapter 14
Debugging and Deployment

Debugging is a process in software development that aims in making your application more robust and defect-free. The good news for OpenLaszlo developers is OpenLaszlo comes with a sophisticated debugging tool. Debugging is the main topic of this chapter. The second topic is deployment. Deploying OpenLaszlo applications is a very easy and straightforward process.

Debugging

OpenLaszlo provides a sophisticated tool for debugging purpose. This tool allows you to view runtime error messages, evaluate variable values, etc

When developing an OpenLaszlo application, you can display the Debugger window. It looks like the one in Figure 14.1.

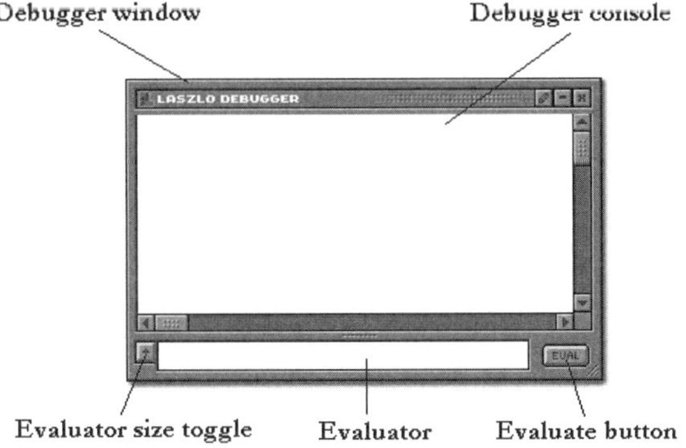

Figure 14.1: The Debugger Window

You can activate the Debugger window by doing one of the following.

1. Setting the **debug** attribute of the **canvas** tag to **true**:

```
<canvas debug="true">
```

2. Appending the query parameter **debug=true** at the end of the URL used to request the OpenLaszlo application. For instance:

```
http://localhost:8080/lps-4.0.x/app14/debugTest.lzx?debug=true
```

3. Clicking the Debug radio button and clicking the Compile button. See Figure 14.2.

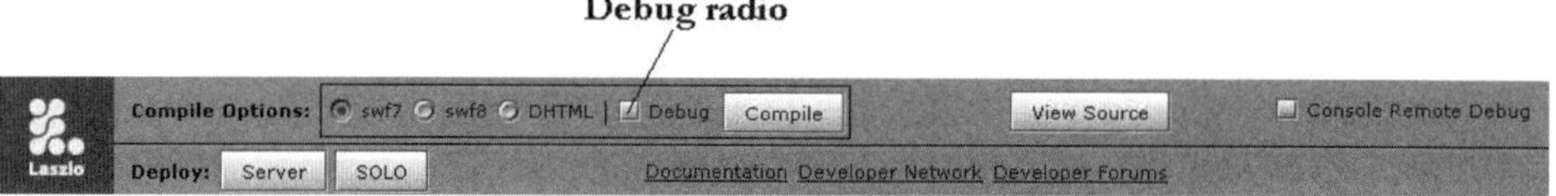

Figure 14.2: The Debug radio button

When activated, you can control the Debugger window as you would other views. The Debugger window is an instance of the **Debug** class, which is a subclass of **LzView**. Therefore all attributes in the **LzView** class are also available in the **Debug** class. This means, you can specify the **x**, **y**, **width**, **height**, and other attributes. Some attributes, such as **bgcolor**, cannot be changed.

To change the appearance of the Debugger window, use the **debug** tag. Here is an example:

```
<canvas width="580" height="400" debug="true">
    <debug width="200" height="100" x="10" y="10"/>
```

Note also that the **debug** tag can only be a direct child of **<canvas>**.

The **Debug** class is the topic of discussion of the next section.

Debug Class

The **Debug** class has one attribute, **showInternalProperties**. This attribute is described in Table 14.1.

Name	Usage	Type	Default	Accessibility
showInternalProperties	Tag and JS	boolean		read-write
	Description. Indicates whether or not the internal properties should be shown.			

Table 14.1: The attribute of the Debug class

The following are the methods defined in the **Debug** class.

`backtrace(frameCount)`
> Copy the snapshot of the current call stack into a **LzBacktrace** object, which can then be printed or inspected. This method is only available if if the application is compiled with --option debugBacktrace=true. The frameCount argument specifies the number of frames to omit from the backtrace (the default is 1).

`error(control, args)`
> Displays an error on the console. The *control* argument specifies a format control and the *args* argument represents any number of arguments.

`format(control, args)`
> Formats the output using the **formatToString** method. The control argument specifies a format control and the *args* argument represents any number of arguments.

`formatToString(control, args)`
> This method is similar to the **printf** function in the C language. The *control* argument specifies a format control and the *args* argument represents any number of arguments.

`inspect(object, reserved)`
> Displays the properties of the specified object on the debug console. The *reserved* argument is reserved for future use.

`log(message)`
> Sends the message to the log file.

`monitor(object, property)`
> Monitors the specified property of the specified object. Every time the value of the property changes, a message will be displayed in the Debugger window.

`pad(string, length, dec, pad, sign, radix, force)`
> Pads or trims a string to the specified length. The following are the arguments:
> *string*. The value to pad.
> *length*. The minimum width. If the value is negative, pad on the right.
> *dec*. Ensure that dec characters to the right of '.', padding with 0.
> *pad*. Character to pad on left.
> *sign*. One of the following: ' ', '-', '+'. The default is '-'.
> *radix*. The radix to represent numbers in. The default is 10.

force. A boolean value that indicates whether or not numbers always have a decimal.

```
trace(object, method)
```
Monitors the use of the specified method in the specified object. Every time the method is invoked, a message will be printed in the Debugger window.

```
unmonitor(object, property)
```
Cancels the monitoring of the specified property on the specified object.

```
untrace(object, method)
```
Cancels the monitoring of the specified monitor on the specified object.

```
warn(control, args)
```
Displays a warning message on the console using the specified format control. The *args* argument represents any number of arguments.

Formatting Output

The **write** method is handy for writing messages quickly to the Debugger window. If the output needs formatting, however, you need to use the **format** method of the **Debug** class.

Here is the signature of the **format** method:

```
format(control, args)
```

where *control* is the format control, a string that contains the text to be printed and can contain format tags to be substituted by the values specified in *args*. The *args* argument represents any number of arguments. For example, the following uses format with two arguments:

```
Debug.format("%*d", 15, 10);
```

This prints 10 preceded by 15 spaces.

The **format** method is similar to the **printf** function defined in ANSI C. All standard **printf** conversions are accepted, except for 'a', 'n', and 'p'. 'e', 'f', and 'g' conversions, which are accepted but equivalent to 'f'. The 'h' and 'l' length modifiers are accepted but ignored. No errors are signaled for invalid format controls or insufficient arguments.

For instance, the LZX code in Listing 14.1 shows the power of **Debug.format**.

Listing 14.1: Using the format method

```
<canvas width="580" height="400" debug="true">
    <debug width="400" height="200" x="10" y="10"/>
    <script>
        Debug.format("100 in hexadecimal: %#x", 100);
    </script>
</canvas>
```

The output in the Debug console is

```
100 in hexadecimal: 0x64
```

In this case, the control argument is assigned "%*d" and the args argument consists of two arguments, 15 and 10.

The format tags in the control argument has the following format:

```
%[flags][width][.precision][modifiers]type
```

Tables 14.2, 14.3, 14.4, 14.5, and 14.6 summarize the type, flag, width, and precision values you can use with the format method.

Type	Description	Example
c	Character	A
d or I	Signed decimal integer	125
e or E	Scientific notation (mantise/exponent)	1.24c2, 1.24E2
f	Decimal floating point	124.42
o	Signed octal	342
s	string	"Holla"
u	Unsigned decimal integer	3911
x or X	Unsigned hexadecimal integer	DEF0

Table 14.2: Type values

Flag	Description
-	Left align within the given width
+	Forces to preceed the result with a + or − sign.
blank	Insert a space if the argument is a positive signed value.

#	Used with o, x, or X type to indicate that the value should be prefixed with 0, 0x or 0X. If used with e, E, or f forces the output value to contain a decimal point even if only zeros follow. If used with g or G the result is the same as e or E but trailing zeros are not removed.

Table 14.3: Flag values

Width	Description
number	The minimum number of character to be printed. If the length of characters to be printed is shorter than number, the result will be padded with spaces.
0number	Similar to number, except 0s are used instead of spaces.
*	The width is not specified in the control string but by an integer value preceding the argument that has to be formatted.

Table 14.4: Width values

Precision	Description
number	If the type is one of d, I, o, u, x, X, the precision specifies the minimum number of decimal digits to be printed. If the value to be printed is shorter than the specified precision, the result is padded with spaces. If the type is e, E, or f, the precision specifies the number of digits to be printed after the decimal point. If the type is s, the precision specifies the number of character to be printed. If the type is c, the precision value has no effect.

Table 14.5: Precision values

Modifier	Description
h	The argument is to be interpreted as a short integer.
l	The argument is to be interpreted as a long integer or double..
L	The argument is to be interpreted as a long double (floating point type)

Table 14.6: Modifier values

The Evaluator

In addition to displaying runtime error messages and writing debug info, the Debugger window can also be used for evaluating JavaScript global variables and expressions and executing JavaScript statements. The evaluator is the text field and the EVAL button at the bottom of the Debugger window. Figure 14.3 shows the use of the Debugger window for evaluation.

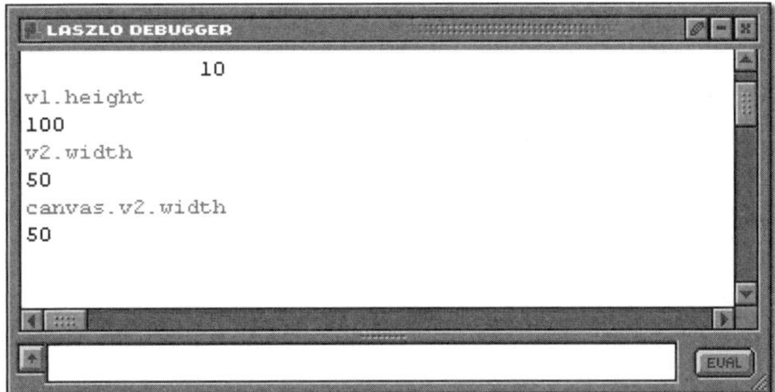

Figure 14.3: Using the Debugger window to evaluate values

To use the evaluator, you just need to type an expression or statement and click the EVAL button. If it is an expression, the expression value will be displayed on the Debug console. If it is a statement, the statement will be executed.

For example, if you type **canvas.width**, the value of the canvas's width attribute will be printed. Assuming there is a view named **v1**, typing **v1.height** prints the view's height in pixel.

The evaluator recognizes special characters. An underscore (_) refers to the value of the previous expression. Two underscore characters (__) refers to the result prior to the previous expression. Three underscore characters (___) refers to the result prior to the __ expression.

Deployment

Now that you have learned how to develop OpenLaszlo applications, it's time to focus on deployment. There are two deployment modes in OpenLaszlo:

- Proxied deployment. In this mode, your application runs on the OpenLaszlo server that in turns runs on a J2EE server or a servlet/JSP container. In this deployment mode, you just need to make sure that your lzx file(s) reside in the right directory. Nothing more.
- Stand-alone OpenLaszlo Output (SOLO) deployment. In this mode, you compile your application to a Flash file or an AJAX application and deploy it and its related resources. No J2EE container or servlet/JSP container is involved as the application file will be called from an HTML file. This mode is often called the server-less deployment.

SOLO applications are easier to deploy and often perform better. This is the better choice for production. Proxied deployment is suitable for development because in this deployment you can compile your code simply by requesting the application from within a Web browser.

Summary

A debugging tool is a valuable feature in a programming language. OpenLaszlo programmers are lucky to have one. A powerful one. This chapter has shown how you can use the Debugger window to perform various debugging tasks. The last section of this chapter discussed application deployment, a very simple process in OpenLaszlo.

Chapter 15
Google Maps Application

This chapter presents an OpenLaszlo application that uses the Google Maps API. The code for this application was written by Manabu Togawa, the webmaster of laszlo.jp. I'd like to thank Manabu for his great work and for granting us permission to reprint it here.

Signing Up

Google wants to know who are using their services. Therefore, before they allow you to download maps from their site, they want you to sign up. You can do this from here:

```
http://www.google.com/apis/maps/signup.html
```

As long as you do not use more than 50,000 page views per day, you are free to use it. In this page you can also read the terms and conditions of use.

Upon registration, you will be assigned a key. This key is linked to your domain. For testing this application, enter http://localhost:8080.

Google Maps API

You use Google Maps API to display a map. For example, the code in Listing 15.1 shows a map of Palo Alto.

Listing 15.1: A Map of Palo Alto

```
<!DOCTYPE html PUBLIC "-//W3C//DTD XHTML 1.0 Strict//EN"
    "http://www.w3.org/TR/xhtml1/DTD/xhtml1-strict.dtd">
<html xmlns="http://www.w3.org/1999/xhtml">
<head>
```

```
<script src="http://maps.google.com/maps?file=api&v=1&key=
ABQIAAAAIgThCNv3JZ4GZTXeVZlXLxTwM0brOpm-
All5BF6PoaKBxRWWERT1zOfmjyhFP8UxLMMX1EFUICYGmg"
        type="text/javascript"></script>
</head>
<body>
<div id="map" style="width: 500px; height: 400px"></div>

<script type="text/javascript">
    //<![CDATA[
    var map = new GMap(document.getElementById("map"));
    map.addControl(new GSmallMapControl());
    map.centerAndZoom(new GPoint(-122.1419, 37.4419), 4);

    //]]>
</script>
</body>
</html>
```

Examine the first **script** tag. The **src** attribute points to
http://maps.google.com/maps. The URL is followed by three query
parameters, **file**, **v**, and **key**. The **v** query parameter specifies the version of the
API. The application uses version 1. However, version 2 is also available.
When a new version is released, Google posts a notice on Google Code
(http://code.google.com/) and the Maps API discussion group
(http://groups.google.com/group/Google-Maps-API). Google does not
promise backward compatibility.

The **key** query specifies the user key. You should replace this key with
your own. To run the example, invoke it using this URL:

```
http://localhost:8080/lps-4.0.x/gmaps/gmapsTest1.html
```

Figure 15.1 shows the map.

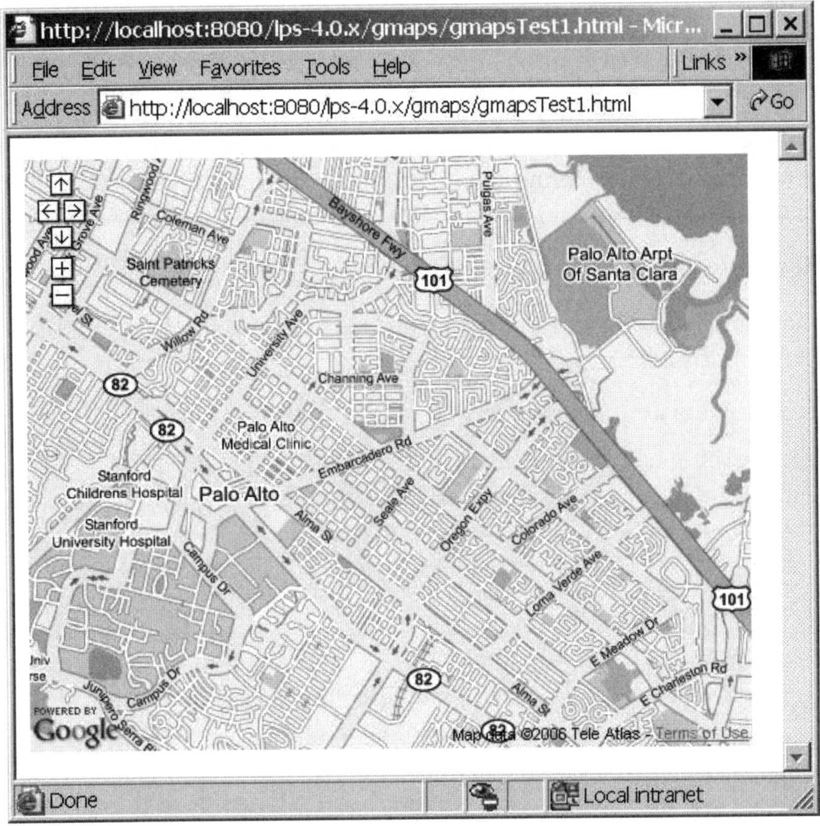

Figure 15.1: The Google map of Palo Alto

Before we delve into more details, let's study the main classes in the Google Maps API.

GMap

A **GMap** object represents a map on the page. To create a **GMap** object, you use the **GMap** class's constructor, whose signature is as follows:

```
GMap(container, mapTypes?, width?, height?)
```

A question mark after an argument indicates that the argument is optional.

The *container* argument specifies a container in which the map will nest. It is typically a **div** tag. The *mapTypes* argument specifies the map types. The default set of map types is ([**G_MAP_TYPE**, **G_HYBRID_TYPE**, or **G_SATELLITE_TYPE**]). The *width* and *height* arguments specify the width and height of the map, respectively. If no width or height is present, the container's width or height will be used.

For example, the following line of code constructs a **GMap** object within a **div** element named **map** and assigns the instance to the **map** variable.

```
var map = new GMap(document.getElementById("map"));
```

There are various methods defined in the **GMap** class. These methods are displayed here by category.

The following are methods related to configuration.

```
enableDragging()
```
> Enables dynamic dragging. Dragging is enabled by default but can be disabled by calling the **disableDragging** method.

```
disableDragging()
```
> Disables dynamic dragging.

```
draggingEnabled()
```
> Indicates whether or not dynamic dragging is enabled.

```
enableInfoWindow()
```
> Enables the info window on this map. The info window is enabled by default but can be disabled by calling the disableInfoWindow method.

```
disableInfoWindow()
```
> Disables the info window on this map.

```
infoWindowEnabled()
```
> Indicates whether or not the info window is enabled on this map.

These are methods related to controls:

```
addControl(control)
```
> Adds the specified map control to this map.

```
removeControl(control)
```
> Removes the specified control from this map.

These are methods related to state:

```
getCenterLatLng()
```

Returns the latitude/longitude coordinate of the center point of the map viewport.

`getBoundsLatLng()`

Returns the latitude/longitude bounds of the map viewport.

`getSpanLatLng()`

Returns the width and height of the map viewport in latitude/longitude ticks.

`getZoomLevel()`

Returns an integer specifying the map zoom level.

`centerAtLatLng(point)`

Centers the map at the specified point.

`recenterOrPanToLatLng(point)`

Center the map at the specified point, performing a fluid pan to the point if it is within the current map viewport.

`zoomTo(zoomLevel)`

Zooms to the specified zoom level.

`centerAndZoom(point, zoomLevel)`

Atomically centers the map to the specified point and zooms the map to the specified zoom level.

`getMapTypes()`

Returns an array of map types supported by this map (currently it is **G_MAP_TYPE**, **G_HYBRID_TYPE**, and **G_SATELLITE_TYPE**).

`getCurrentMapType()`

Returns the map type in use.

`setMapType(mapType)`

Assigns the specified map type of this map.

The following are methods related to overlays:

`addOverlay(overlay)`

Adds the specified overlay object (either an instance of **GMarker** or **GPolyline**) to this map.

`removeOverlay(overlay)`

Removes the specified overlay from this map.

`clearOverlays()`

Removes all overlays from this map.

These are methods related to the info window:

```
openInfoWindow(point, htmlElement, pixelOffset?, onOpenFn?,
    onCloseFn?)
```
> Displays the info window with the given HTML content at the specified latitude/longitude point. The *htmlElement* argument should be an HTML DOM element. If the *pixelOffset* argument is present, the info window will be offset by the given number of pixels. If the *onOpenFn* argument specifies a JavaScript function that will be invoked when the window is displayed. The *onCloseFn* argument specifies a JavaScript function that will be called when the window is closed.

```
openInfoWindowHtml(marker, htmlStr, pixelOffset?, onOpenFn?,
    onCloseFn?)
```
> This method is similar to **openInfoWindow**, but takes an HTML string instead of an HTML DOM element.

```
openInfoWindowXslt(marker, xmlElement, xsltUri, pixelOffset?,
    onOpenFn?, onCloseFn?)
```
> This method is similar to **openInfoWindow**, but takes an XML element and the URI of an XSLT document to produce the content of the info window.

```
showMapBlowup(point, zoomLevel?, mapType?, pixelOffset?, onOpenFn?,
    onCloseFn?)
```
> Shows a blowup of this map at the specified **GPoint**. If the *zoomLevel* and *mapType* arguments are not present, the map will default to a zoom level of 1 and the current map type.

```
closeInfoWindow()
```
> Closes the info window if it is open.

GMarker

A **GMarker** object is a type of map overlay that shows an icon at a single point on the map. The constructor takes an instance of **GIcon**, which indicates the point at which it should be displayed. You create a **GMarker** point by using its constructor:

```
GMarker(point, icon?)
```

The following are the methods defined in the **GMarker** class.

```
openInfoWindow(htmlElement)
```

Opens an info window with the specified HTML element over this marker. The *htmlElement* argument should specify an HTML DOM element.

```
openInfoWindowHtml(htmlString)
```
This method is similar to **openInfoWindow**, but takes an HTML string instead of an HTML DOM element.

```
openInfoWindowXslt(xmlElement, xsltUri)
```
This method is similar to **openInfoWindow**, except that it takes an XML element and the URI of an XSLT document to produce the content of the info window.

```
showMapBlowup(zoomLevel?, mapType?)
```
Shows a blowup of the map over this marker. If the arguments are not present, a default zoom level of 1 and the current map type will be used.

GPolyline

A **GPolyline** object represents a vector polyline overlay on the map. You construct a **GPolyline** object by using this constructor:

```
GPolyline(points, color?, weight?, opacity?)
```

The *points* argument should be assigned an array of latitude/longitude points. The color argument specifies a hexadecimal HTML color (such as #ff0000 for red), the weight argument specifies the thickness of the line in pixels, and the opacity argument specifies the opacity with a value between 0.0 and 1.0.

GIcon

A **GIcon** object represents an icon used to display a marker on the map.. You use this constructor to create a **GIcon** object:

```
GIcon(anotherIcon?)
```

The *anotherIcon* argument must be an instance of **GIcon**. If this argument is present, the properties of *anotherIcon* are copied to the new instance.

The **GIcon** class has the following attributes:

```
image
```
The foreground image URL of the icon.

shadow
>   The shadow image URL of the icon.

iconSize
>   The size of the foreground image of the icon in pixels.

shadowSize
>   The size of the shadow image in pixels.

iconAnchor
>   The pixel coordinate relative to the top left corner of the icon image at which this icon should be anchored to the map.

infoWindowAnchor
>   The pixel coordinate relative to the top left corner of the icon image at which the info window should be anchored to this image.

printImage
>   The URL of the foreground icon image that should be used for printed maps.

mozPrintImage
>   The URL of th eforeground icon image that should be used for printed maps in Firefox/Mozilla.

printShadow
>   The URL of the shadow image that should be used for printed maps. A GIF image should be used as most browser cannot print PNG images.

transparent
>   The URL of a virtually transparent version of the foreground icon image used to capture IE click events. This image should be a 24 bit PNG version of the main icon image with 1% opacity, but have the same shape and size as the main icon.

imageMap
>   An array of integers representing the (x, y) coordinate of the image map that should be used to specify the clickable part of the icon image in non-IE browsers.

GEvent

The **GEvent** class handles all event registration and triggering. It has these methods, all of which are static.

```
addListener(source, eventName, listenerFn)
```
Invokes the specified *listenerFn* function when the given event is raised on the specified source object.

```
removeListener(listener)
```
Removes the specified listener.

```
clearListeners(source, eventName)
```
Removes all listeners that have previously been registered to listen on the specified event on the source.

```
trigger(source, eventName, args...)
```
Raises the specified event on the source with the given list of arguments.

```
bind(source, eventName, object, method)
```
Binds the specified method of the specified object to the specified source event.

GXmlHttp

The **GXmlHttp** class provides a static no-argument method for creating cross-browser **XmlHttpRequest**. This method is appropriately called **create**.

GPoint

A **GPoint** object represents a point. The constructor is as follows.

```
GPoint(x, y)
```

where (x, y) is a 2-dimensional coordinate or a pair of longitude/latitude.

The **GPoint** class has two properties:

x

The x coordinate or the longitude of the point

y

The y coordinate or the latitude of the point

GSize

An instance of **GSize** represents a two-dimensional size. Here is its constructor:

```
GSize(width, height)
```

If a **GSize** represents a latitude/longitude span, *width* represents the number of longitude degrees and *height* represents the number of latitude degrees.

The **GSize** class has two properties:

```
width
```
The width of the **GSize**.

```
height
```
The height of the **GSize**.

GBounds

A **GBounds** object represents a two-dimensional bounding box. Here is the **GBounds** class's constructor:

```
GBounds(minX, minY, maxX, maxY)
```

The attributes of the **GBounds** class are as follows:

```
minx
```
The x coordinate of the top left corner of the bounds.

```
minY
```
The y coordinate of the top left corner of the bounds.

```
maxX
```
The x coordinate of the bottom right corner of the bounds.

```
maxY
```
The y coordinate of the bottom right corner of the bounds.

The Example

Now, let's review an LZX application that employs the Google Maps API. This application shows how to use the classes in the Google Maps API and how to control JavaScript control from inside an OpenLaszlo application.

The application shows a list of prominent cities in Japan with their longitudes and latitudes. When you click a city, the map of the city is displayed.

There are several parts of this application:

1. The **ken.xml** file that lists all locations.
2. The LZX application.
3. The HTML wrapper application

The **ken.xml** file is given in Listing 15.2. Note that ken means location in Japanese. The longitude is given by the **lon** element and the latitude by the **lat** element.

Listing 15.2: The ken.xml file

```xml
<?xml version="1.0" encoding="utf-8" ?>
  <lists>
   <items>
     <ken>Hokkaido</ken>
     <lon>141.35046</lon>
     <lat>43.06197</lat>
   </items>
   <items>
     <ken>Aomori</ken>
     <lon>140.74365</lon>
     <lat>40.82178</lat>
   </items>
   <items>
     <ken>Akita</ken>
     <lon>140.10626</lon>
     <lat>39.71539</lat>
   </items>
   <items>
     <ken>Iwate</ken>
     <lon>141.15547</lon>
     <lat>39.70096</lat>
   </items>
   <items>
     <ken>Yamagata</ken>
     <lon>140.36702</lon>
     <lat>38.23746</lat>
   </items>
   <items>
     <ken>Miyagi</ken>
     <lon>140.87549</lon>
     <lat>38.26594</lat>
   </items>
   <items>
     <ken>Hukushima</ken>
     <lon>140.47157</lon>
```

```
    <lat>37.74733</lat>
  </items>
  <items>
    <ken>Nigata</ken>
    <lon>139.02640</lon>
    <lat>37.89942</lat>
  </items>
  <items>
    <ken>Tokyo</ken>
    <lon>139.69487</lon>
    <lat>35.68627</lat>
  </items>
  <items>
    <ken>Gunma</ken>
    <lon>139.0638</lon>
    <lat>36.38779</lat>
  </items>
  <items>
    <ken>Totigi</ken>
    <lon>139.88673</lon>
    <lat>36.56242</lat>
  </items>
  <items>
    <ken>Ibaragi</ken>
    <lon>140.45047</lon>
    <lat>36.33791</lat>
  </items>
  <items>
    <ken>Saitama</ken>
    <lon>139.65221</lon>
    <lat>35.85421</lat>
  </items>
  <items>
    <ken>Tiba</ken>
    <lon>140.12637</lon>
    <lat>35.60131</lat>
  </items>
  <items>
    <ken>Kanagawa</ken>
    <lon>139.64578</lon>
    <lat>35.44445</lat>
  </items>
  <items>
    <ken>Yamanashi</ken>
    <lon>138.57152</lon>
    <lat>35.66302</lat>
```

```
</items>
<items>
  <ken>Sizuoka</ken>
  <lon>138.38623</lon>
  <lat>34.97353</lat>
</items>
<items>
  <ken>Nagano</ken>
  <lon>138.18398</lon>
  <lat>36.64779</lat>
</items>
<items>
  <ken>Toyama</ken>
  <lon>137.21463</lon>
  <lat>36.69237</lat>
</items>
<items>
  <ken>Isikawa</ken>
  <lon>136.62853</lon>
  <lat>36.59171</lat>
</items>
<items>
  <ken>Gihu</ken>
  <lon>136.72688</lon>
  <lat>35.38808</lat>
</items>
<items>
  <ken>Aichi</ken>
  <lon>136.90973</lon>
  <lat>35.17691</lat>
</items>
<items>
  <ken>Mie</ken>
  <lon>136.51149</lon>
  <lat>34.72701</lat>
</items>
<items>
  <ken>Hukui</ken>
  <lon>136.22368</lon>
  <lat>36.06207</lat>
</items>
<items>
  <ken>Siga</ken>
  <lon>135.87238</lon>
  <lat>35.00097</lat>
</items>
```

```
<items>
  <ken>Kyoto</ken>
  <lon>135.75781</lon>
  <lat>35.01786</lat>
</items>
<items>
  <ken>Osaka</ken>
  <lon>135.52233</lon>
  <lat>34.68347</lat>
</items>
<items>
  <ken>Nara</ken>
  <lon>135.83568</lon>
  <lat>34.68179</lat>
</items>
<items>
  <ken>Wakayama</ken>
  <lon>135.17028</lon>
  <lat>34.22273</lat>
</items>
<items>
  <ken>Hyogo</ken>
  <lon>135.18575</lon>
  <lat>34.6878</lat>
</items>
<items>
  <ken>Tottori</ken>
  <lon>134.2408</lon>
  <lat>35.50033</lat>
</items>
<items>
  <ken>Okayama</ken>
  <lon>133.93787</lon>
  <lat>34.65815</lat>
</items>
<items>
  <ken>Simane</ken>
  <lon>133.05305</lon>
  <lat>35.46919</lat>
</items>
<items>
  <ken>Hiroshima</ken>
  <lon>132.46188</lon>
  <lat>34.39309</lat>
</items>
<items>
```

```
  <ken>Yamaguti</ken>
  <lon>131.47297</lon>
  <lat>34.18288</lat>
</items>
<items>
  <ken>Kagawa</ken>
  <lon>134.04599</lon>
  <lat>34.33718</lat>
</items>
<items>
  <ken>Tokushima</ken>
  <lon>134.56094</lon>
  <lat>34.06277</lat>
</items>
<items>
  <ken>Ehime</ken>
  <lon>132.76865</lon>
  <lat>33.83861</lat>
</items>
<items>
  <ken>Kouchi</ken>
  <lon>133.53367</lon>
  <lat>33.55634</lat>
</items>
<items>
  <ken>Fukuoka</ken>
  <lon>130.41806</lon>
  <lat>33.60078</lat>
</items>
<items>
  <ken>Saga</ken>
  <lon>130.30139</lon>
  <lat>33.24616</lat>
</items>
<items>
  <ken>Nagasaki</ken>
  <lon>129.87575</lon>
  <lat>32.74123</lat>
</items>
<items>
  <ken>Ooita</ken>
  <lon>131.61493</lon>
  <lat>33.23479</lat>
</items>
<items>
  <ken>Kumamoto</ken>
```

```
      <lon>130.7438</lon>
      <lat>32.78617</lat>
    </items>
    <items>
      <ken>MIyazaki</ken>
      <lon>131.42601</lon>
      <lat>31.90745</lat>
    </items>
    <items>
      <ken>Kagoshima</ken>
      <lon>130.5600</lon>
      <lat>31.55750</lat>
    </items>
    <items>
      <ken>Okinawa</ken>
      <lon>127.68269</lon>
      <lat>26.20836</lat>
    </items>
  </lists>
```

The LZX application consists of two LZX files, **gmaps.lzx** and
googlemaps_sample1.lzx, given in Listings 15.3 and 15.4, respectively.

Listing 15.3: The gmaps.lxz file

```
<library>
    <class name="gmaps">
        <attribute name="mapname" type="string" value="map" />
        <method name="centerAndZoom" args="lat, lon, zoom">
            evalscript(mapname + ".centerAndZoom(new GPoint(" + lat
        + "," + lon +
"))," + zoom + ")");
        </method>


        <method name="centerAndZoomJp" args="lat, lon, zoom">
            var nlat = lon - lon * 0.00010695  + lat * 0.000017464 +
        0.0046017;
            var nlon = lat - lon * 0.000046038 - lat * 0.000083043 +
        0.010040;
            evalscript(mapname + ".centerAndZoom(new GPoint(" + nlat
        + "," + nlon +
"))," + zoom + ")");
        </method>


        <method name="openInfoWindowHtmlAtMapCenter" args="msg">
            evalscript(mapname + ".openInfoWindowHtml(" + mapname +
```

```
                    ".getCenterLatLng(),'" + msg + "')");
        </method>

        <method name="openInfoWindowHtmlJp" args="lat, lon, msg">
            var nlat = lon - lon * 0.00010695  + lat * 0.000017464 +
    0.0046017;
            var nlon = lat - lon * 0.000046038 - lat * 0.000083043 +
    0.010040;
            evalscript(mapname + ".openInfoWindowHtml(new GPoint(" +
    nlat + "," +
nlon + "),'" + msg + "')");
        </method>

        <method name="evalscript" args="script">
            var str = "evalscript(\"" + script + "\")";
            LzBrowser.loadJS(str);
        </method>
    </class>
</library>
```

Listing 15.4: The googlemaps_sample1.lzx file

```
<canvas>
    <include href="gmaps.lzx/" />
    <gmaps name="map"/>

    <class name="kenitem" extends="view" focusable="true"
        bgcolor="#9999CC">
        <attribute name="ken" value="$path{'ken/text()'}" />
        <attribute name="lat" value="$path{'lat/text()'}" />
        <attribute name="lon" value="$path{'lon/text()'}" />

        <simplelayout axis="y"/>

        <text text="${classroot.ken}" />
        <view name="hint" height="0" clip="true" x="5">
            <simplelayout axis="y"/>
            <text text="${'lat:' + classroot.lat}" />
            <text text=" ${'lon:' + classroot.lon}" />

            <animator name="open" attribute="height" to="30"
                    duration="100" start="false"/>
            <animator name="close" attribute="height" to="0"
                    duration="50" start="false"/>
        </view>

        <method event="onclick">
```

```
                map.openInfoWindowHtmlJp(lat, lon, getHtmlMsg());
        </method>

        <method name="getHtmlMsg">
        <![CDATA[
            var msg ='<nobr>'+ this.ken +' is selected.<br />'
                    + '<b>lat: </b>'+ this.lon +'<br />'
                    + '<b>lon: </b>'+ this.lat +'<br /></nobr>'
            return msg;
        ]]>
        </method>

        <method event="onblur">
            this.hint.close.doStart();
            this.setBGColor(0x9999CC);
        </method>

        <method event="onfocus">
            this.setBGColor(0xFFFFFF);
            this.hint.open.doStart();
        </method>
    </class>

    <dataset name="ken" src="ken.xml" />

    <view width="200" height="400" datapath="ken:/lists"
        clip="true">
        <view name="contents">
            <simplelayout axis="y" spacing="2" />
            <kenitem datapath="items" />
        </view>
        <scrollbar/>
    </view>

</canvas>
```

To test this application, you need a wrapper, which for this application is the index.html file in Listing 15.5

Listing 15.5: The index.html file

```
<!DOCTYPE HTML PUBLIC "-//W3C//DTD HTML 4.01 Transitional//EN"
        "http://www.w3.org/TR/1999/REC-html401-19991224/loose.dtd">
<html>
<head>
<title>LaszloJapan - Google Maps + OpenLaszlo Demo</title>
```

```
<script language="JavaScript1.1"
src="/lps-4.0.x/lps/includes/vbembed.js" type="text/javascript">
</script>

<script src="/lps-4.0.x/lps/includes/embed.js"
      type="text/javascript">
</script>

<script
      src="http://maps.google.co.jp/maps?file=api&v=1&key=ABQIAAAAI
      gThCNv3JZ4GZTXeVZlXLxTwM0brOpm-
      All5BF6PoaKBxRWWERT1zOfmjyhFP8UxLMMX1EFUICYGmg"
      type="text/javascript"></script>

<body>
    <div id="map" style="width: 500px; height: 400px; float:
      left"></div>

    <div id="laszloapp" style = "margin:0px">
    <script type="text/javascript">
        lzLPSRoot = '/lps-4.0.x;
        lzCanvasRuntimeVersion = 7 * 1;
        if (lzCanvasRuntimeVersion == 6) {
            lzCanvasRuntimeVersion = 6.65;
        }
        if (isIE && isWin || detectFlash() >=
      lzCanvasRuntimeVersion) {
            lzEmbed({url:
      'googlemaps_sample1.lzx.swf'+window.location.search.substring
      (1), bgcolor: '#ffffff', width: '200', height: '400', id:
      'lzapp'}, lzCanvasRuntimeVersion);
            lzHistEmbed(lzLPSRoot);
        } else {
            document.write('This application requires Flash player '
      + lzCanvasRuntimeVersion + '. <a
      href="http://www.macromedia.com/go/getflashplayer"
      target="fpupgrade">Click here</a> to upgrade.');
        }
    </script>
        </div>

        <script type="text/javascript">
          var map = new GMap(document.getElementById("map"));
          map.addControl(new GLargeMapControl());
          map.centerAndZoom(new
        GPoint(139.69512732988332,35.685483113982414), 0);
```

```
function evalscript(str){
    eval(str);
}
</script>
```

```
<noscript>Please enable JavaScript in order to use this application.
</noscript>
</body>
</html>
```

Note that you need to edit the value of the **lzLPSRoot** variable (in the bold line) if you're not using OpenLaszlo 4.0.x when testing this application.

To compile and run this application, use this URL:

```
http://localhost:8080/lps-4.0.x/gmaps/index.html
```

Figure15.2 shows the application.

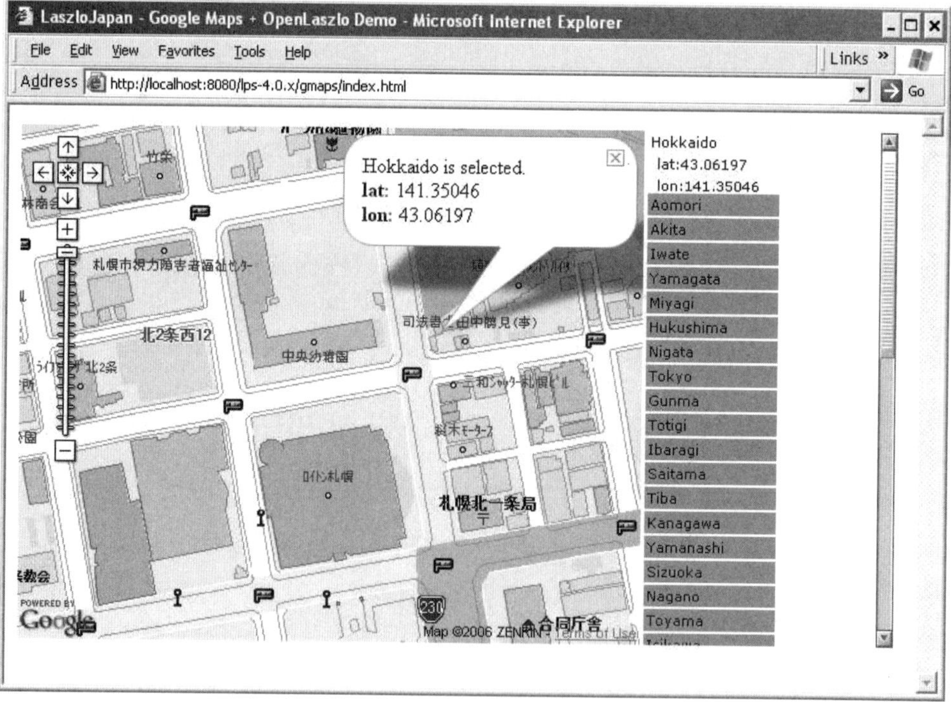

Figure 15.2: The Google Maps application

Summary

The sample application in this chapter demonstrates how an LZX application can interact seamlessly with the browser. The application reads the locations of dozens of cities in Japan and show their respective Google maps.

Appendix A
Introduction to XML

This appendix provides a brief tutorial on XML. It is by no means complete, as XML is a very broad and a thorough discussion would require a book of its own. If you are new to XML, however, this tutorial should provide you with the basics for you to understand the sample applications accompanying this book and write your own.

Benefits of XML

An XML document is a plain text file, and you can use any text editor to write, view, and edit it. When you see an XML document for the first time, you will immediately notice that some words are enclosed in brackets: < … >. The words in brackets are called *tags*. If you already know Hypertext Markup Language (HTML), you'll feel at home learning XML. However, unlike HTML, there are no predefined tags in XML. Every tag is tailor-made—in other words, you create your own!

The main use of XML is to store data, just like relational databases do. If relational databases work so well, why do you need XML at all? XML has the following advantages over relational databases.

- XML uses a standard and open format from the W3C (www.w3c.org), making data exchange easy. Compare this with proprietary data formats of relational databases that make exchanging data a complex process.
- XML can represent hierarchical data.
- You must comply with rules when writing XML. These rules make it possible to check the data integrity of an XML document.
- The same rules make it possible to validate XML documents.
- XML is extensible. You create your custom tags to accommodate any type of data you have.

Note

You can find the XML recommendation version 1.0 (the latest version) at http://www.w3.org/TR/REC-xml.

Consider, for example, a table containing product information as given in Table A.1.

ProductId	Name	Description	Price	SupplierId
1	ChocChic	Mint chocolate 100g	1.50	1
2	Chocnuts	Chocolate with peanuts, 200g	2.95	2

Table A.1: A Products table

If the two records in Table A.1 is to be written in XML, you will get the XML document in Listing A.1.

Listing A.1: An XML document that contains product information

```xml
<?xml version="1.0" standalone="yes" encoding="UTF-8"?>
<products>
    <product>
        <product_id>1</product_id>
        <name>ChocChic</name>
        <description>Mint Chocolate 100g</description>
        <price>1.50</price>
        <supplier_id>1</supplier_id>
    </product>
    <product>
        <product_id>2</product_id>
        <name>Chocnuts</name>
        <description>Chocolate with peanuts, 200gr</description>
        <price>2.95</price>
        <supplier_id>2</supplier_id>
    </product>
</products>
```

The first line tells you that it is an XML document that is compliant with version 1.0, it is a stand-alone document (meaning it does not refer to any external entity), and it uses UTF-8 encoding.

The second line begins the data, which is represented as a collection of elements. The first element in the XML document is **products**, which indicates a collection of products. The first element is called the *root*. So, <products> is the root of the XML document in Listing A.1.

An element can contain other elements, which are called the *child elements* of the first element. As previously mentioned, XML is suitable for hierarchical data. Therefore, elements with child elements with child elements are common in XML. For example, the **product** element is the child element of the **products** element. The **product** element has the child elements **product_id**, **name**, **description**, **price**, and **supplier_id**.

An element in an XML document can contain *attributes*, which are similar to attributes in an HTML tag. For example, the following is a **product** element to which an **in_stock** attribute has been added:

```
<product in_stock="yes">
```

Note
Element names and attribute names are case sensitive.

Well-Formed XML Documents

Let's define a term that you will often encounter when working with XML: *well-formed-ness*. A well-formed XML document follows the syntax rules governed by the World Wide Web Consortium (W3C) in the XML 1.0 Specification. Well-formed-ness means the following:

- An XML document must contain at least one element, the root element.
- There can be only one root element. All other elements are nested inside the root element, either directly or indirectly.

The XML document in Listing A.1 is well-formed, but that in Listing A.2 is *not* because the closing **name** element appears after the **description** opening tag.

Listing 2-2. A not well-formed XML Document

```
<product>
    <name>
        ChocChic
    <description>
        chocolate with mint 100g
    </name>
    </description>
</product>
```

What does it take to write a well-formed XML document? The short answer is that the document must meet all the well-formedness constraints specified in the W3C's XML 1.0 recommendation: an XML document has three parts—the prolog, an element part, and a miscellaneous part.

The Prolog

The prolog starts an XML document. It contains an XML declaration, miscellaneous part, and DTD. (I'll explain about DTD later). All the parts in the prolog are optional. Therefore, an XML document can still be well-formed even if the prolog is empty. However, an XML document with an empty prolog is not valid.

The XML declaration part of the prolog contains the version information, optional encoding declaration, and optional stand-alone document declaration. These prolog examples contain only the XML declaration part:

```
<?xml version="1.0"?>
<?xml version="1.0" encoding="UTF-8"?>
<?xml version="1.0" standalone="yes"?>
<?xml version="1.0" encoding="UTF-8" standalone="yes"?>
```

The only valid version number for an XML document is currently 1.0. The encoding declaration is the language encoding for the document. The default value for the encoding declaration is UTF-8. A value of "yes" for the stand-alone declaration means the XML document does not refer to any external document; "no" means otherwise.

The Element Part

Right after the prolog comes the element part. An XML element begins with a start tag and ends with an end tag. A start tag begins with < and ends with >. An end tag starts with </ and ends with >. Here is an XML element, the tag name is **productId**:

```
<productId>1</productId>
```

A tag name starts with a letter, an underscore, or a colon. Following the first character are letters, digits, underscores, hyphens, periods, and colons. A tag name can contain no white space.

Empty elements are also possible. For example:

```
<bodyNumber></bodyNumber>
```

Empty elements can be written using only one tag:

```
<bodyNumber/>
```

An element can have *attributes*, which are name-value pairs containing additional data for the element. You separate the name and the value in an attribute with the equal sign. Attribute names follow the same rule as tag names. You must enclose attribute values in quotation marks, either double quotes or single quotes. Using double quotes is more common, but you can use single quotes if the value itself contains double quotes. In the case where an attribute value contains both single quotes and double quotes, you can encode the single quote and double quote characters. **'** represents a single quote and **"** represents a double quote.

Note

The <, >, and & characters are special characters that must also be encoded. You can use **&** for the ampersand (&), **<** for <, and **>** for >.

For example, the following **product** element has an attribute called in_stock. The attribute has the value of 6.

```
<product in_stock="6">
    <name>ChicChoc</name>
</product>
```

Confusion often arises whether or not to write data related to an element as an attribute or as a child element. For example, you can rewrite the preceding **product** element as follows:

```
<product>
    <in_stock>6</in_stock>
    <name>ChicChoc</name>
</product>
```

Whether to use an attribute or a child element is entirely up to you. However, the general rule of thumb says that you should not have more than 10 attributes in one element.

The Miscellaneous Part

This part can contain comments or processing instructions. An XML comment starts with <!-- and ends with -->.

Validating XML Documents

One of the benefits of XML is you can verify the data integrity of an XML document by validating it. A valid XML document must be well-formed and follows a set of rules. You can check the validity of an XML document against one of two types of rules: Document Type Definitions (DTDs) and schemas.

A valid XML document must have a DTD or a schema associated with it, against which the correctness of the XML document can be verified. For example, an XML document that contains the data structure for some products may define that the root element is **<products>** and there are five child elements under it: **<name>**, **<description>**, **<product_id>**, **<price>**, and **<supplier_id>**. If a document has a **products** element as its root, but the **supplier_id** element is missing, the document is not valid, even though it may be well-formed.

Specifications for DTDs were published earlier than those of schemas, but schemas are more powerful than DTDs. Both are still widely in use today and we will look at both in turn.

Document Type Definition

You can define a DTD or DTDs in the XML document itself, in an external file, or in both. In the following sections, we first look at DTD basics in an internal DTD, then we discuss documents that have external DTDs. The last subsection talks about entities and attributes.

Note
You can find the formal rules for DTDs in the XML 1.0 at www.w3.org/TR/REC-xml.

The first thing to note is that you use **<!DOCTYPE>** to write a DTD, which always appears in the XML document prolog. There are a few syntaxes for **<!DOCTYPE>**, this appendix uses the following:

```
<!DOCTYPE rootName [DTD]>
```

where *rootName* is the name of the root in the document and [DTD] is the part that defines all elements—in other words, the root itself and all other elements nested inside the root. Each element is defined by <!ELEMENT>. Because an XML document must have a root, the DTD must have at least one element that defines the root itself. For example, the following is an XML document with an internal DTD. The DTD dictates that the document must have a root called **products**, and **<products>** can have no elements nested inside it:

```
<?xml version="1.0" standalone="yes"?>
<!DOCTYPE products [
<!ELEMENT products (#PCDATA)>
]>
<products/>
```

Note that the XML declaration in the prolog contains the **standalone** attribute with the value of "yes". This means this XML document does not refer to any external document. Note also that the DTD defines the **<!ELEMENT>** for products. **#PCDATA** stands for parsed character data and means text that does not contain markup.

You can also declare that an element must be empty using the **EMPTY** keyword. An empty element cannot have a value or a child element, but it can have attributes. For example, the following is the previous XML document with a DTD that states that the root element (**products**) must be empty:

```
<?xml version="1.0" standalone="yes"?>
<!DOCTYPE products [
<!ELEMENT products EMPTY>
]>
<products></products>
```

An XML document with only the root and no other elements is not very useful. The **<!ELEMENT>** in a DTD allows you to define another element. For instance, the following is a DTD that states that the XML document must have **<products>** as its root and **<products>** must have a **product** element. The DTD also states that the **product** element must have the **name** and **product_id** elements:

```
<!DOCTYPE products [
<!ELEMENT products (product)>
<!ELEMENT product (name,product_id)>
<!ELEMENT name (#PCDATA)>
<!ELEMENT product_id (#PCDATA)>
]>
```

Listing A.3 shows a valid XML document that uses the previous DTD.

Listing A.3: A valid XML document with an internal DTD

```
<?xml version="1.0" standalone="yes"?>
<!DOCTYPE products [
<!ELEMENT products (product)>
<!ELEMENT product (name,product_id)>
<!ELEMENT name (#PCDATA)>
<!ELEMENT product_id (#PCDATA)>
]>
<products>
    <product>
        <name>ChicChoc</name>
        <product_id>10</product_id>
    </product>
</products>
```

When declaring child elements, you can use the following operators that have special meanings. Here *x* denotes a child element:

- x*: Zero or more instances of x
- x+: One or more instances of x
- x?: Zero or one instance of x
- x, y: x followed by y
- x | y: x or y

For example, if you want to say in a DTD that **<products>** can have zero or more **product** elements and a **product** element can have an optional **name** element but must have a **product_id** element, use this DTD:

```
<!DOCTYPE products [
<!ELEMENT products (product)*>
<!ELEMENT product (name?,product_id)>
<!ELEMENT name (#PCDATA)>
<!ELEMENT product_id (#PCDATA)>
]>
```

External DTDs

Using an external DTD makes sense if the DTD is to be used by multiple XML documents. Also, for a long DTD, an external DTD makes the XML document that uses it tidier.

There are two kinds of external DTDs: private and public. Private DTDs are to be used privately by certain people or applications in a group. You specify an external private DTD using the **SYSTEM** keyword in the <!DOCTYPE>. On the other hand, a public external DTD can be used by anyone. To make an external DTD public, use the **PUBLIC** keyword in the <!DOCTYPE>.

Practically the only differences between using an external DTD from an internal DTD are that with external DTDs you have a separate file for the DTD and this DTD file is referenced from inside the XML document. Listing A.4 shows an XML document that uses a private DTD called **products.dtd**. Because the **products.dtd** file is referenced without any information about its path, it must reside in the same directory as the XML document.

Listing A.4: A valid XML document referencing a private, external DTD

```
<?xml version="1.0" standalone="no"?>
<!DOCTYPE products SYSTEM "products.dtd">
<products>
    <product>
        <name>ChocChic</name>
        <product_id>12</product_id>
    </product>
    <product>
        <name>Waftel Chocolate</name>
        <product_id>15</product_id>
    </product>
</products>
```

And, the following is the **products.dtd** file.

```
<!ELEMENT products (product)+>
<!ELEMENT product (name, product_id)>
<!ELEMENT name (#PCDATA)>
<!ELEMENT product_id (#PCDATA)>
```

You can also reference a private external DTD using its Uniform Resource Locator (URL). In this case, you just specify a URL after the SYSTEM keyword:

```
<!DOCTYPE products SYSTEM
    "http://www.brainysoftware.com/dtd/products.dtd">
```

A public external DTD is similar to a private DTD, except that you must define a Formal Public Identifier (FPI) after the **PUBLIC** keyword in the <!DOCTYPE>. The FPI has four fields, each of which is separated from each other by double forward slashes (//). The first field in an FPI indicates the formality of the DTD. For a DTD that you define yourself, you use a minus (-) sign. If the DTD has been approved by a nonstandard body, you use a plus (+) sign. For a formal standard, use the reference to the standard itself. The second field in an FPI is the name of the organization that maintains the DTD. The third field indicates the type of document being described, and the fourth field specifies the language that the DTD uses. For example, EN stands for English.

This is an example of a <!DOCTYPE> that references an external public DTD:

```
<!DOCTYPE products PUBLIC "-//bs//Exports//EN"
    "http://brainysoftware.com/products.dtd">
```

Entities

You can define *entities* in a DTD. You will probably ask then, what is an entity? To explain it to a programmer like yourself, it is best to draw an analogy between an entity in an XML document and a constant in a computer program. You declare a constant (using the keyword **Const** in Visual Basic) and assign it a value so that you can reference the value through the constant from within your code. Likewise, you define an entity in a DTD so that you can use it from anywhere in the XML document. You define an entity using the following syntax:

```
<!ENTITY name definition>
```

When the XML document is parsed, the entity will be replaced by the value of the entity. To use the entity, you precede the entity name with the ampersand and add a semicolon after the name. For example, to refer to an entity called **myEntity**, you write **&myEntity;**.

As an example, Listing A.5 shows an XML document in which an entity named **company** is declared in its DTD. The value of the entity is "Cooper Wilson and Co."

Listing A.5: An XML document with an entity

```
<?xml version="1.0" standalone="yes"?>
<!DOCTYPE products [
<!ELEMENT products (manufacturer, (product)*)>
<!ELEMENT manufacturer (#PCDATA)>
<!ELEMENT product (name, product_id)>
<!ELEMENT name (#PCDATA)>
<!ELEMENT product_id (#PCDATA)>
<!ENTITY company "Cooper Wilson and Co.">
]>
<products>
    <manufacturer>&company;</manufacturer>
    <product>
        <name>ChocChic</name>
        <product_id>12</product_id>
    </product>
    <product>
        <name>Waftel Chocolate</name>
        <product_id>15</product_id>
    </product>
</products>
```

When an XML parser reads this XML document, it replaces the entity with its value, like the one in Listing A.6.

Listing 2-6. An XML document with an entity's value

```
<?xml version="1.0" standalone="yes" ?>
<!DOCTYPE products (View Source for full doctype...)>
<products>
    <manufacturer>Cooper Wilson and Co.</manufacturer>
    <product>
        <name>ChocChic</name>
        <product_id>12</product_id>
    </product>
    <product>
        <name>Waftel Chocolate</name>
        <product_id>15</product_id>
    </product>
</products>
```

You can use five predefined entities in your XML document without declaring them in the DTD: **'**, **"**, **&**, **<**, and **>**.

Attributes

You specify attributes that an element has using the following syntax:

```
<!ATTLIST elementName
    attributeName_1 type_1 defaultValue_1
    attributeName_2 type_2 defaultValue_2
        .
        .
        .
    attributeName_n type_n defaultValue_n>
```

For example, to define that the **product** element must have the **id** attribute, you write the code in Listing A.7.

Listing A.7: An XML document with elements and attributes

```
<?xml version="1.0" standalone="yes"?>
<!DOCTYPE products [
<!ELEMENT products (product)*>
<!ELEMENT manufacturer (#PCDATA)>
<!ELEMENT product (name, product_id)>
<!ELEMENT name (#PCDATA)>
<!ELEMENT product_id (#PCDATA)>
<!ATTLIST product
    supplier_id CDATA #IMPLIED>
]>
<products>
    <product supplier_id="1">
        <name>ChocChic</name>
        <product_id>12</product_id>
    </product>
    <product supplier_id="2">
        <name>Waftel Chocolate</name>
        <product_id>15</product_id>
    </product>
</products>
```

The default value **#IMPLIED** means that the attribute is optional.

Schemas

Like DTDs, schemas validate XML documents. However, schemas are more powerful. Schemas provide the following advantages over DTDs:

- Additional data types are available using a schema.
- Schemas support custom data types.
- A schema uses XML syntax.
- A schema supports object-oriented concepts such as polymorphism and inheritance.

Note

Schemas are basically XML documents. By convention a schema has an .xsd extension. The term *instance document* is often used to describe an XML document that conforms to a particular schema. A schema does not have to reside in a file, though. It may be a stream of bytes, a field in a database record, or a collection of XML Infoset "information items."

When discussing schemas, it is convenient to refer to elements as *simple types* and *complex types*. Elements that contain subelements or carry attributes are complex types, whereas elements that contain numbers (and strings, and dates, and so on) but do not contain subelements are simple types. Some elements have attributes; attributes always have simple types.

The W3C recommendation defines schemas in a three-part document at the following locations:

```
http://www.w3.org/TR/xmlschema-0/
http://www.w3.org/TR/xmlschema-1/
http://www.w3.org/TR/xmlschema-2/
```

Each of the elements in the schema has the prefix **xsd:**, which is associated with the XML Schema namespace through the declaration xmlns:xsd="http://www.w3.org/2001/XMLSchema" that appears in the schema element. By convention, the prefix **xsd:** denotes the XML Schema namespace, although you can use any prefix. The same prefix, and hence the same association, also appears on the names of built-in simple types—for example, **xsd:string**. The purpose of the association is to identify the elements and simple types as belonging to the vocabulary of the XML Schema language rather than the vocabulary of the schema author. For clarity, we just mention the names of elements and simple types and omit the prefix.

Note

Like DTDs, schemas can appear inside an XML document or as external documents. The **schemaLocation** and **xsi:schemaLocation** attributes specify the location of an external schema referenced to by an XML document. Interested readers should read the document at http://www.w3.org/TR/xmlschema-0/.

In XML Schema, there is a basic difference between the complex types that allow elements in their content and can carry attributes and the simple types that cannot have element content and cannot carry attributes. There is also a major distinction between definitions that create new types (both simple and complex) and declarations that enable elements and attributes with specific names and types (both simple and complex) to appear in document instances. In this section, we focus on defining complex types and declaring the elements and attributes that appear within them.

You define new complex types using the **complexType** element; such definitions typically contain a set of element declarations, element references, and attribute declarations. The declarations are not themselves types, but rather an association between a name and the constraints that govern the appearance of that name in documents governed by the associated schema. You declare elements using the **element** element, and you declare attributes using the **attribute** element. Listing A.8 is an example of an XML document that uses an inline schema.

Listing A.8: Using an inline schema

```
<xs:schema
  xmlns:xs='http://www.w3.org/2001/XMLSchema'
  xmlns='xsdBook'
  targetNamespace='xsdBook'
>
  <xs:element name='Book'>
    <xs:complexType>
      <xs:sequence>
        <xs:element name='Title' type='xs:string' maxOccurs='1'/>
        <xs:element name='Author' type='xs:string' maxOccurs='1'/>
      </xs:sequence>
      <xs:attribute name='Edition' type='xs:string' use='optional'/>
    </xs:complexType>
```

```
    </xs:element>
</xs:schema>

<hc:Book Edition='1' xmlns:hc='xsdBook'>
  <Title>Dogs are from Mars, Cats are from Venus</Title>
  <Author>T. Sakhira</Author>
</hc:Book>
```

Related XML Resources

To conclude the discussion of XML basics, the following are links to useful documents to help you work with XML and understand it better:

- http://www.w3c.org/xml: The official Web site of XML
- http://www.w3c.org/TR/REC-xml: The W3C XML 1.0 recommendation
- http://www.w3c.org/DOM/: The W3C Document Object Model
- http://www.w3.org/TR/REC-xml: The formal rules for DTDs in XML 1.0
- http://www.w3.org/TR/xmlschema-0/: XML Schema Part 0: Primer
- http://www.w3.org/TR/xmlschema-1/: XML Schema Part 1: Structures
- http://www.w3.org/TR/xmlschema-2/: XML Schema Part 2: Datatypes
- http://www.xml.com: A site dedicated to providing XML resources, discussions, and so on
- http://msdn.microsoft.com/xml/tutorial/default.asp: Microsoft's XML tutorial

Appendix B
Introduction to JavaScript

JavaScript is a very popular scripting language that works in virtually all modern browsers in use today. Since the LZX language in OpenLaszlo has the same syntax as JavaScript, mastering JavaScript is a prerequisite for writing robust and efficient OpenLaszlo applications.

This appendix provides you with a brief tutorial on JavaScript.

Your First Script

You use the **script** tag to embed JavaScript in an HTML page. For example, Listing B.1 shows a simple script.

Listing B.1: A simple JavaScript script.

```
<html>
<head>
<title>Your First Script</title>
<body>
<script type="text/javascript">
    document.write("Hi there! I am JavaScript!")
</script>
</body>
</html>
```

In this case, the script consists of just one line of code:

```
document.write("Hi there! I am JavaScript!")
```

It uses one of the available objects, **document**, which will be discussed later and which is basically the page you see in your browser. Open this HTML page in any browser and you should see an empty page with "Hi there! I am JavaScript!" printed on it.

If you are a Java or C++ programmer, you will be tempted to put a semicolon in the end of the line of code. All right, do it! Semicolons are optional in JavaScript unless you have multiple statements in the same line of code. It is recommended to always use a semicolon at the end of your statement.

Have you ever looked at the source code of a web page with JavaScript embedded in it? If yes, then most probably you've seen some unusual comments, like the one here:

```
<script type="text/javascript">
<!--
  document.write("Hi there! I am JavaScript!")
//-->
</script>
```

This is for Web browsers that do not support JavaScript. These very old browsers do not understand what <script> means and would just print your JavaScript code on the page. With comments after **<script>**, older browsers will not display the script.

If your script is long, it is good practice to put your script in a separate file and then reference it from the HTML file by using the **src** attribute of the **script** tag. For example, the following **script** tag references an external file named **try.js**.

```
<script type="text/javascript" src="try.js"></script>
```

Variables

Like other programming languages, JavaScript works with variables, which are basically named pieces of memory used to store data. Variables help you manipulate and change the data in your code.

It is important to remember that JavaScript is case-sensitive, so **myVar** is different from **myvar**.

When it comes to declaring a variable, JavaScript is a rather forgiving language. You can declare a variable, like this:

```
var aVariable;
```

or, you can declare and assign a value at the same time.

```
var aVariable = someValue
```

Bear in mind that JavaScript doesn't care about the type of data stored in a variable. You can put into the same variable a string, an integer, a floating point number, or even an object. For example, consider the code in Listing B.2.

Listing B.2: Using variables

```
var myVar = 100;
document.write("myVar is an integer: " + myVar);
myVar = myVar + 23;
document.write("<br/>Now its value is: " + myVar);
myVar = "one hundred";
document.write("<br/>And now it is a string: " + myVar);
myVar = myVar + 23;
document.write("<br/>Finally, the string is modified: " + myVar);
```

The output of this script is this:

```
myVar is an integer: 100
Now its value is: 123
And now it is a string: one hundred
Finally, the string is modified: one hundred23
```

Arrays

Arrays are handy if you need to store a collection of values/objects. In JavaScript, an array is represented by the **Array** class. For example, this code constructs a JavaScript array:

```
var averageTemps = new Array()
```

Once you have an instance of **Array**, you can add to it as many elements as you wish. JavaScript arrays can grow as needed. Remember though that the numbering in JavaScript arrays starts from zero:

```
averageTemps[0] = 10
averageTemps[1] = 12
averageTemps[2] = 8
```

If you know that the exact number of values you are going to store in your array is, say, 30, you can declare the array like this:

```
var averageTemps = new Array(30)
```

This will make your script slightly more efficient, but in most cases the difference will not be noticeable.

Yet another way to create an array is to just list all its members, like this:

```
var averageTemps = new Array(10, 12, 8, 15, 11, 10, 9)
```

Once an array is created, you can retrieve the values stored in its members, or you can assign them new values, like here:

```
averageTemps[1]
averageTemps[2] = 14
```

Operators

JavaScript comes with operators for various operations. This section discusses those operators.

Arithmetic Operators

These are probably the most often used operators. I'll use examples to explan them. Here is the first example.

```
var result;
var a = 5;
var b = 17;
var c = "some string";
var d = "another string";

result = a + b; // Addition
document.write("The result of addition is " + result);

result = a - b; // Substraction
document.write("<br/>The result of subtraction is " + result);

result = a * b; // Multiplication
document.write("<br/>The result of multiplication is " + result);
```

```
result = b / a; // Division
document.write("<br/>The result of division is " + result);

result = b % a; // Modulus
document.write("<br/>The division remainder is " + result);

// Increment
document.write("<br/>The incremented value of a is " + ++a);

// Another way to increment a value
document.write("<br/>The value of a is " + a++);
document.write("<br/>And now it is " + a);

/* And two ways to decrement a value
(this also demonstrates a different kind
of comment)*/
document.write("<br/>Decremented b: " + --b);
document.write("<br/>Another way, b = " + b--);
document.write("<br/>And now b is " + b);

// Concatenating strings
document.write("<br/>Concatenating strings: " + c + d);
document.write("<br/>Same with an integer: " + b + c);
```

Here is the result you should see on your browser:

```
The result of addition is 22
The result of subtraction is -12
The result of multiplication is 85
The result of division is 3.4
The division remainder is 2
The incremented value of a is 6
The value of a is 6
And now it is 7
Decremented b: 16
Another way, b = 16
And now b is 15
Concatenating strings: some stringanother string
Same with an integer: 15some string
```

Everything is simple with addition, subtraction, multiplication and division. The modulus operator is also straightforward if you know what it does. It produces a remainder of division.

The increment and decrement operators are a little bit tricky because they can be used in two ways. If you put the operator before the variable, as in **++a** and --**b**, the variable is first incremented or decremented, and then used in the expression (in our case it is displayed on the web page).

But if you put the operator after the variable, like this: a++, b--, then the variable's value first used in the expression and only after that it is incremented or decremented. To understand how it works, have a look at the code examples and their results.

If the addition operator is used for strings, these strings are joined together (concatenated). And, even if only one of the operands is a string, all the other operands are also treated as strings. In fact, we were using this concatenation operator in many of our examples, like this:

```
document.write("myVar is an integer: " + myVar);
```

Two types of comment are also shown in this example. One of them, double slash, makes a comment everything which goes on the right of it in the same line.

Another way to write a comment, most useful for multiline comments, is the combination of /* and */ symbols. Everything which goes in between them is a comment.

Assignment Operators

The basic assignment operator is very simple, it evaluates the expression on the right hand side and assigns the resulting value to the variable on the left hand side. For example, in this statement:

```
a = 3 + 4;
```

the expression on the right hand side is evaluated, which produces 7, and then this result is stored in variable **a**.

The other versions of the assignment operator look a little strange, but are really convenient in many cases. It is easier to explain how they work with an example:

a += b is the same as a = a + b

a -= b is the same as a = a − b

a *= b is the same as a = a * b;

a /= b is the same as a = a / b;

a %= b is the same as a = a % b

Comparison Operators

Comparison operators are used to compare two values and returns a boolean value, i.e. **true** or **false**. As you will see it shortly, they are normally used in looping and conditional constructs in JavaScript.

To see how these operators work, run the following script:

```javascript
// Equality
document.write("5 == 5 returns " + (5 == 5));
document.write("<br/> 7 == 3 returns " + (7 == 3));
document.write("<br/> '5' == 5 returns " + ('5' == 5));

// Strict equality
document.write("<br/> 5 === 5 returns " + (5 === 5));
document.write("<br/> 7 === 3 returns " + (7 === 3));
document.write("<br/> '5' === 5 returns " + ('5' === 5));

// Not equal
document.write("<br/> 10 != 1 returns " + (10 != 1));
document.write("<br/> 5 != 5 returns " + (5 != 5));

// Greater than and less than
document.write("<br/> 10 > 1 returns " + (10 > 1));
document.write("<br/> 10 < 1 returns " + (10 < 1));

// Greater than or equal, less than or equal
document.write("<br/> 10 >= 10 returns " + (10 >= 1));
document.write("<br/> 10 <= 11 returns " + (10 <= 11));
```

Here is the result.

```
5 == 5 returns true
7 == 3 returns false
'5' == 5 returns true
5 === 5 returns true
7 === 3 returns false
'5' === 5 returns false
10 != 1 returns true
5 != 5 returns false
10 > 1 returns true
```

```
10 < 1 returns false
10 >= 10 returns true
10 <= 11 returns true
```

Everything should be pretty obvious here, except for the **===** (strict equality) operator, which checks the equality of both the value and the type. Two strings can be equal to each other, as can two numbers. But a string and a number cannot be equal, with this operator.

Logical Operators

There are only three of them, && (logical AND), || (logical OR) and ! (logical NOT). Again, it will be easier to just demonstrate how they work with an example. Try the following code in your browser:

```
// && operator which means AND
// Returns true if both conditions are true
document.write("(5 > 3) && (7 > 1) returns " + ((5 > 3) &&
        (7 > 1)));
document.write("<br/> (5 > 3) && (7 < 1) returns " + ((5 > 3) &&
        (7 < 1)));

// || operator which means OR
// Returns true if at leas one of the conditions is true
document.write("<br/> (5 > 3) || (7 > 1) returns " + ((5 > 3) ||
        (7 > 1)));
document.write("<br/> (5 > 3) || (7 < 1) returns " + ((5 > 3) ||
        (7 < 1)));
document.write("<br/> (5 < 3) || (7 < 1) returns " + ((5 < 3) ||
        (7 < 1)));

// ! operator which means NOT
// Changes true to false and vice versa
document.write("<br/> !(7 > 1) returns " + !(7 > 1));
document.write("<br/> !(7 < 1) returns " + !(7 < 1));
```

The result should look like this:

```
(5 > 3) && (7 > 1) returns true
(5 > 3) && (7 < 1) returns false
(5 > 3) || (7 > 1) returns true
(5 > 3) || (7 < 1) returns true
(5 < 3) || (7 < 1) returns false
!(7 > 1) returns false
```

```
!(7 < 1) returns true
```

Conditional Operator

The syntax of the conditional operator is as follows.

```
aVariable = (condition)? value1 : value2
```

If *condition* is true then *value1* is assigned to *aVariable*. Otherwise, *value2* is assigned to *aVariable*.

Now, try this.

```
var t = -5;
var weather;
weather = (t > 10)? "warm": (t >= 0)? "cold" : "freezing!";
document.write(weather);
```

Loops

Computers are very good at doing the same thing repeatedly. They never get bored. To ask a computer to repeat the same piece of code again and again, programmers use loops. There are three kinds of loops available in JavaScript.

The while Loop

The **while** loop executes the code which goes inside of it while a certain condition remains true. In a generic way, it can be shown like this:

```
while (condition) {

    // The code you want to be repeated

}
```

And here is a real example of this kind of loop:

```
var i = 3;

while (i < 10000) {
```

```
    document.write(i + " ")
    i *= i
}
```

Try this code in your browser, and it should display four numbers: 3 9 81 6561. So it kept displaying the value of the **i** variable while it was less than 10000.

The **while** loop is most useful when you don't know how many times the code should be repeated. You just allow it to iterate while some condition is true. Note however that it is you, the programmer, who is responsible for defining when the loop ends. If you make a mistake, the loop can become endless. For example, try to comment out the line, where the value of **i** is changed, like this:

```
while (i < 10000) {
  document.write(i + " ")
  // i *= i
}
```

If you try to run this code, then depending on which browser you are using, the browser will freeze at first, but then its internal anti-fault mechanism will figure out that something is wrong with your loop, and it should report the problem in one or the other way.

If the looping condition is false from the very beginning, for example if the initial value of **i** was 10001, the code inside the loop will never run. Depending on the logic of your script, you might want the code to run at least once before the condition is checked. In this case, another variety of looping construct will be useful, it looks like this:

```
do {

// The code to be repeated

} while (condition)
```

And, here is an example you can run in your browser:

```
var i = 33333;

do {
  document.write(i + " ")
  i *= i
```

```
} while (i < 10000)
```

You will see that the value of **i** is displayed once.

The for Loop

Let's say you have ten numbers in an array, and you want to find their average. One of the ways to achieve this is by using the **for** loop, which repeats the code inside of it the specified number of times. This is how its structure looks:

```
for (initialization; condition; incrementing) {

  // The code to be repeated

}
```

The **for** loop uses a variable to count how many times it has already executed the code. In the very beginning, before doing anything else, this variable receives its initial value. Then the condition of the loop is checked, and if it is true, the code inside the loop is executed. Afterwards, the variable is incremented, and the condition is checked again, and if it is true, the code is executed again, and so on. Let's look at an example:

```
var numbers = new Array(10, 12, 37, 54, 23, 6, 73, 59, 28, 81);
var sum = 0;
var i;

for (i = 0; i < 10; i++) {
    sum += numbers[i]
}

document.write("The simple average is " + sum / 10);
```

We use the **for** loop here to add all the numbers in the array, one by one, to the **sum** variable, and then just divide it by 10, which is how many numbers we have. The **i** variable is used as a counter, and since array members are numbered from 0, we initialize it to 0, and then increment it after the code inside the loop runs. This is the most common way to use the **for** loop, but you can be quite creative with it, like here:

```
var i = 100;

for (; i > 1; i /= 3) {
```

```
   document.write(i + " ")

}
```

The for ... in Loop

The **for ... in** loop is used to iterate over all the elements of an array or the properties of an object. Consider this.

```
var sum = 0;
var numbers = new Array(10, 12, 37, 54, 23, 6, 73, 59, 28, 81);
for (i in numbers) {
  sum += numbers[i]
}
document.write("The average is " + sum / numbers.length)
```

This code doesn't look very different from the previous version. First of all, we don't need to know how many elements there are in the array to iterate through all of them.

And since we might not know that there are ten elements in this array, we used the **length** property of the **Array** object, which tells us the number of elements.

Branching in JavaScript

In many cases you will need to decide in your script whether to execute some piece of code or some other piece, depending on some condition. This is exactly when branching constructs are used in programming. In JavaScript, there are two of them: **if ... else** and **switch**.

If and If ... Else Statements

The simplest way to decide whether to execute some code is to use the **if** statement. It is very simple:

```
if (condition) {

  // The code to be executed if the condition
```

```
  // evaluates to true

}
```

For example:

```
if (temp > 20) {
  document.write("I like when it's warm!")
}
```

If you want to execute one version of code if the condition is true and another version of code otherwise, use the **if ... else** statement:

```
if (condition) {
  // The code to be executed if the condition
  // evaluates to true

}
else {
  // The code to be executed if the condition
  // evaluates to false
}
```

As an example,

```
if ((temp > 20) && (temp < 30)) {
  document.write("I like it when it's warm! ")
}
else {
  document.write("No, this is not comfortable! ")
}
```

Finally, we can chain **if ... else** statements:

```
if (temp < 0) {
  document.write("It is freezing!")
}
else if (temp < 10) {
  document.write("It is cold")
}
else {
  document.write("It is warm enough")
}
```

The switch Statement

This statement allows us to literally switch execution of a script between different options depending on the value of a variable. Check this example out.

```
var x = 1;

switch (x) {
  case 1:
      document.write("The value is one.")
      break
  case 2:
      document.write("The value is two.")
      break
  case 3:
      document.write("The value is three.")
      break
  default:
      document.write("Some other value.")
}
```

The **switch** statement evaluates the value in its brackets (in our case, the variable **x**) and then compares the result with the value for each **case** entry. As soon as it finds a match, the code inside that case entry is executed. If no match is found, the code under the **default** entry is executed.

You see the **break** statement which terminates the code after each case entry. What is it for? Try to remove or comment out the **break** statements in the code shown above and then run it in your browser. This is what you'll get:

```
The value is one.The value is two.The value is three.Some other
      value.
```

This means that if after choosing a **case** entry the execution doesn't encounter the **break** statement, it just "falls through", i.e. continues to execute the code of the next entry. In some cases this might be exactly what you want from your program. But if not – just use the **break** statements where needed.

When execution comes to such a **break** statement inside of **switch** construct, it just exits the whole **switch** block and continue to the next line of code after the switch block.

Interrupting a Loop

In some cases you might want to interrupt a loop before it terminates naturally, i.e. before the value of its condition changes to **false**. This can be achieved using one of two ways.

First, you can use the same **break** statement. If it is met inside the loop, the execution will just leave the loop and continue with the next line of code after it. Let's see how this happens.

```
var i = 0;
while (i < 10) {
    if (i == 5) break
    document.write(i + " ")
    i++
}
```

Here is the result which you should see after running this code in your browser:

```
0 1 2 3 4
```

When the value of **i** is equal to 5, the **break** statement is executed. As a result, our **while** loop is left behind and since there is no more code in our simple script, it comes to its end.

But there is also another option we might choose: the **continue** statement. Modify the previous code like this:

```
var i = 0;

while (i < 10) {
    i++
    if (i == 5) continue
    document.write(i + " ")
}
```

And then run it in your browser. This is what you should see:

```
1 2 3 4 6 7 8 9 10
```

Can you figure out what is happening here? When the value of **i** was equal to 5, the **continue** statement was executed. As a result the execution of the code inside the loop was stopped, and 5 wasn't printed out. However, the loop wasn't terminated either, it just *continued* with the next iteration.

Functions

In many programs we need to use the same piece of code again and again. It makes sense not to rewrite it, but to put that code in a special place, give it a name, and then use that name to call our code when needed. This is exactly how functions are declared and used in JavaScript.

Consider the following example:

```
<html>
<head>
<title>JavaScript Function Test</title>

<script type="text/javascript">
function simpleFunction(x) {
  var y = "Your simple function says: " + x;
  return y
}
</script>

</head>
<body>

<script type="text/javascript">
var aVar = "hi there!";
document.write(simpleFunction(aVar))
</script>

</body>
</html>
```

Not a very useful example of a function, but still, it demonstrates all the important points.

First, functions are normally declared in the <head> portion of an HTML page. As a result, they are guaranteed to be loaded into the memory before anything happens in the body. And there, in the body, the functions are normally used.

Our function accepts a parameter which is shown in its declaration as **x**. When calling the function, we pass it through this parameter some value, or some variable. The function, when called, performs some logic. And then, using the **return** statement, it sends back the result of its work. In our case, we are just printing the result onto the page.

Run this code in your browser and you should see:

```
Your simple function says: hi there!
```

Objects

An object is a set of values and methods (which are actually a special kind of function) used to deal with these values. **Array** is an example of an object, with its elements as a set of values and predefined functions like **sort()**, which can do something with its elements. **Array** also has a useful property, **length**, which can tell us a number of elements in our array.

But there are more important built-in objects in JavaScript. First of all, strings are treated as objects in JavaScript. A **String** object has the **length** property and a number of useful methods. Try the following code to see some of them in action:

```
var aString = "hi there!"
document.write(aString.length + " " + aString.toUpperCase() +
      "<br/>" + aString.bold() + "<br/>" + aString.blink() +
      "<br/>" + aString.toUpperCase().sub());
```

Date is a very useful object which allows you to easily display or modify a date. Try the following code:

```
// Creates a new Date object
// with the current date and time already in it
var aDate = new Date()

// Displays the date in the default format
document.write(aDate + "<br/>");

// Returns the number of a week day (0 for Sunday etc.)
document.write(aDate.getDay() + " ");

// Return the current hour, minute and second
document.write(aDate.getHours() + " ");
document.write(aDate.getMinutes() + " ");
document.write(aDate.getSeconds() + "<br/>");
```

```
// You can set some other date
aDate.setFullYear(2007, 6, 12)
document.write(aDate + "<br/>");
```

And, here is the output which I just had (yours will be different, of course):

```
Sun Feb 26 2006 13:12:03 GMT+0000  (GMT Standard Time)
0 13 12 3
Thu Jul 12 2007 13:12:03 GMT+0100  (GMT Daylight Time)
```

Index

Java™ 5

A Beginner's Tutorial
by Budi Kurniawan
448 pages, April 2005
ISBN: 0-9752128-5-0
US $39.95

Java is an easy language to learn. However, you need to master more than the language syntax to be a professional Java programmer. For one, object-oriented programming (OOP) skill is key to developing robust and effective Java applications. In addition, knowing how to use the vast collection of libraries makes development more rapid.

This book introduces you to important programming concepts and teaches how to use the Java core libraries. It is a guide to building real-world applications, both desktop and Web-based. The coverage is the most comprehensive you can find in a beginner's book. Here are some of the topics in this book:

- Java language syntax
- Object-oriented programming
- The Collections Framework
- Working with numbers and dates
- Error handling
- Input Output
- Swing
- Database access
- Internationalization
- Networking
- Applets
- Multithreading
- Servlet and JavaServer Pages
- API documentation
- Security
- Application deployment

This book In addition, Java 5 new features are also discussed. They are:

- Enum type
- Boxing/unboxing
- Varargs
- Static import
- Annotations

Struts Design and Programming

A TUTORIAL
by Budi Kurniawan
448 pages, April 2005
ISBN: 0-9752128-1-8
US $44.99

The first book on both design and programming of Apache Struts. The first part provides a complete reference on the latest version of Struts and teaches how a beginner can start coding with Struts. The second chapter discusses best practices and popular design patterns and teaches how Struts developers/architects should design their applications.

Here are some of the programming and design issues this book addresses:

- Action forms and how to choose the type of an action form's property
- How Struts processes action forms
- Input validation and the Validator plug-in
- Data conversion with Jakarta Commons BeanUtil class
- HTML, Bean, Logic tag libraries
- The Expression Language and JSTL
- The Data Access Object design pattern
- Earlier session invalidation
- Caching, paging, and sorting
- Request wrappers

How Tomcat Works:

A Guide to Developing Your Own Java Servlet Container
by Budi Kurniawan and Paul Deck
464 pages, April 2004
ISBN: 0-9752128-0-X
US$49.99/C$77.99

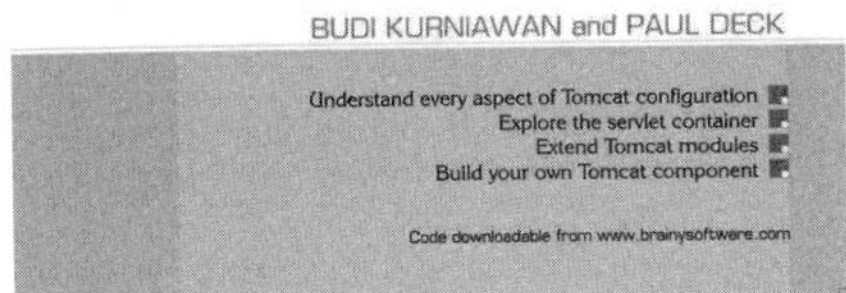

How Tomcat Works is the only book that explains the internal workings of Tomcat, the open source project used by millions of Java developers. Unlike other Tomcat titles, it is unique because it does not simply covers the configuration or servlet development with Tomcat. Listed on the official Tomcat website (http://jakarta.apache.org/tomcat/resources.html) and featured on Java Pro online (the most prestigious Java magazine), this book is meant for advanced readers interested in writing their own Tomcat modules or in understanding more beyond servlet/JSP programming. The publication of this book has generated tremendous interest as indicated by the fact that more than 3,000 people have downloaded the accompanying applications.

The authors of this book have cracked open Tomcat 4 and 5 and revealed the internal workings of each component. Upon understanding the contents of this book, you will be able to develop your own Tomcat components or extend the existing on